Palgrave Studies in Economic History

Series Editor
Kent Deng
London School of Economics
London, UK

Palgrave Studies in Economic History is designed to illuminate and enrich our understanding of economies and economic phenomena of the past. The series covers a vast range of topics including financial history, labour history, development economics, commercialisation, urbanisation, industrialisation, modernisation, globalisation, and changes in world economic orders.

More information about this series at
http://www.palgrave.com/gp/series/14632

Jason Begley · Tom Donnelly ·
David Jarvis · Paul Sissons
Editors

Revival of a City

Coventry in a Globalising World

palgrave
macmillan

Editors
Jason Begley
Coventry University
Coventry, UK

Tom Donnelly
Coventry University
Coventry, UK

David Jarvis
Coventry University
Coventry, UK

Paul Sissons
Coventry University
Coventry, UK

Palgrave Studies in Economic History
ISBN 978-3-030-22821-7 ISBN 978-3-030-22822-4 (eBook)
https://doi.org/10.1007/978-3-030-22822-4

Cover illustration: Trinity Mirror/Mirrorpix/Alamy Stock Photo

This Palgrave Macmillan imprint is published by the registered company Springer Nature Switzerland AG
The registered company address is: Gewerbestrasse 11, 6330 Cham, Switzerland

Contents

Notes on Contributors

Jason Begley is a an Assistant Professor at Coventry University and Academic Director for Postgraduate Researchers in the Centre for Business in Society. He has published in the fields of Economic History, Business History and Local Economic Development. His most recent research, looking at occupational change in the Nineteenth Century, has been published in the *Cambridge Journal of Economics*, while he has also recently co-authored an article on the history of the Rootes Group for the journal, *Business History*. He is currently a member of the European Network for the Comparative History of Population Geography and Occupational Structure 1500–1900.

Malte Busch is an Associate Lecturer in the School for Strategy and Leadership at Coventry University. His research focuses on the relationships between multinational companies, public actors and non-governmental organisations and how a variety of stakeholders influence corporate social responsibility (CSR) approaches of companies, especially in the automotive industry. He has presented his research at different international and national CSR and management conferences and symposiums. Prior to the completion of his Ph.D. in 2018, Malte gained degrees at Strathclyde Business School and the Deggendorf

Institute of Technology. In addition to his academic activities, Malte has been playing a part in various projects for the consulting and trade company MayConsult for many years.

Clive Collis is an Emeritus Professor at Coventry University where he was formerly Head of the Department of Economics and Director of the Centre for Local Economic Development. He has published widely in the fields of local and regional development with particular reference to FDI, the automotive industry, retail decline and the labour market role of older workers. He has acted as consultant to the OECD and advisor to the UK Department of Employment.

Tom Donnelly is an Emeritus Professor at Coventry University. His research focuses on the international automotive industry with particular reference to Western Europe and China. Tom was a founder member of the Centre for Local Economic Development, the Centre for Business History and the Motor Industry Observatory, with all three now forming part of the Centre for Business in Society at Coventry University. Tom has also been a Visiting Professor at the Institut d'Administration des Entreprises at the University of Caen, Oulu University of Applied Sciences in Finland, and Silesian University in the Czech Republic. Finally, he has been active as an Associate Editor of the Dictionary of National Biography.

Dr. Michael Haynes is an economic historian who is Emeritus Professor of International Political Economy at the University of Wolverhampton and a former Joint head of the Management Research Centre in its Business School. Living in a neighbouring county, he regularly visited Coventry as a schoolchild after his parents acquired a car in the late 1950s. Professionally, he has written extensively on the economic and social development of Britain and Europe in the nineteenth and twentieth centuries.

David Jarvis is Reader in Local and Regional Economic Development and Co-Director of the Centre for Business in Society (CBiS) at Coventry University. David is also founding Academic Programme Director for the University's Professional Doctorate (DBA), and sits on the Management Group of the University's Future Transport and Cities (FTC) Research Centre. Alongside his academic leadership roles, David has secured, managed and delivered more than 70 research or evaluation projects for clients across the public, private and charitable sectors. Particular areas of focus have been: Economic development and economic impact; Manufacturing sectors, clusters and economies; and Neighbourhood regeneration, faith and community.

Dr. Jonathan Kershaw graduated with his Ph.D. from Coventry University in 2016. His thesis appropriated the notions of affect and non-representational theory to explore the socio-cultural 'consumption' of the car and how our relationship with the car might impact upon the uptake of low carbon vehicles. His work applying affect theory to everyday activity has been published in the *Journal of Geography in Higher Education* and in *Transportation Part D: Transport and Environment.* He has also contributed to the e-book *Dialogues of Sustainable Urbanisation: Social Science Research and Transitions to Urban Contexts*, published in 2015 by the University of Western Sydney, and written more generally online about affect theory in automobility.

Myles Mackie, M.A., M.Sc. after teaching applied economic statistics at Cambridge University, he worked in the food industry before joining Coventry City Council. At the Council, he worked on business support and inward investment during the Thatcher years. From 1993, he was engaged on broader economic development issues, alternative fuelled vehicles use with Coventry businesses and key research on a wide range of policy issues. He retired in 2011 but continues to research and write articles for clients.

David Morris is a Professor of Business Development at Coventry University. He has been researching the automotive industry for over thirty years and has over sixty publications in the field. He was the founding Dean of Coventry Business School. Professor Morris also founded the Motor Industry Observatory which undertakes independent strategic analysis of the automotive industry worldwide. The MIO has been consulted by many major industry players and provides informed comment to the media. His current research activities are in the development of "smart mobility" strategies, connected cars and electric vehicles. His team are also working on the cybersecurity implications of developments in "connected cars".

Dr. Paul Sissons is a Reader in Employment Studies in the Centre for Business in Society, Coventry University. Paul's research focuses on spatial aspects of labour markets, low-wage work, labour market disadvantage, and local and regional economic development. His recent work has examined wage inequality in British cities, the links between economic growth and poverty reduction, policies to facilitate in-work progression, and employer approaches to productivity and pay.

List of Figures

List of Tables

1

Introduction

Jason Begley, Tom Donnelly, David Jarvis and Paul Sissons

Coventry is city with an important economic history. This may sound surprising, that a medium sized city in the Midlands of England has such a rich and varied past, socially and economically. Yet it remains true that throughout the city's existence it has been at the centre of, or subjected to, a slew of economic events that have served to repeatedly and fundamentally alter its character and structure. The city's fortunes have fallen and risen so frequently in the last hundred years or so that the symbol of the city, a phoenix, has become indelibly linked with its identity. While Coventry's residents take pride in this symbol

J. Begley (✉) · T. Donnelly · D. Jarvis · P. Sissons
Coventry University, Coventry, UK
e-mail: Jason.Begley@coventry.ac.uk

T. Donnelly
e-mail: aa5962@coventry.ac.uk

D. Jarvis
e-mail: ecy037@coventry.ac.uk

P. Sissons
e-mail: Paul.Sissons@coventry.ac.uk

J. Begley et al. (eds.), *Revival of a City*, Palgrave Studies in Economic History,
https://doi.org/10.1007/978-3-030-22822-4_1

of recovery, it's sometimes easy to forget that before rebirth must come fire. The symbolism can also be misleading, since what has emerged from the ashes of Coventry's economic past bears little resemblance to what came before. For example, as will be discussed in the pages that follow, industrialisation at the turn of the twentieth century has given away to a service-based local economy, heavily embedded in regional, national and global networks of economic and commercial activity. This shift was punctuated by two world wars, during which Coventry acted as a major centre of munitions production and, latterly, aero and vehicular production. For its efforts the city suffered in both post-war periods, from depression after the first conflict, to significant structural damage after World War Two. Rebuilding after the war wrought enormous changes to the physical landscape of the city, as it transformed from a medieval city in shape to a modern urban centre, with new spaces created for retail, industry and a road network for an emerging mass transport revolution, the passenger car.

Arguably, however, it would be another international force that would bring even greater changes and impact the city, namely globalisation. During the nineteenth century an enormous decline in transport costs across sea lanes allied to declining tariffs and the opening-up of the Americas and the Indian subcontinent encouraged British and European exporters to pursue greater trade and increase opportunities for the exchange of goods and services. Innovations in transportation technologies and improved efficiency of institutional structures further drove this process (Williamson 2008). However, it was by the beginning of the next century where globally integrated commodity and factor markets were truly in evidence, and as O'Rourke and Williamson note, by 1914 there was no area of the globe influenced or untouched by foreign markets, by foreign capital or traded expert skills (1999). Those who lost out, such as farmers who saw a sharp fall in food prices and domestic firms suffering from international competition voiced their opposition and set the stage for what would become the defining economic concern of the last century, but also, arguably, the most potent economic force for positive change and development. Two world wars and an intervening period of protectionism saw the rollback of many of the gains made by closer, integrated markets, but the post second-world war years saw a return to globalisation with a new vigour, along with successive waves of growth and decline.

For the city of Coventry, the opening up of post-war markets provided some of the richest and most successful years of its history, with specialised workers receiving significant rewards as the demand for their products took off. What followed though was a city which would become better known for its decline in the face of rival producers than for the quality of its work. Starting from the 1960s onwards the main industrial sector, the automotive industry in Coventry, would be subject to increasing competition from international rivals, as well as waves of Foreign Direct Investment that would begin to absorb or outperform domestic firms. In a comparatively short span of time Coventry's most important economic activity would be reduced to a negligible presence. To fill the vacuum created by deindustrialisation the city authorities sought, with the support of national government, to encourage replacement activities. The result of these efforts saw an increase in tertiary activities in the local economy. These were not support services to industrial actors, rather they were often low skill and low wage employment opportunities meeting the needs of the population, such as retail and cleaning.

As the economic base of the city changed so too did occupations, as industrial workers gave way, increasingly, to professional jobs but also elementary activities and a more polarised labour market. Arguably what has emerged in the decades since the collapse of the motor industry and driven by globalising processes are two visible tiers of growth in the city's workforce; skilled, mobile professionals locating often within travel-to-work corridors at the city's edge, and less qualified workers based around the commercial centre of the city and performing a range of jobs in comparatively low-paid occupations. In an attempt to reverse this trend city officials and national policymakers have attempted to follow a triple helix model of innovation, promoting educational opportunities within Coventry's two main higher education institutions (Coventry University and the University of Warwick) and intersecting these efforts with the development of Science Parks and Enterprise Parks. Encouraging close relations between industry, academia and government has brought considerable success to Coventry, but has not been without challenges, not least related to the mobility of new graduates. In an era when globalisation encourages the movement of capital and labour, it has proven difficult to anchor this talent pool in the city, with low rates of graduate retention. Whereas is the past Coventry attracted migration through the offer of high pay and the potential of upskilling on site, there is now considerably more churn associated with attending education in the city (but often not remaining afterwards).

This is the story of how globalisation has changed and continues to change the nature of Coventry city in terms of social and economic character. This is partly a product of Coventry's economic history and partly a product of new systems of economic organisation associated with globalisation mirrored in other medium-sized cities throughout the world. In the year when Coventry has successfully been awarded City of Culture for 2021, a tribute to its inventiveness and resilience, it is particularly timely to reflect and asses the social and economic changes wrought by globalising forces that help explain how Coventry has become the city it now is, how these winds of change have revitalised it, but with certain costs accrued. To do so, this book is arranged in two parts; Part one offers a chronological overview of the economic history of Coventry from the late nineteenth century up until the period of decline and deindustrialisation associated with the collapse of the motor industry in the city. The second part of the book looks thematically at how the city has changed and altered since this traumatic event, buffeted by globalising forces, but also shaped by local and national intervention, as well as the actions of key actors in emerging sectors of the local economy.

The origins of these changes can be found in the watch-making and ribbon manufacturing enterprises that brought the first waves of industrialisation to Coventry at the end of the nineteenth century. In Chapter 2, Donnelly explores these businesses, showing how these sectors provided the basis for volume manufacturing of first bikes and then machine tools, but more significantly later, auto manufacturing. What Donnelly also captures so well is the impact of rapid growth on the city, as inflows of migrant labour, attracted by new employment opportunities, brought pressure to bear on services and infrastructure. Growing pains would be a recurring theme for the city, whenever it underwent rapid expansion. Ribbon and watch-making were ultimately out-competed by cheaper but effective foreign producers with better production methods and access to plentiful, inexpensive labour, not the last example in Coventry's history of the city's main economic base being unable to maintain parity with its rivals for a host of reasons related to size, structure and location. As each wave of international competition came forth, Coventry's industries were forced to respond, either by cutting costs or diversifying.

Arguably international competition created a dynamic, entrepreneurial environment, a positive churn in the economic base of the city. Although of course there were significant difficulties for those employers and labourers impacted by these events, and this is well documented here. For those that diversified into automotive manufacture, the inter-war period proved a golden era and Coventry could be seen to prosper. Important to this success was the protected nature of the market, a consequence of government intervention during WWI. The role of policy-making in the fortunes of the City's key industries is the central theme of Busch's chapter, exploring as he does the growing interconnectedness of business and government during the years of war and those in between.

Busch focuses in particular on the operation of the Shadow Factory Scheme(s) from the mid-1930s onwards. Echoing Donnelly, he shows how rapid growth impacted on the city's residents, seen through the increasingly irate eyes of the local authorities. The picture that emerges is of an urgent, at times chaotic, atmosphere of development, heightened in its intensity by the threats posed by the international geopolitical situation. The sense of purpose shown by those involved is tempered by the realisation that many of the post-war problems encountered by Coventry city can be located in these actions. In particular, planning was not optimal, particularly post-conflict planning. Furthermore over-specialisation into a narrow range of economic activities had been encouraged by intervention, leaving the city vulnerable to shocks to core sectors, most notably automotive. Busch also stresses that the suspension of normal activities may have also created a sense of complacency amongst the city's industrialists, meaning that by 1945 Coventry was not as well placed to take advantage of new and growing markets as has sometimes been understood. In fact, a protracted period of protection with limited opportunity to invest in research and design mean that once domestic and international demand for vehicles had been sated, Coventry's automotive sector was not well-prepared to compete on the world stage.

The post-war boom was ultimately built on weak foundations. Subsequent interpretations of these halcyon years are difficult to disaggregate from the malaise and deep depression that followed. Here Haynes assesses the years before the downturn with a balanced view on growth and success measured against the social impacts of economic development on the residents of the city. By exploring the changes to culture he demonstrates how the opening up of the local economy brought new vistas to the life of its people. By the 1970s, however, the economic engine of Coventry was beginning to struggle, with waves of Foreign Direct Investment bringing more and more competition for local manufacturers. The opening-up of markets after the war also brought renewed competition. Collis details the decline of Coventry's major firms, using shift-share analysis to place this decline in a broader context. The impact of globalising forces in Coventry is best exemplified by the motor industry, the change in its structure and organisation being brought about by inflows of not just capital but new ideas and means of production. With the support of new regional agencies, such as the West Midlands Regional development Agency, Coventry began to change, economically, but also in terms of labour skills, mobility of labour and its organisation.

It is this latter process, the reorganisation of the workplace and, in particular, the shifting emphasis to a services within the economy, which preoccupies the thematic debates in the latter part of the book. The first of these chapters focuses on the sectoral and structural changes Coventry underwent during these years. Mackie, complementing the work of Collis, offers a different insight to the processes of sectoral change, viewing through the prism of local authorities' attempts to grapple with the unfolding challenges facing policymakers at a time when key industries were collapsing and unemployment was rising steeply in the city. Insights into the planning of a new Coventry, emphasising emerging advanced manufacturing opportunities and anchoring these concerns into an economy that was increasingly embedded in international networks of corporate actors are valuable; so too are the discussions around the new understandings reached between education, government and industry, the development of the knowledge economy in the city that has come to dominate its core activities.

Begley also returns to the theme of the new knowledge economy in his complementary analysis of occupational change and structure after the war. Sectoral change in Coventry was accompanied by new work modes and new skillsets being required by the labour force. Tracked over approximately a sixty year period, what emerges is a picture of population growth driven by young migrant graduates and labour attracted to managerial and professional opportunities in the city. In parallel has been the increase in elementary occupations with more low-paid service sector work. This has manifested in a concentration of workers in high skilled and low skilled jobs in the city, with fewer employment opportunities between these two tiers.

The mobility of the Coventry workforce is also a theme explored by Sissons, who focuses on migrant labour as well as the movement of those seeking an education in the city. Looking at travel to work patterns, he shows how the more highly qualified component of Coventry's workforce is located significantly outside the city, not fully embedded within its environs but rather commuting there daily for work, before returning to residences in a belt around the city. The potential for a silo effect is high, a point considered by Kershaw in his work looking at the built environment of Coventry since the war, as he considers the lived experiences of the City's residents, and how these have changed over time since the Second World War. Driven by globalising forces and mobile labour Coventry has enjoyed waves of inward migration, domestic and foreign, that have located in communities around the city, changing both its character and structure. The Coventry of the boom era is no longer a recognisable identity, with the city much changed due to open markets and mobile investment.

The final theme examined in this book is where Coventry's future lies. Has the move toward a local economy more embedded in regional, national and international networks of economic activity, driven by globalising forces, proven to be a positive shift for the city? Here Morris focuses on clusters of activity and smart specialisation as hallmarks of modernising economies. In particular he places Coventry's recent development in the global, a combination of linear local development in parallel to global and exponential growth. This is best exemplified by the development of the education sector in the city. Universities are becoming major social, economic and political forces in city centres and this is equally true for Coventry. These institutions act as anchors for local growth and development even as they become more international in scope and reach. By assessing the impact of both Coventry University and the University of Warwick on the local Coventry economy a true appreciation for the impact of the triple helix arrangement of business, government and education is reached. Morris then asks and answers the intriguing question of whether the motor industry is set to make a return to prominence in the fortunes of the city once more.

What comes through strongly across all the chapters is the transformation of Coventry wrought by globalising forces. This can be traced back to the beginnings of Coventry's industrial origins when foreign competition forced firms to diversify to survive. However, it was during the latter half of the twentieth century that the growing impact of mobile capital and labour began to really manifest, shaping Coventry's structures physically, economically and socially. As will be shown in the following pages, the concept of rebirth is perhaps less appropriate than that of renewal, a city growing and developing in different ways to take advantage of new circumstances of organisation. Ultimately then what must be assessed is whether Coventry, in a globalising world, has been revitalised by waves of capital, labour and goods flowing into the city, or has it instead been weakened by these forces? Has the process of globalisation created a more diverse, resilient local economy less impacted by fluctuations in the market, or has it in fact made the city more vulnerable to future shocks? Will Coventry, once more, have to endure the deep trough of a downward cycle of development before recovering in an oscillating cycle of growth and decay?

References

O'Rourke, K. H., & Williamson, J. G. (1999). *Globalization and History: The Evolution of a Nineteenth-century Atlantic Economy*. MIT Press.

Williamson, J. G. (2008). Globalization and the Great Divergence: Terms of Trade Booms, Volatility and the Poor Periphery, 1782–1913. *European Review of Economic History, 12*(3), 355–391.

2

Coventry: A Growing City

Tom Donnelly

Coventry's growth dates from the Roman occupation of these islands. Allegedly the Roman outpost was followed by the establishment of a convent of nuns, though the exact origins of the city remain obscure. In medieval times the city was bound up with the cloth industry and not only sold kerseys and the like in London, but exported to nearby Europe through ports such as Boston. By the eighteenth-century, however, Coventry was gaining a reputation for fine quality watches and ribbon making, which were to dominate the city's economy for most of the following century. In time these also fell into decline and Coventry progressed to the cycle trade, then motor cycles and eventually motor cars and, to a much lesser degree, aeronautics after 1914. The city became the main centre of car building in Britain. This, however, was not a linear progression as many firms made variants of all at roughly the same time.

Along with the changing structure of industry, Coventry's population seems to have grown and declined according to the census. Population

T. Donnelly (✉)
Coventry University, Coventry, UK
e-mail: aa5962@coventry.ac.uk

J. Begley et al. (eds.), *Revival of a City*, Palgrave Studies in Economic History,
https://doi.org/10.1007/978-3-030-22822-4_2

levels doubled to 49,730 by 1851. Thereafter, it fell mainly due to the decline of the older industries with many of the city's inhabitants seeking work elsewhere. Throughout the ensuing decade, Coventrians in the 1860s chose to leave and seek work in London or Lancashire where trade was brisker (Lancaster 1985). By 1871 the population was no more than 30,474, rose to 45,116 in the following decade and then to 53,004 in 1891 before peaking at 118,004 in 1911 (Census Reports).

Such an increase in demographics put pressure on schools and housing. Much of this was due to inwards migration which was an important factor between 1901 and 1911. A great deal of this originated outside Warwickshire, coming from Worcestershire, Northamptonshire, London and beyond. This was primarily a young population which had an impact on marriage and birth rates which were above UK average levels. The middle years of the nineties saw the level of immigration coincide with peak years of rising demand for cycles and so create a housing crisis. According to the local officer of Health, houses were not being built fast enough to satisfy demand, but by 1906 supply had risen to 800 per annum and even this was insufficient. Similar difficulties affected education as schools struggled to cope with the growth in child population. The Coventry School Board which had been slow in responding to the problems of over-crowding, was replaced by the Local Education Authority in 1903. It found that even as late as 1908, 28% of children suffered from the effects of over-crowded premises. Incomes were high in Coventry compared to other parts of the economy, but were seasonal in nature with firms being subject to trade fluctuations in the cycle and motor industries. Nevertheless, in 1910 local children were well nourished and clothed adequately, which is symbolic of rising living standards (Thoms and Donnelly 2000).

By the outbreak of War in 1914, Coventry with its back courts and narrow medieval street pattern, was tied into the world economy. It had prospered due to the emergence of the textile industries, fell away due to its own failings, the quicker evolvement of the French ribbon industry and the Cobden Treaty. The watch trade failed partly because of the rise of the American and Swiss overseas trade in watches and partly due to its own conservatism. The economy revived with a successful growth of the cycle, motor cycle and motor industries so that by the outbreak of World War One the city was well integrated into the global economy.

Ribbon Weaving

Ribbon weaving was introduced to Coventry, Atherstone, Nuneaton and surrounding areas at some point in the eighteenth century or even earlier by Huguenot refugees, escaping persecution and gradually spread out to nearby country towns such as Atherstone and Nuneaton, though earlier evidence suggests otherwise (Noon 2013; Hemsley 2013). About 1770 the weaving of silk became a fast growing industry but its heyday was short lived, lasting from 1813 until the end of the Napoleonic wars two years later. For most of the century the industry experienced decline as the following Table 2.1 illustrates.

Searby is surely correct in the view that between 1815 and 1860 the industry suffered severe competition from other parts of England such as Derby where steam looms were introduced. Coventry was a place of small concerns and independent craftsmen whose main aim was to resist modern modes of production. They harboured the opinion that they had done reasonably well for a considerable time and, for as long as the industry was protected against the import of French products they had nothing to fear. Whenever there was any threat of lifting the prohibition on French ribbons there was an outcry from Coventry. This was surely a protest to delay invention or retard improvement (Stephen 1969).

Table 2.1 Silk workers in Coventry 1821–1901

	1821	1841	1851	1861	1871	1991	1901
Males	4973*	3232	4170	3988	1904	896	506
Females		3106	6472	6955	3706	2512	1671

*This figure refers to 1818 and is drawn from an unofficial census compiled by the ribbon weavers. It includes both males and females (Searby 1976).

Coventry was even against the introduction of the Dutch engine loom or later the Jacqard loom on which several ribbons could be woven at the same time. Switching to the latter would have increased production, lowered costs and paved the way for the factory system. The conflict between those who favoured the factory system and the outworkers lasted decades. There was nothing that could be done to prevent the enactment of the Cobden-Chevalier Treaty of 1860 which abolished the 15% tariff on ribbons and silk which revealed that the Coventry product was far behind the French in design and methods of production. It was then that decline set in as imports grew, leaving thousands of weavers unemployed. There was brief revival during the Franco-Prussian war but it was too late to have more than a marginal effect. Many weavers directed their offspring after 1870 to trades where their prospects were better served (Stephen 1969; Thoms and Donnelly 2000). The industry however did not die entirely. Thomas Stevens, inventor of the 'Stevengraph', a pictorial bookmark, demonstrated it successfully at the Crystal Palace exhibition of 1868, in Europe and New York, extending the life of the industry. Cash's, which had been formed in 1857 almost as an experiment, survived by turning to a conventional factory system. Coventry's remaining weavers found salvation in chenille, most of which was sent to London, but as has been shown the number of workers was considerably smaller than it had been in 1860. By 1935 the number of manufacturers had dwindled to thirteen, the most renowned of which was J. & J. Cash (Stephen 1969).

Watchmaking

As ribbon weaving fell away, it was replaced by watchmaking as the city's premier industry. Watchmaking in the area dates from the seventeenth century when a local trade began to appear. John Patson and Joseph Huet, for example, were responsible for the running of the clocks in the market and the grammar school respectively. In the 1680s new clocks were installed at the New Gate and at the school. In 1706 the Council or Leet declared that no payments should made for the upkeep of the clocks until the middle of the century when it changed tack. At that juncture watch making was beginning to emerge as one of the city's trades. Samuel Vale and others founded Rotherhams which specialised in setting up the trade with John Bottrill and certain others (Stephen 1969).

In 1830 the city boasted some fifty-three watchmakers at least. Of these twenty remained among the 142 named individuals or possibly employers twenty years later. The years of expansion were clearly those between 1830 and 1850. Watch making and ribbon weaving did not vie for labour. The former demanded a higher level of skill than the latter and, because of higher wages and better prospects, weavers were apprenticing their sons to watchmakers. However, it should be remembered that in excess of two thousand were employed in the watch trade (ibid.). Throughout the period from the eighteenth to the nineteenth century, work was minutely subdivided with each member of the trade being responsible for only one part of the operation. The many parts of the watch were installed by specialist fitters considered to be expert finishers. All parts were made by using hand tools which were often not interchangeable. Journeymen often worked from home or in the shops of small masters who employed no expensive equipment. As can be imagined, there was a great deal of coming and going between the various houses and shops and so it is little wonder that they were situated in close proximity to each other. Initially watch making began around Spon St before spreading to Spon End and then to Chapelfields as the trade expanded but after the mid-fifties a decline set in. Several attempts were made to try and improve the situation by raising standards of craftsmanship and operating a fixed price list. These were in 1843, 1848 and 1859. In the latter year over six hundred watchmakers joined the movement but within even six months the engravers, dial-makers and case makers withdrew their support, arguing that their interests would be better served elsewhere, but doing nothing to fill the void. The employers argued in turn that there was nothing they could do to bring prices down to compete with imports led especially from Switzerland. A hammer blow was the government decision to opt for an economic policy of Free Trade under the previously mentioned Cobden-Chevalier Treaty of 1860 by which goods of foreign origin could enter the UK free of quotas or tariffs. Between March and August of 1859 and similarly in 1860, imports from France alone increased from 54,000 to 83,000 (Searby 1976). Coventry was forced to concentrate on making high quality watches maintaining an excellent small niche market but having to forego competing with the Swiss and to a lesser degree the French for the mass market. English watches were often unornamented unlike many of their European counterparts as UK makers were more intent on making an accurate piece of equipment. This gives rise to important questions which has been answered by Church (1975).

Church points out that in the eighteenth century, Britain enjoyed a considerable reputation in the production of clocks and watches but that in the following century, this leadership was lost to the United States due to standardisation and the assembly of interchangeable parts, and this was even before Eli Whitney had introduced the mass production of weapons. The crux of the case is that watches and clocks would have standardised anyway as America concentrated on standardisation through large sections of its economy. Emphasis was laid on the efforts of Browne and Sharp and also of Terry and Dennison in spreading a knowledge of a new manufacturing system as distinct from simply the passing on of craftsmanship skills as English concerns had been doing throughout the period. Dennison is singled out for his foundation of the Waltham Watch Company in 1840. By 1859 he had reduced the time taken to produce a watch from twenty-one days to four with craftsmen being replaced by machines so raising productivity in the process of producing cheap watches.

Also analysed were the Swiss, who had also made advances in producing cheap watches. Compared to Waltham's twenty-one days around 1859 the Swiss pace lay between eight and eleven days. Though the English rate is not discussed, most commentators were agreed that the Swiss were the driving seat before the Waltham revolution. In the opening years of the nineteenth century the Swiss expanded their markets in Britain and America for both relatively cheap and good quality watches and by the 1880s supplied three quarters of imports of clocks and watches to American ports. By the same year imports of watches to English markets had risen by a factor of four to reach a figure of one hundred and sixty thousand. Though the English did succeed in retaining a grip on their upper market segment, they made no impression on either sector of the American market. The increase in Swiss exports were directly due to attempts to diversify their economy which was being subject to competition from English cotton textiles. The Swiss had little choice but to expand their clock and watch industries, taking advantage of lower labour costs.

One reason why the Swiss were more successful was that they mechanised quicker than their English counterparts, though by not as much as the Waltham works. They initially passed their watches off as English and evaded weakly enforced British customs duties. More importantly, they employed agencies and agents to study overseas markets, disseminated information and trained apprentices to be engineers as well as watchmakers. In such an environment it was more likely that innovation could occur. The outcome was that the slimline Swiss product found a niche at the lower end of the market. In the meantime, the Swiss introduced the key as the means of winding and setting the time in low priced segment watches. Continued improvement and development allowed them to be used in the higher echelons of the market in search of higher unit profits. Exhibitors were also prominent at trade exhibitions in the 1870s. Some ten years on, English production stood at two hundred and twenty thousand while the European and American figures were three and a half million and one and a half million respectively; the popular cheaper end of the trade. Basically, the English had been too conservative in their ways and, for example, avoided winding to the right in keyless watches, thereby saving on the cost of new machines. The Swiss treated watch and clock making as an industry. The English did not. They failed to mechanise until the beginning of the twentieth century and even then they seemed unenthusiastic about the process of going after the cheaper end of the market as evidenced by the numbers who sought other outlets for their talents notably in Coventry's bicycle industry. Even Rotherham's and The Coventry Movement Company turned to producing bicycle and car parts. What contribution the English made to interchangeable parts was left to other areas of life (Wood 1988).

What has been exposed here in the role of the ribbon and watch industries in the city is how they clung to craft traditions of a conservative nature and how both failed to take cognisance of the facts that their respective industries and the world they operated in was changing.

Bicycles, Cars and Components

As has been suggested before, industrialisation came late to Coventry, but it was not the type of coal, iron, steel cotton and shipbuilding structure that had dominated the North of England, Wales and Scotland for most of the nineteenth century. It was the new light engineering industries of cycles, cars, machine tools and components that were to thrive throughout the twentieth century. The fall of the ribbon and watch industries was offset by the emergence of the cycle and car industries and to a lesser extent the motor cycle industry. The number of cycle firms in the city peaked at around seventy-five in 1898, and by the outbreak of the First World War, Coventry was home to around twenty car manufacturers out of one hundred and thirteen for all of Britain or roughly 28% of the national total. Most of Coventry's output was controlled a few firms such as Daimler, Humber, Rover, Swift and Standard. Of these, Humber was the largest, producing two and a half thousand vehicles per annum, whereas Ford turned out five thousand in Manchester. Other Coventry firms were much smaller and included in these were Hillman, Maudslay and Riley whose total output did not exceed one hundred and fifty cars a year (Saul 1962).

Generally, Britain was late in coming to the car industry compared with the Americans and to a lesser degree the French. First imports to Britain and Coventry by English agents included the Panhard-Levassor, Peugeot, De Dion, Bouton and Bollee models (Adeney 1988). Thus, the early development of British cars depended on vehicles and components from the Continent. One reason for this may have been that the heavy engineering concerns concentrated on the higher rates of return on capital available in their own areas of activity rather than devote time and money investing in an emergent industry whose future was uncertain. It was not until a rough agreement on what constituted a clear car design with engines at the front, passengers facing forward, and the basic power train agreed upon that the fledgling industry began to attract capital in sufficient amounts. Even then, larger producers dominated the industry, some of whose origins lay in the cycle trade (Church 1994). Lastly, redundant watchmakers looked on the cycle industry as a saviour. The precision engineering skills of the watchmakers especially were highly regarded by the enthusiastic entrepreneurs. Others increasingly were recruited from beyond the city attracted by the prospects of higher wages than those offered by most rural occupations.

The cycle industry was by far more attractive to investors than the city's traditional industries and so with comparatively little capital, entrepreneur/engineers set up cycle making businesses cheaply, using premises vacated by unemployed textile workers. As one might imagine, output and productivity was small (Thoms and Donnelly 1985). Even firms such as Rover and Centaur began in limited-sized accommodation. Early firms often began as partnerships, bringing together money and skill. For example, the firm of J.K. Starley and William Sutton in 1873 brought together Starley's innovatory mind and Sutton's money in the Meteor Works to produce the 'Safety Cycle'. Partnerships were a common form of commercial relationships, but the last years of the nineteenth century witnessed the reconstruction of the larger cycle firms into private and public companies with local capital still to the fore. Thomas Mercer, for instance, a leading watchmaker, became managing director of the Quinton Cycle Company when it was overhauled in 1891. George Woodcock, a solicitor, was involved in several reconstructions, gaining control of the Wolverhampton firm of Dan Rudge in 1885 which he merged with his own Coventry Cycle Company renamed as Rudge-Whitworth and Company (Thoms and Donnelly 2000).

At around the same time, the industry tried to extend the market by inventing the tricycle and quadricycle. The former was meant to appeal to men of advanced years as well as other professionals who placed a value on the element of speed. It was really the coming together of the pneumatic tyre and the 'safety cycle' that propelled the growth and boom of the nineties. Many firms were experimenting with knowledge flowing relatively freely between firms who copied each other though their inability and lack of finance to defend and protect their innovation in court.

Though occasional companies such as Rudge-Whitworth persevered with making cycles, what must not be overlooked is the role of component suppliers in supporting the cycle and ultimately the motor industry. Components were mainly obtained locally or either from nearby Birmingham's engineering industries or those in the Black Country. Many former watchmakers such as the Coventry Watch Movement Company, not finding trade brisk enough from 1903 onwards, especially with falling profits and depressed trade, began to supply cycle and motor firms with parts, including lubricators and radiator tubes. Coachbuilders also got involved with trade, but more so with the motor rather than the cycle trade. In 1881 Hollick and Pratt supplied the bodywork for J.K. Starley's electrically driven tricar. Other examples include Thomas Pass and that of Hawkins and Peake, who hailed from Birmingham. At first, the latter supplied several firms, but from 1904 their main client was Rover.

Some of the cycle firms and motor firms developed links, often through motor cycles. The move to motor cycles was a form of diversification and offered new engineering problems surrounding the generation and transmission of power. The Riley tricar is a fine example of technical progress in this area as the company developed a motorised example of such a vehicle which lasted from 1898 until production ended in 1907 before switching to conventional motor cars to fit in with evolving market conditions. Additionally, numerous firms preferred to try their luck at making motor cars and bought out complete engines or components from outside firms such as White and Poppe, suppliers of engines to Swift and Singer, for instance. Others relied on obtaining expertise from consulting engineers as it was less expensive to employ their services intermittently.

The remaining cycle firms further assisted the move to motor production by building a supply chain to provide components to the larger firms such as Humber and Rover. Some of the pioneer cycle firms such as Bayliss Thomas and Company produced some two thousand cycles per annum in 1878, but by 1896 Swift and Humber were averaging seven hundred to two thousand cycles per week. This increasing volume led inevitably to the demand for the introduction of interchangeable parts. Rover changed to flow production, while Rudge-Whitworth used a similar system to dwarf its smaller rivals in terms of output (Lewchuk 1987). The pace of change varied from firm to firm, notably among those who had begun to concentrate on cars. The boom in cycle sales came and ended in the middle nineties both at home and abroad. The recession which followed was the consequence of other countries' efforts in cycle development in conjunction with a falling off in interest in cycling among the upper classes. German and French output grew as exports fell particularly in 1897. In America, rising output, backed by imports tariffs, led to a fall in British imports and market share for British firms. In contrast American firms succeeded in obtaining advances in British imperial markets, while German and French machines were in a dominant position at home. Britain by 1897 had fallen to third behind the United States in the export tables. These were followed by spectacular company failures and a subsequent rise in the number of bankruptcies in Coventry (Harrison 1969, 1981).

This new competitive environment had an impact on Coventry in that it resulted in dropping sales and dwindling dividends. Though there are no output figures, the number of cycles sent from the city by the London and North Western Railway fell from sixty-three thousand to thirty thousand between 1896 and 1900 (ibid.). By the turn of the century even New Premier and Calcott were registering losses, whereas some of the larger firms, having augmented their premises or plant during the boom, had overcapitalised in the hope of increased profits. Losses were inevitable. The situation was not helped by the use of debentures or fixed interest securities which were attacked by ordinary shareholders. They viewed such practices as reducing profits, making it difficult to expand sales through price cuts in periods of poor trade endemic in the industry's natural cycle. The main problem was that debentures were often used to obtain bank loans. By 1900, however, the local banks were becoming increasingly wary of the cycle industry Midland Bank, Coventry (Day Book) (1900). A number introduced economies, but such measures could not stop failure from occurring. From a peak figure of seventy-five in 1898, the number of cycle firms dropped to forty-nine in a mere fourteen years and included in those who fell by the wayside were Bayliss Thomas and Coventry Cross firms (Harrison 1969). There was still no great incentive to move wholesale into motors until such times as the future seemed more certain.

However, there was a need to face American competition. The only successful way of meeting it in the home market was to cut prices yet still produce efficient machines. Rudge-Whitworth in 1887 managed to achieve this by catering for the cheap end of the market through cutting the price of its Special and Standard cycles. Such a move was followed albeit reluctantly by Singer and others. Inexpensive machines helped stave off the U.S. competition yet other firms stuck with high price high quality cycles. Why some followed one policy and some another remains a mystery. It may be that the management of some companies such as Rudge-Whitworth were less conservative in their style of management than others, who pursuing a more conservative line were still imbued with the idea of a craft culture. Reminiscent perhaps that a proportion of the city's cycle makers were traditionalists with an engineering background. Even Lea-Francis persisted with the high price-quality policy right into the opening decade of the twentieth century. Whilst maintaining its reputation for high standards of production, aiming only at the upper end of the market until the coming of the First World War, cycles remained their main concern (Thoms and Donnelly 2000; Price 1978).

Diversification into cars was rewarding for some firms, but not for all as a great deal seems to have depended on when the move was made. By 1913 the successful car firms were Swift, Singer, Rover and Calcott Brothers. These were however somewhat tardy in concentrating almost exclusively on cars and may have profited from those who had gone before them or when the market for cars was buoyant. The switch from cycles to motor cars seemed to rely on several factors. One key factor was the level of profit. For example, Swift and Rover persisted in selling cycles in sufficient quantities to ensure a satisfactory balance sheet until the industry fortunes seemed secure.

No single company represents the industry, although Rover seems to come closest as an illustration. Under the stewardship of J.K. Starley, Rover was formed as a limited cycle company in 1896 with capital of £150,000 which was too much in relation to the firm's assets and subsequently being reduced by half on Starley's death in 1901. The secretary,

Harry Smith, was appointed managing director and under his guidance matters improved. After avoiding the debacle of falling profits of the late nineties, Rover, apart from recording a deficit in 1904 did well in comparison with many of its competitors. It followed in the footsteps of Rudge-Whitworth in reducing prices and was quick to produce the Meteor, a cheap cycle for the lower sector of the market and mounted an advertising campaign in Europe and in Australia. In addition, a bank loan was secured to allow the firm to manufacture machines during the winter months in readiness for the springtime season. Favourable discounts were also agreed with suppliers. In 1898 Rover registered patents for a motor-gearing mechanism and a year later several Peugeot motor cycles were bought for research. No motor cycles were made before 1902 and it was another two years before motor car production was started (Foreman-Peck 1983).

On assuming his position, Smith started to cut production costs by replacing labour with machines, buying equipment from a Yorkshire firm which had entered liquidation. He sought greater economies of scale in production through expanding depots and even negotiated a volume deal with the War Office for cycles. Perhaps more importantly, Smith faced down his Board of Directors to pursue his ambition to make motor cars. The company offered stiff opposition, but Smith persisted, and eventually, extra factory space was made available. Moreover, at the same time he encountered some difficulty in receiving suitable engines for his vehicles leaving him with little choice but to make his own units. In itself this was no bad thing, helping to cement the firm's position and ensuring that motor production would follow even if opposition continued. Again, the influence of Smith was of significance, having secured earlier in the year the leading engineer, Edmund Lewis from Daimler. Rover's first car was an immediate success and established the company firmly in the motor market (Foreman-Peck 1983; Thoms and Donnelly 2000).

Other firms such as Daimler and Standard could be discussed here along with extensive biographies of the Harry Lawson and Charles Friswell for example, but space precludes, and it is more apt and, hopefully rewarding, to discuss how the early motor trade was organised. As explained earlier in this chapter, the growth of the car industry was uneven, but gradually from the turn of the twentieth century it gathered its own momentum. By 1913 Coventry was producing in the region of 9000 motors. Testament to this is the extension and addition to factories. Firms such as Daimler invested in a large new factory, finished in 1905 and Humber's new building was completed three years later on a site comprising of twenty-two acres. Several car and for that matter cycle concerns now employed large numbers. Daimler employed some five thousand workers and Humber around three thousand. Almost all the others began operating from modest premises and productivity was consequently low. Apart from firms, such as Standard, and Siddelely-Deasy, these made very little impact on the industry. For example, even Crouch cars succeeded in producing only some three thousand units in its entire lifetime between 1912 and 1927 when it ceased to exist. Though the products were sound, it could not survive against larger firms (Thoms and Donnelly 2000).

The rise of the car industry increased the size of the components industry in the West Midlands and, of course, in Coventry. A great deal of the latter was based in the general area, doubtless assisted by the metal working of the region which provided axles, brakes and other parts. Excellent transport links by water, road and rail supported the logistics involved. Just before the outbreak of hostilities in 1914, the city had eight body builders, eight engine assemblers and a host of manufacturers of general and specific components for cars and commercial vehicles (Saul 1962; Gallagher 1974). A good illustration of this was Morris-Lister Magnetos, founded by two electrical engineers, who had worked previously at Birmingham University. More important was the firm of White and Poppe, a firm of engine makers who formed a partnership in Lockhurst Lane, making shell fuses during the first Boer War in 1899. Their contribution really started in 1903 through the manufacture of engines for motor cycles. Two years later, Swift's order to them for petrol engines was followed up by a similar order by other firms (Lane 1977). The firm also exhibited at the Olympia motor show and in 1913 produced roughly 2000 engines, some of which were for commercial vehicles. The company was not averse to diversifying into carburettors which proved profitable when demand for engines was low.

William Morris of Oxford was insistent on using White and Poppe carburettors when necessary (Adeney 1993).

From what has been said, the relationship between the manufacturers and the component suppliers was close though the depth of this relationship was varied. Some component makers sold their goods to a select few manufacturers which eventually led to mergers and takeovers, particularly during the inter-war years. Harbingers of this before 1914 were Rover's acquisition of Hawkins and Peake, the coachbuilders, in 1907 and then Daimler's offer of £30,000 to the Coventry Chain Company to fund a move to new premises. These were attempts at a degree of vertical integration. Daimler, it must be emphasised, had been dealing with Coventry Chain firm for a considerable time having been impressed by the quality of its output. The car firm itself merged with Birmingham Small Arms Company three years later as the latter was keen to move from cycles to cars. Daimler, like its counterpart, Rover, was anxious to raise the quality of nuts and bolts which it had found unreliable and this explains both why the firm tried to merge Coventry Chain and why it established a facility for testing all bought-out components in 1902 (Tripp 1956). Others who set up workshops to control the quality of component supply included Standard and Rover (Foreman-Peck 1979, 1983).

Such close relationships proved advantageous to both sides, allowing the saving of capital, sharing of research expenses, product development with each side being prepared to share relevant expertise and developmental costs as well as the holding of stock and possibly granting credit. The car assemblers all underwent periods of shortages of ready capital and so had little choice but to approach their suppliers for extended credit. White and Poppe, for example, held stock in 1907 worth about £9000 above their requirements as customers refused to take delivery of the firm's products because of slack trade (LBC, 5 November 1907). The component firm did, however, attempt to control the period of credit by insisting upon John Siddeley accepting goods within a specified time. This was necessary because it affected the purchase of new plant by White and Poppe (LBC, 7 September 1907).

In the opening months of 1906 the motor industry was busy, but by the following year, a depression had set in and even the larger firms had resorted to price cutting, making it difficult for much smaller outfits to flourish and survive. Humber, Daimler, Rover and Singer reported losses in 1907 (Thoms and Donnelly 2000). Three years later, there was an upswing in fortunes. In the same year Swift was hard pushed for work space with cars taking up places normally used for cycles. Daimler also struggled to meet orders for cars due to lack of space but did not increase its premises. Demand for cars was changing considerably. There had been a latent demand for light vehicles mainly from the professional classes for some time, but it was now becoming more vibrant, as will be shown, especially in the years immediately prior to 1914.

The rise of the car industry in Coventry was often effected by inputs of capital, frequently in modest sums from local sources such as family, friends and business associates. Some came from as far away as Kidderminster, Birmingham, London, Wales and even Scotland. Alfred Herbert, of machine tool fame, raised funds through his family which had agricultural and building interests in Leicestershire. The mobilisation of money was perhaps eased by the Coventry and County Club in the city where many manufacturers met their suppliers and financiers in a relaxed environment over a drink and discussed business (Brittain 1989; Davies 1983, 1986; Batchelor 2009). While this may have sufficed for the small to medium sized firms, it was not enough for the larger firms whose requirements were such that they had to seek public funding. Deasy went public in 1906 and seven years later Standard followed likewise to attract investment for its strategy of producing lighter cars. Rover went to the market on several occasions to obtain investment funds. Its capital was ultimately raised to £200,000 helping it to switch from cycles and concentrate on cars once the War was over. Daimler was rescued from impending bankruptcy in 1904 when it was totally reconstructed to put it on a firm financial footing after the Lawson years of uncertainty. Such an injection was essential if the firm was to meet production targets to produce income for the future (Davy 1964; Saul 1962).

There were firms which remained undercapitalised in Coventry and as one would expect these were the firms with less than basic resources, some working only from back courts. Some, with only a capital of £5000, a tiny sum, made a couple of vehicles and then declared bankruptcy, leaving customers bereft of spares or a resale value. In itself, this helps to explain the volatility that plagued the industry in its early years. Even Standard was not aloof from this during its early years causing it to go public in 1914 and then only managing to raise £50,000 compared with £650,000 for Austin at Longbridge in Birmingham (Church 1979, 1994). There were also large firms which suffered from under subscription and among these were Siddeley-Deasy and Maudslay. The latter in 1907 was 60% undersubscribed by the public and Cyril Maudslay's own part of this was only made possible by a bank loan (Harrison 1981). In the following year the firm had a shortage of capital and was refused funds by Midland Bank. Siddeley-Deasy was however eventually financially assisted by the Rothchilds but both firms, having failed to have their issues formally underwritten to save on costs, had to pay an appropriate penalty (Thoms and Donnelly 2000).

Obviously, a number of firms needed working capital, essential for paying utility bills, wages and component suppliers, especially as the industry suffered from being seasonal. Bank support was often necessary if cash flow problems were to be overcome, particularly for those smaller firms whose survival was at stake. Even large firms had recourse to bank lending from time to time. Overdrafts normally lasted for a period of twelve months, though assets and personal security could lead to a time extension. In 1909, the London and Westminster Bank arranged a loan of £10,000 for Daimler. The banks, however, did not throw money at the industry, proving less than accommodating to small and medium sized firms. There were no set criteria for making a judgement on which loans were based, but financial history and whether past advice was followed were reputedly looked at in detail. Bank managers could act autonomously, but sometimes they bowed to advice from head office. The banks were as a rule unwilling to lend money for capital projects as was the norm for British banks. As Thoms and Donnelly have quoted the manager of the Midland Bank in 1908 made it abundantly clear that 'no part of the bank's money was put into bricks and mortar' (Thoms and Donnelly 2000).

Survival also depended on the availability of labour which was recruited quite easily to the motor vehicle industry. Skill transferability from cycles to motors was common as was migrant labour and more importantly it was young. Many came from nearby Warwickshire, others from Birmingham, London, Cheshire or Lancashire, all places with an engineering tradition. Local schools proved a source of fertile recruitment as there was very little tradition of going on to university in Coventry. Bablake, albeit a grammar school, offered instruction on the industry and the local technical college, which had been started in 1888 offered evening classes. Few motor firms paid much attention to education as most seemed to prefer 'learning on the job'. Only a small number of boys had a formal education apart from following the apprenticeship route; few manufacturers, Daimler apart, showed much interest in either an in-house system of education or of sending boys to a technical college. The employers' preference was for hiring design engineers, an area in which the industry was particularly deficient. As noted earlier, most of the early vehicles built in Coventry were of French design. British design engineers were in great demand and changed employers with relative frequency, doubtless to find a new challenge or perhaps chasing money. Indeed, the success of individual firms might have rested on the skills of such engineers which may explain why Edmund Lewis was recruited by Rover from Daimler in 1904 (Thoms and Donnelly 2000).

High wages acted as a magnet for workers. Reward was what mattered on the shop floor. In their turn the employers tried to raise quality, quantity and productivity through manipulation of methods of payment and, also, as a means of controlling the work force. Well-paid workmen were less likely to affiliate to a union. Life in the car factories varied between firms. In most establishments the normal working day was from 6 a.m. to 6 p.m. or from 7 a.m. until 7 p.m. On a Saturday the day shift ceased at 12 noon (Donnelly and Durham 1989). Not all shifts ran smoothly. If a firm was recorded in the Amalgamated Society of Engineers (ASE) minutes, it was usually indicative of a fall in orders or short time. The Minute books of the ASE are replete with complaints from workers over piecework and premium bonus rates, in other words, the work effort required. New equipment and machine tools introduced by Harry Smith at Rover and John Siddeley at Deasy, made work more intensive. By 1906, however, this led to production costs falling. In that year Daimler argued costs per unit of output had dropped by nearly 15%. An increase in productivity was therefore anticipated in subsequent years. However, in the years leading up to the First World War, the introduction of machinery and a shortage of skilled labour had led to local de-skilling. This caused upset among the highly skilled men who fearful of pay and status erosion complained bitterly. Faced with a shortage of highly skilled men, the employers argued, as did Tolliday, it was axiomatic that semi-skilled men could do all the tasks required to operate the machines. Therefore, where possible the employers allowed semi-skilled men to be used in the workshops and proposed that rates be attached to the man rather than the machine, especially if the work involved was of a repetitious nature. At first the ASE resisted. They were successful in the north of England but made little progress in Coventry. It proved difficult to fight the issue as there was no displacement of skilled men and the ASE could not supply skilled labour for the new machines. There was frequently little choice but to cease resistance (Tolliday 1984) The men had little option but to concentrate then on conditions of work.

In addition to bringing in new machines and powered tools the employers had introduced piecework and premium bonus. Both systems were open to abuse in that bonuses were deemed unfair and that often the foremen claimed the lion's share of the bonus if a Gang system was in operation. In 1898 the ASE minute noted that a charge-hand getting 10% of the preferential bonus was unjust (ASE, 2 September 1898). In 1901 the Daimler works manager agreed to mutuality in pricing with all payments being made through the office and making it clear that he would not tolerate a piece-master system (AES, 9 October 1901). This system meant essentially that the time taken to complete a particular task was set by the piece-master or rate fixer along with the operative mutually. If the operative finished the job in hand he received a bonus. Often, however, these were so tightly timed that completion within the time specified was nigh impossible and the worker had to work off the time in the next task. As can be imagined, this was an issue of serious contention as the operative often worked in deficit (ASE, 1898–1914). Work in the factories was hard and demanding, but, as said before, the money was good.

Just prior to the outbreak of War the light car appeared (Caunter 1957). Basically, light cars were smaller versions of their larger brethren and enjoyed a capacity of no more than 1.500 cc. and proved popular with the middle and professional classes. Some Coventry firms succeeded in cornering a slice of the market. These included Singer, Standard and Humber, but the leader was Ford at Trafford Park. Before the beginning of hostilities, output of light vehicles grew quite fast. What helped the development of such vehicles was the image and influence of the motor car agents whose advice was often followed. The car was viewed as a custom-made body which was fitted to platform or chassis for the upper classes or wealthier sectors of society. Perhaps this opinion hampered development, or was it the innate conservatism of manufacturers? A range of views probably influenced thinking before 1914. Daimler, for instance, enjoyed a reputation for large cars, but as far back as 1899 it had produced light cars. These however were never seen as main line features as they had come from Germany and only a few were manufactured. Daimler remained with large cars for the luxury market and royalty. Diluting the brand was not a route the company wished to take as it had to compete with the likes of Lanchester and Rolls-Royce. Light cars were produced by Rover from 1910 with Owen Clegg's appointment as works manager. His light car, a Rover 12, recovered the firm's fortunes, but two years later he quit to assume a position with the French firm, Darracq.

The early Standards were quite heavy and so the firm was one of the first to bring in a six-cylinder engine. This was boosted by the entrepreneurial chairman Charles Friswell. Being enthusiastic about cars in general, he sought patronage from the aristocracy and even royalty. His London premises were lavish, but Friswell's preference was for larger vehicles. This was opposed by other board members and his ultimate departure in 1912 was followed by the emergence of the 9.5 hp Standard light car, which sold for £185. It was successful with 2000 being manufactured before War broke out. The light car was here to stay as Alfred Herbert claimed in 1913.

The First World War

The path that Coventry had followed since the 1890s soon brought it to prominence. Its industrial structure of cars, motor cycles, machine tools and latterly its ordnance factory provided the essential equipment which would be required to meet the demand for transport, armaments and guns, necessary to fight a war of this type. The first thing to catch the eye was the near frenetic pace of building work as premises were built or extended to meet the demands of the military. Accommodation, too, was at a premium as the city's population swelled to over 128,000 in 1921 rising from 106,349 a decade earlier, due primarily to inwards migration (Richardson 1972). Many migrants settled in the city, others travelled daily by commute, while others found accommodation through employers. White and Poppe, helped by government finance, built hutted accommodation for migrant females. By 1916 the company had thirty-two such buildings, each housing up to a hundred women and girls. This type of accommodation was very basic but gave rise to feelings of isolationism. Future blocks of this nature were appointed in a more comfortable manner yet for young couples, accommodation was a continual problem being, one of the issues raised in the 1917 strike (Thoms and Donnelly 2000; Hinton 1973). Immediately from the outbreak of hostilities the nature of Coventry's industry meant that involvement in the war could not be avoided. By 1915 the majority of engineering firms were involved in meeting Britain's strategic objectives. The Ordnance works, for example, quickly became a major supplier of motor components because, from its founding in 1905, it had not received substantial orders for field or naval guns. So only a relatively small number of men had knowledge of military weapons. However, the works were commanded to turn towards military guns and to direct attention to aviation (Beavan 1993). The Ordnance's War years output included 710 aircraft, 92 anti-aircraft guns, nearly 400.000 cartridge cases and some millions of fuses and detonators (ibid.; Trebilcock 1977).

The experience of firms during the War differed according to their readiness and whether or not their manpower or their management for that matter was capable of turning to military products, thereby availing themselves of the advantages offered through profitability of wartime contracts. By late 1916, with the exigencies of War, many Coventry firms were under state control although owners and managers still met from time to time at the Coventry and County Club to discuss matters of interest (Batchelor 2008). Singer, for example, made substantial profits through government munitions contracts. As Rover's 12 was too light a vehicle for military use, the firm had little alternative but to work on shells, fuse mortars and transmissions. Additionally, the firm carried out work on lorries and ambulances. This permitted motor output and motor cycle output to continue (Foreman-Peck 1981). Triumph supplied some thirty thousand of its motor cycles to the military, making it a major supplier of motorised transport.

Although it was one of the largest firms in the car industry, Daimler had little choice other than turning to munitions. Its primary contribution was a vast array of motorised transport to Allied forces. Additional pressure from the authorities gave the firm no option but to direct its attention to aviation work, tank engines, telegraphy stations as well as the three-ton lorries used as workshops in the event of failure elsewhere. The firm was also assigned the task of coordinating the building of the BR2 aero-engine, later used in the Sopwith Snipe. By the end of the War some eighty aircraft per annum were being produced (Thoms and Donnelly 2000). As noted by Batchelor, Daimler was supported by its parent company, the British Small Arms Company of Birmingham with whom it had merged in 1910, putting the company in a strong position to enter the aero industry (Batchelor 2008).

Siddeley-Deasy, too, became part of Coventry's war machine. Though not as large as Daimler as a whole, much of its effort was devoted to aircraft and continued to do so after the war ended. John Siddeley was regarded as the major figure in the aircraft industry having been involved since the War broke out. His factories were under War Office control and with the help of public funds and bank loans, he extended his premises and purchased new equipment. Within two years he had rented from Calcott Brothers and Swift premises for aircraft and motors. The building of land vehicles, lorries and field kitchens continued, but the firm's main interest lay in aircraft and aviation related items. Until 1917 most of Siddeley's output was dictated by the air force but a change in government policy allowed him to produce the Siddeley Puma aeroplane, which was widely used as it rolled off the line. Siddeley persevered with aircraft after the War and to some extent neglected cars which had very little development even after peace returned (Richardson 1972; Morewood 1990, 2004).

When War broke out, Standard concentrated on turning out munitions. Vast quantities of shells were made, and it was only in 1915 that it received its initial aircraft contract under which it became a controlled establishment. This first order was for fifty tubular-framed BE12s. By the time the peace was signed at Compiegne, the firm had made some 1600 aircraft, the most famous of which, the Sopwith Pup, proved popular with the Australian and Japanese air forces in the following decade (Richardson 1972). Its War-time operations brought Standard many benefits in that it was able to advance the assets of the company by purchasing premises in Leamington Spa and in the City of Coventry. But none of these compared with the purchase of Canley in 1915 for aircraft construction which turned out to be of great value to the firm when it reverted to normal car output. Further new premises were forthcoming and a hundred and ten-acre site was purchased beside the Canley works thanks to debentures, bank loans and profits made from government contracts. After the War, Canley became the prime site for motor production and remained so until its eventual closure when British Leyland collapsed in the 1970s (Thoms and Donnelly 2000; Gomes et al. 2010).

Though there were other firms and groups involved in the Coventry war effort, all were aware of the need to increase output and productivity. From time to time during the war, shortages of labour or materials hampered production. The labour situation was not helped either by enlistment procedures in the opening months of the war. This meant that factories soon had a shortage of skilled workers and employers were having to openly advertise for recruits despite their earlier encouragement for men to enlist. Such shortages soon affected engineering of all types as firms competed for labour. Migrant workers eased the situation somewhat. Batchelor has demonstrated how the council, the admiralty, the firms and to some extent, the government responded by building hostels and canteens to accommodate the workers to hopefully offset declining housebuilding from its low figure of nine hundred and seventy-seven in 1914. The response was still woefully inadequate to meet the requirements of a population which had swollen by around thirty-two thousand by 1917 (Batchelor 2008).

The problem of labour supply would be solved only by dilution and the subsequent employment of women and girls as neither of the main unions could meet the increased demand for skilled labour. The engineering fraternity had little option, but to employ females such was the shortage of men. Employing women had advantages in that labour costs were lower. It meant that some men were fired to enable their replacement by women deemed capable of carrying out work of a repetitive nature. The percentage of working-women rose during the war and narrowed thereafter. As men returned to their place of work, women remained an important part of the work force. Standard and Swift, for instance, kept women on the shop floor, thereby keeping hold of some jobs formerly the stronghold of their male counterparts. The employment of women in Coventry was relatively easy. Dilution had already taken place before war broke out. The ASE were willing to compromise because it could not supply the labour any more than could the National Union of Vehicle Builders (NUVB) (Thoms and Donnelly 2000; Donnelly and Thoms 1989).

Although the ASE had supported the Workers Union (WU), a relatively unskilled and new union, in its pre-war struggle for recognition, low wages and poor conditions, they had reservations about the narrowing of differentials. The WU was very strong on socialist rhetoric but had no history. The war-time ASE was more concerned with wages and conditions (Friedman 1977; Hinton 1973). Cooperation between the main unions became fraught. The ASE feared the rise of the WU might encroach on their areas of territory or jurisdiction as the war trundled on. For example, there was a refusal to submit joint pay claims and each usually insisted on separate conferences. Women gave the ASE a commitment to withdraw from male jobs at the close of hostilities but not to the WU. Most enmities remained below the surface and it was not until 1918 that trouble broke out between the unions when the WU refused to support the ASE's strike. Under the Occupations Act, both unions might have had members operating the same machinery. The ASE member would avoid conscription by being declared 'reserved' whereas the other would not. A great deal then depended on which union claimed their loyalty. Peace brought a type of compromise, but little else. Inter-Union rivalry continued throughout the inter-war period to the detriment of all unions and may explain why the area was a 'trades union desert' until the late thirties with power resting mainly with the employers (Tolliday 1984; Church 1994).

Conclusion

It is not without reason that the symbol of the City of Coventry is that of the Phoenix bird which immerses itself in flames only to rise again from the ashes into new life. So, too, with Coventry as it seems that every so often the city must reinvent itself to cope with economic change. This is undoubtedly true of the ribbon weavers and the watchmakers, both of whom suffered from Free Trade policies of the then government, but more importantly from their clinging to their own conservatism in failing to mechanise production and modernise. These hit the weavers and watchmakers hard. It exposed both to foreign competition, superior design and the factory system with its lower costs. In the latter case too much attention was paid to the upper end of the market which fits well with a philosophy of making a perfect timepiece rather than to one which produced a less expensive, perhaps slightly less accurate product which satisfied by far the majority of customers.

In 1860 Coventry had no tradition of engineering, relying on its craftsmen and other workers. By the end of that decade and in the years thereafter the city had to revitalise itself and turned to sewing machines, cycles and later to motor cars and machine tools. In other words, the City, given its resources, had little choice but to turn way from the traditional industries of cotton, coal, iron steel and shipbuilding upon which so much of Britain's wealth and position in the world was based and take its chance with the type of industry that was to dominate the country for most of the twentieth century. This meant embracing the emerging technologies of the period, namely light engineering, machine tools, interchangeable parts and increasing the size of industrial units alongside the ultimate demise of personal capital. By the outbreak of the First World War, the old back court type of operations was disappearing with a few leading cycle and motor firms dominating their respective industries as is common in emergent sectors. The days of the pioneer industrialist were almost over, being replaced by boards of directors and professional managers.

Externally, Coventry was forced to play its part in the world economy. Though cycles were designed and improved upon locally, early car design came from Europe, notably France. Cars initially were 'the rich man's toy' remaining that until around 1912. On the eve of hostilities, the light car appeared and brought vehicles within the purchase range of the middle and professional classes. Also, the City in exporting its products to the USA and Europe encountered foreign competition and import penetration, forcing the industries to react through lowering the price of cycles and latterly producing light vehicles.

Neither of the Boer wars had upset life in Britain, which had not fought a European War since the Crimean War, let alone a World War. Britain was changed as was Coventry. Population swelled, housing problems worsened, civilian production of cars declined rapidly and within a short space of time the city's economy was devoted to the War effort with government controlling what the major concerns produced, switching to producing munitions, lorries, tanks and ambulances. What is remarkable is how firms such as Siddeley's had little trouble in turning to aircraft production, how the machine tool sector responded, how quickly communications grew and how crucial the whole of the light engineering industries was to the British economy. Coventry was destined to be the fastest growing City in Britain between the two World Wars, symbolic of modern industry and a magnet to inwards migration.

Bibliography

Adeney, M. (1988). *The Motor Makers*. London: Collins.

Adeney, M. (1993). *The Motor Makers: The Turbulent History of Britain's Car Industry*. London: Collins.

Batchelor. L. A. (2008). *A Great Munitions Centre: Coventry's Armaments and Munitions* (Unpublished M.Phil. thesis). Coventry University.

Batchelor, L. A. (2009). *A Great Munitions' Centre: Coventry's Arms and Munitions Industry, 1914–1918* (Unpublished M.Phil.). Coventry University, Coventry.

Beaven, B. J. (1993). Reconstructing the Business Community; the Small Firm in the No. 72.

Beavan, B. J. (1994). *The Growth and Significance of the Coventry Car Components Industry 1885–1939* (Unpublished Ph.D.). De Montfort University.

Brittain, R. R. (1989). *The Machine Tool Industry in Coventry 1880–1939* (Unpublished). Coventry University, Coventry.

Caunter, C. F. (1957). *The History and Development of Light Cars*. London: HMSO.

Census Reports, 1801–1911.

Church, R. A. (1975). Nineteenth Clock Technology in Britain, United States and Switzerland. *Economic History Review*, 2nd Series, *XXXVIII*(4), 616–630.

Church, R. A. (1979). Markets and Marketing in the British Motor Industry Before 1914. *Journal of Transport History, 3,* 1–20.

Church, R. A. (1994). *The Rise and Decline of the British Motor Industry*. London: Macmillan.

Davies. J. McG. (1983). *Social Relations in an Engineering Factory (Alfred Herbert Ltd., 1887–1992)* (Unpublished Ph.D.). University of Warwick, Coventry.

Davies, J. McG. (1986). A Twentieth Century Paternalist: Alfred Herbert and the Coventry Workman. In W. Lancaster & T. Mason (Eds.), *Life and Labour in a Twentieth Century City*. Coventry: Cryfield Press, University of Warwick.

Davis, M. (1985). *Everyman His Own Landlord*. Coventry: Coventry Building Society.

Davy, J. (1964). *The Standard Motor Car 1903–1963*. Coventry: Sherbourne Press.

Donnelly, T., & Durham, M. (1989). *Labour Relations in the Coventry Motor Industry 1896–1939: A Guide to the records of the AUEW*. Coventry: Coventry Polytechnic.

Foreman-Peck, P. (1979). *Tariff Protection and the Economies of Scale: the British Motor Industry Before 1939* (New Series, Vol. 31). Oxford: Oxford Economic Papers.

Foreman-Peck, J. (1981). *Exit, Voice and Loyalty as a Response to Decline: The Rover Company in the Inter-War Years*. Business History, Vol. XXIII.

Foreman-Peck, J. (1983). *Diversification and the Growth of the Firm: The Rover Company to 1914*. Business History, Vol. XXV.

Friedman, A. (1977). *Industry and Labour*. London: Macmillan.

Gomes, E., Collis, C., Donnelly, T., & Morris, D. (2010). *Mergers and Acquisitions as Strategic Methods of Business Development in the Global Automobile Industry*. Lampeter and New York: Edwin Mellen Press.

Harrison, A. E. (1969). The Competitiveness of the British Cycle Industry. *Economic Review*, 2nd Series, *XXII*(2), 287–303.

Harrison, A. E. (1981). Joint Stock Company Flotation in the Cycle, Motor Vehicle and Related Industries. *Business History, XXIII*, 165–190.

Hemsley, B. (2013). *Riots, and Ribbon, Part 1, Heritage and Culture*. www.ourwarwickshire.org.uk.

Hinton, J. (1973). *The First Shop Stewards Movement*. London: Allen and Unwin.

Lancaster, B. (1985). Who's a Real Coventry Kid? Migration into Twentieth Century Coventry. In B. Lancaster & T. Mason (Eds.), *Life and Labour in a Twentieth Century City*. Coventry: Cryfield Press, University of Warwick.

Lane, J. (1977). *A Register of the Business Records of Coventry and Related Areas*. Department of Politics and History, Coventry Polytechnic, Coventry.

Langley, A. (2015). *Former Silk Ribbon-Weaving Factory in Coventry*. Our Warwickshire. www.ourwarwickshire.org.

Lewchuk, W. (1987). *American Technology and the British Motor Vehicle Industry*. Cambridge: Cambridge University Press.

Lloyd's Bank Coventry. (1907, November 5 and 7). White and Poppe Accounts.

Lowe, J. (1982). *A Guide to Sources in the History of the Cycle and Motor Industries in Coventry 1880–1939*. Centre for Business History, Coventry Polytechnic, Coventry.

Morewood, S. (1990). *Pioneers and Inheritors, 1896–1972: Top Management in the Coventry Motor Industry*. Centre for Business History, Coventry University.

Morewood, S. (2004). *John Siddeley, First Baron Kenilworth*. Dictionary of National Biography. Oxford: Oxford University Press.

Noon, S. (2013). *Silk Ribbon Weaving*. Nuneaton: Nuneaton Memories.

O'Gallagher, C. (1974). *Payne and Bates of Coventry: Pioneer Motor Manufacturers*. Warwickshire History, Vol 5.

Perkin, H. (1979). *The History of the Cycle Industry in Coventry 1896–1912* (Unpublished Dissertation: Degree of B.A. Modern Studies). Coventry Polytechnic, Coventry.

Price, B. (1978). *The Lea Francis Story*. London: Batsford.

Richardson, K. E. (1972). *Twentieth Century Coventry*. Coventry: City of Coventry.

Saul, S. B. (1962). The Motor Industry in Britain. *Business History, 5*(1), 22–44.

Saul, S. B. (1968). The Engineering Industry. In D. H. Aldcroft (Ed.), *The Development of British Industry and Foreign Competition 1875–1914*. London: Allen and Unwin.

Searby, P. (1976). Watchmaking in Coventry, Warwickshire Local History Society, Warwick, Vol. 3.

Stephen, W. B. (Ed.). (1969). *The City: Crafts and Industries, Modern Industry and Trade in a History of the County of Warwick, Vol. 8, the City of Coventry and Borough of Warwick*. London: VCR.

Thoms, D., & Donnelly, T. (1985). Coventry's Industrial Economy. In B. Lancaster & T. Mason (Eds.), *Life and Labour in a Twentieth Century City*. Coventry: Cryfield Press, University of Warwick.

Thoms, D., & Donnelly, T. (2000). *The Coventry Motor Industry: Birth to Renaissance*. Aldershot: Ashgate.

Tolliday, S. (1984). *Trade Unions and Collective Bargaining in the Motor Industry 1896–1870*. Paper presented to the Conference on the International Automobile Industry and its Workers. Dept. of Politics and History, Coventry (Lanchester) Polytechnic, Coventry.

Trebilcock, C. (1977). *Vickers Brothers: Armaments and Enterprise*. London: Europa.

Tripp, D. (1956). *Renold Chains*. London: Allen and Unwin.

Whyte, K. (1979). *Company Heritage: Chrysler U.K.* (Unpublished Dissertation: Postgraduate Diploma in Managerial Studies). I am grateful to the late John D. McIntyre, Head of Department of Management Studies at Coventry Polytechnic for giving me a copy of the afore mentioned Dissertation.

Wood, J. (1988). *Wheels of Misfortune: The Rise and Fall of the British Motor Industry*. London: Sidgwick and Jackson.

3

Coventry at War: Industrial Relations, Ownership and Production

Malte Busch

One of the key arguments posited to explain the demise of the motor industry in Coventry and the subsequent deindustrialisation experienced by the city as whole focuses on the role of international competition and the opening up of global markets. The failure of motor manufacturers across the UK, but in particular in Coventry, to adequately respond to the challenges posed at the end of the 1960s by an influx of new technologies, processes and Foreign Direct Investment from international rivals, served to fatally undermine the sector and lead to a period of dramatic change in the economic base of the city. The reasons for this failure to compete has been widely discussed in the literature, usually in terms of management, structural challenges, weak product development, intransigent trades unions and national policy considerations (Dunnett 1980; Whisler 1999; Thoms and Donnelly 2000). Perhaps less appreciated and discussed was the role of wartime production and government intervention during a critical period for Coventry's industrial base from the mid-1930s to the end of the Second World War. During these years the use of shadow

M. Busch (✉)
Coventry University, Coventry, UK

J. Begley et al. (eds.), *Revival of a City*, Palgrave Studies in Economic History,
https://doi.org/10.1007/978-3-030-22822-4_3

factories to increase production and the means by which they were operated served to skew the normal operations of the market for key industrial actors within the city. What will be demonstrated here is that the rapidity of the rollout of the scheme itself, allied to war pressures led to growing overspecialisation.

This chapter explores the economic development of Coventry City and its environs during the interwar and post-war years. In particular it seeks to understand how the economic focus of the local economy that emerged after the war's end, with its emphasis primarily on metal engineering, vehicle manufacturing and the aero industry, contributed to later deindustrialisation. The decline of Coventry's industrial base reached its peak in the 1970s when the effects of increasing globalisation and market competition became more palpable. The reasons for the erosion of Coventry City's advantageous position in terms of manufacturing output may be traced back to the shape of Coventry's industrial base in the 1930s and its expansion of these activities up to and during the Second World War.

This chapter focuses on Coventry's economic development by providing insights into the operations of the Shadow Factory Scheme(s), an integral component of British plans for rearmament after 1935, and other related factors, for example the suppression of market activities due to the monopsony relationship that emerged between industrialists and government officials. Other factors considered include the logistical and organisational challenge of managing the influx of 50,000 new workers to the city. Arguably this injection of labour, which increased the presence of skilled specialists in a particular sphere of manufacturing, also impacted post-war decision-making around industrial specialisation and market exports.

The reaction of key figures in local authorities to the rapidly growing labour force serves to contextualise the impact of the arrival of the new labour force. It will be shown how the interactions and the different interests of some local officials potentially anticipated future problems with the local economy and attempted to plan for these eventualities as early as 1940. While producing goods to win the war remained the key focus of all concerned, the views offered by local officials give some valuable insights into the challenges of shifting from a war economy back to peacetime operations. They also cast post-war industrial specialisation in the city in a more revealing light.

Context of Industry

The manufacture of cars and their components developed slowly in the 1890s but accelerated quickly after the turn of the century. By 1907 there were 5372 workers involved in cycle and motor manufacturing (excluding dealers) out of an occupied population of 22,255 (Richardson 1972). Donnelly explores this transformation in an earlier chapter of this book, but suffice to say by 1913, on the verge of the First World War, the industrialist Alfred Herbert was moved to say "We in Coventry are largely concerned with motors" (Thoms and Donnelly 1985). By this time motor firms in Coventry accounted for one third of total automotive vehicle output in Britain. Maxcy and Silberston (1959) state that this growth was due to easy entry requirements for the industry at this nascent stage of its development. Coventry, with its existing expertise in watch-making, engineering and tool-making, was ideally placed for becoming a major centre of vehicle production in the UK (Maxcy and Silbertson 1959; Richardson 1972).

The outbreak of war in 1914 saw corresponding expansion of industrial premises in Coventry as firms moved to prepare for war production. This capital investment was matched by an influx of labour, as the population grew from 119,000 to 133,000 peoples approximately, despite wartime recruitment. During these years the British government also introduced a range of duties on luxury goods to protect domestic firms. This meant that in the immediate aftermath of the war Coventry firms were able to enjoy burgeoning domestic markets without international competition. At this time the operations of the war had established the worth of the motor vehicle as never before. Thousands of men and women who might never have driven a vehicle had been exposed to their operation during the war, generating fresh demand for affordable vehicles (Adeney 1988). Over the next two decades the British motor industry enjoyed a golden era, only slightly tarnished by the slump in demand in the early 1930s.

By the late 1930s the automotive industry in the UK was the second most successful one in the world after the USA. Coventry had been one of Britain's key motor cities with a strong manufacturing industry that grew for decades until the 1960s. The success of Britain's motor industry in the 1930s went hand-in-hand with a consolidation of automotive producers. While there were around 96 car producing companies in the UK in 1922, there were only 18 manufacturers by the end of the 1930s (Thoms and Donnelly 1985). By the middle of the decade the car market was controlled by the 'Big Six' automotive manufacturers consisting of Singer (which would be eclipsed by Rootes later in the decade) and Standard along with Ford, Vauxhall, Morris and Austin in the volume end of the trade (Donnelly et al. 2001). The presence of so many Coventry firms in the 'Big Six' was indicative of the indelible relationship between motors and Coventry city in the interwar years. However, Rootes and Standard still only accounted for approximately 18–20% of the market share between them in 1939, compared to the industry leader Morris with 26% market share. While the city acquired a strong automotive volume production presence before the war, it did not become the dominant centre of production in the UK that it had the potential to achieve (Thoms and Donnelly 2000).

Growth in the sector also carried with it an inherent danger of narrowing the economic base of a mid-sized city like Coventry. The city's over reliance and dependence on a few industrial areas such as metal engineering, vehicles and other metal industries, all associated with or dependent upon the motor sector, becomes clearly evident when comparing the percentage of employed people in these occupations with the national average in the UK. In 1939, 62% of all employed people worked in the above-mentioned industries, while it was only 15% on average, nationally. In 1946, it even rose to 70% in Coventry, while the national average increased only slightly to 17.4% (Thoms and Donnelly 1985). Crucial to overspecialisation in Coventry too was the involvement of a number of core engineering and automotive firms located in the city in armament production as part of the government's plans for war preparation.

The Shadow Factory Scheme(s)

Shadow factories explain both the use of "duplicated facilities under the direct control of the parent company, as well as distributed facilities managed by other companies with appropriate skills" (Little and

Grieco 2011). These factories were seen as an important pillar of the war economy in the UK. In 1936, the British Cabinet passed Scheme F as a reaction to Nazi Germany's re-armament and expansion efforts. The requirements of the previous schemes A and C could be met by the existing aircraft producers, however there was the insight that additional producers and factories were required for Scheme F (Stone 2017). The objective was to increase the number of aircrafts to 8000 and to achieve parity with Germany's military forces.

In May 1936, representatives of the British government met with key industrialists from Coventry and the Midlands to discuss the plan and the necessity of building additional factories. The result were shadow factories, which were constructed next to the existing automotive factories to facilitate the management of the factories by the automotive manufacturers and to optimise production. Skills transfers of the managerial class and the knowhow of the skilled automotive workers were also facilitated, the latter whose mindset was further shaped by the requirements of mass production. However, with the increasing menace of Nazi Germany, the government required greater volumes from the aircraft producers than in the years before and relied on the competence of the automotive producers. The plants needed to be built quickly and posed major challenges for the car and engine manufacturers who operated the shadow factories, as well as for Coventry Council that had to deal with the infrastructural changes. Challenges such as the shortage of skilled labour and the infrastructural problems, which were accompanied by an increasing influx of people and supply of goods will be discussed later in the chapter.

The decision to organise the scheme utilising private entrepreneurs merits some discussion, explaining as it does the development of Coventry's local economy before and during the war, with the subsequent impact on production and goods in the post war era. Forbes (2015) emphasises the ideological concerns for the British government in how they integrated private firms into nationally and centrally controlled armament production. As Forbes explains it, the challenge for civil servants was to;

> Find a way in peacetime not only to produce armaments and synthetic products but also to lay down the capacity to satisfy, in the event of war, an highly uncertain level of future demand. (2015)

This would require considerable coordination and control over input and output, anathema to the normal operations of the market. In Nazi Germany this took the form of price controls, rationing, reallocation of labour and raw materials, protectionism and foreign exchange control. However, the state did not use coercion to force engagement, preferring voluntary cooperation of firms. In Britain there was a reluctance to emulate such methods and concede the benefits of authoritarian rule in preparing for war. As the leading industrialist William Weir, in his role as Adviser to the Air Ministry, explained it, "it was essential to find a compromise solution rather than copying wholesale the systems of centralised dictatorships" (Shay 1977).

The precursor to the Shadow Factory Scheme(s) was the agency factories from the First World War. During this period the British government had requisitioned and built industrial complexes under the auspices of the Ministry of Munitions to supply the war effort. This process had been expedited after shortfalls in shells and ammunition in spring of 1915 (Wingrove 2015). However, there was a reluctance to introduce a state owned and operated armaments industry for fear it would upset the market and unbalance the economy, or at the very least lose the goodwill and support of private business. Instead the British government were ideologically disposed to factories that were run by private entrepreneurs. The shadow scheme was a way for the state to pay and own munitions factories that would meet the needs of wartime, but have them operated more efficiently by experienced industrialists in the private sector (Forbes 2015). Locating the factories also incurred considerable thought, faced as the government was by an array of geographical challenges, strategic issues, risk factors and opportunity costs. In part, Coventry's reputation as the home of car production in Britain, its readily available automotive engineering presence and core of skilled labour, the well-established industrial base, as well as the low degree of unionisation may be considered as factors that persuaded the government to make Coventry an important location for the Shadow Factory Scheme(s) (Thoms and Donnelly 1985; Thoms 1989).

Operations of the Shadow Factory Scheme(s)

The discussions about producing aircraft in shadow factories had started at the end of the 1920s, but it was in the mid 1930s that the scheme took on a new level of import. In February 1936 intense discussions that had been going since the previous year culminated in the decision to initiate 'Scheme F', which provided for the expansion of the British air force by 8000 front line planes, including aircraft that were just emerging from the design stage. On the government side, Lord Swinton who led the Air Ministry, was in charge of coordinating logistics and output targets for the shadow scheme. Key individuals such as Sir Christopher Bullock, Lord Swinton and Lord William Weir realised that the aero industry alone would not be able to produce the required amount of aircrafts. Therefore, the Air Ministry intended to include major motor vehicle manufacturers such as Austin, Humber (Rootes), Wolseley, Daimler, Standard, Singer, and Rover in the production of aero engines (Thoms 1989).

In May the initiative was put to a meeting of Midland auto manufacturers; Lord Austin, Spencer Wilks of Rover, John Black of Standard and William Rootes. Geoffrey Burton was also in attendance but conspicuous by his absence was William Morris. The proposal put to the group by the government was to use their skills, experience and organisational know-how to enter into the aero design and manufacture business. In exchange the government would invest in new plants and equipment, the automakers would manage them and receive a fee for doing so. Auditors would be on site but would not be involved in the running of the factories (Richardson 1972). Herbert Austin was appointed the chairman of the committee that represented these motor-producing companies, effectively putting him in control of production.

This co-ordinating committee was involved in the decision-making process that only the Bristol Aeroplane Company (BAC) and Austin build complete engines, whereas the other companies should produce selected components. This had also accommodated BAC's concerns that the vehicle producers would get their hands on too much industry specific knowhow. However, the decision to split production was not well-received by some members of the committee to oversee aero engine production. Car makers such as Rover, Standard, and Lord Nuffield's Morris were opposed to the split system (Thoms 1989). The problem with a split system of production was that it presumed equal levels of competence amongst all producers. In other words, if one firm was to fall behind in production, it would slow down or halt production across all firms in the chain. Completing engines in totality across a number of plants also meant that if factories were damaged in an air raid, the others could keep operating, albeit at a reduced capacity, whereas in a split system destroying one link in the chain would stop production entirely. Moreover, the split production system was not untested, as vulnerabilities regarding labour strikes, poor processing or air raids in one of the individual components producing firms could lead to interruptions of the production of complete engines. However, Lord Swinton's hope was that measures taken by the committee of the motor vehicle companies would sort out these obstacles.

In 1938, Sir Kingsely Wood took over from Lord Swinton who was Secretary of State for Air from 1935. Wood was installed after MPs such as Winston Churchill heavily criticised Lord Swinton's Air Ministry for the slow progress of the shadow scheme (see e.g. Carverhill 2018). By 1939, the numbers of planes being produced were below expectations. In part this was due to the slower than expected ramping up of production, but equally the impact of new designs for aircraft, such as the Stirling and Lancaster, required new production facilities. The solution was to initiate a second wave of factory buildings. The Czech invasion by Germany expedited this process. Manufacturers already in charge of one factory were offered a second over the phone. A second shadow group, comprised of Daimler, Rootes, Rover and standard, was set up and worked in pairs to produce aircraft engines (Robson 2011; Thoms and Donnelly 1985; Thoms 1989; Richardson 1972). William Rootes took over the running of the second group in 1940 and by the beginning of 1943, all twelve of Coventry's shadow factories were functioning and in the following year their combined output reached 800 engines a month (Richardson 1972; Thoms and Donnelly 1985).

The impact on Coventry in terms of occupational activity as a consequence of the decision to set up the shadow factories was stark. In terms of numbers of workers, there were sharp increases in all employment in manufacturing and ancillary activities. The number of engineers in the city increased from 4165 in 1932 to 8937 just six years later. Those involved in support industries went from 1420 to 1989, while those in vehicle and aircraft manufacture grew from 29,658 to 41,825. These were peace time increases and before the new plant had even begun to reach full production. The influx of workers after the outbreak of war would only make this concentration of specialised labour even more pronounced (Richardson 1972). Initially, however, the greater challenge for the city came with the problems presented by tens of thousands of workers being brought into the city in a very short space of time.

Reaction of Local Authority to Shadow Scheme

The Shadow Factory Scheme(s) posed tremendous challenges to the local authorities and led to tensions between Coventry City officials, industrialists and representatives of Whitehall. Three ministerial departments were involved in locating and building factories for the scheme; the Air Ministry, the Ministry of Health and the Ministry of Labour and National Service. What became very clear from early exchanges was the low priority the City Council held in discussions relating to locating sites for firms, putting in place necessary services to support these firms and dealing with the consequences of the influx of labour associated with the shadow scheme.

An example of such is supplied by the decision to instigate a second wave of factory building that occurred in 1939. Prior to this date the actions of the scheme had prompted few complaints from the Council, at least in the record of minutes from the period. In contrast the rapidity of the second wave of shadow factories, allied to the impending conflict that appeared ever closer triggered much more concern. In April 1939 Daimler Co. Ltd. applied to the City of Coventry Town and planning committee for an extension to their factory for aero engine production. Part of the land was to be designated for immediate use, with the rest subject to use in a national emergency (CCA/1/4/42/4). This prompted a letter from the Coventry Town Clerk to John Keel at the Air Ministry, expressing concern over land purchases around Coventry which the council perceived as related to the Shadow Factory Scheme(s) on 16 May. While the proposed land was outside the immediate boundaries of the city, the council was concerned that existing development plans would be pushed off track (Herbert Archives CCA/3/1/7601/1-4). This letter in turn provoked an exchange between the council and Daimler.

A further letter from the town clerk to Daimler's George Hallyon, dated 29 May 1939, indicated the dismay of Coventry Council's representative considering the lack of notice regarding Daimler's plans build a shadow factory next to the company's Brown Lane plant in Coventry (Coventry Council, letters of correspondence). A week before, on 22 May 1939, the town clerk Smith was informed by Daimler's general manager about the estimate that the corporation's "new factory would require about 2½ times the amount of water, gas, electricity and drainage which our existing factory is now using" (Herbert Archives CCA/3/1/7601/1-4).

The concern for the council was threefold; in the first instance Coventry Council perceived that it was bypassed in the decision-making processes between the companies which participated in the scheme and ministries in London, such as the Air Ministry. The spectre of town planning fifteen years in the making coming undone was a fearful one for the council, a fact driven home by a representation made by the council to members of Parliament (Herbert Archives CCA/3/1/7601/1-4). The second major concern for the council was the anticipated influx of workers and the subsequent strain these workers would have on the city's services; health, education and most importantly housing. It is the latter point that offers a deeper insight into the third major concern for the council. On 7 December 1939, after the conflict had begun, but during a period of prolonged inactivity, the council minutes recorded the following;

> The corporation place on record that they will offer the most strenuous opposition to any scheme for the provision of temporary hutments as a purported solution of the housing problem. Their experience of the

> schemes of this character which were undertaken in Coventry during the war of 1914-18 was lamentable and disastrous. It was only recently, after twenty years of expense and difficulty that the last of the temporary hutments were cleared away as "slums". Under no circumstances will the corporation willingly assent to the repetition of such an unfortunate experiment. (Herbert Archives CCA/3/1/7601/1-4).

This statement of intent resulted from a report from the Coventry Engineering Employers Federation just days before that estimated 35,000 additional skilled workers would need to be brought into Coventry by 1940 to assist with wartime production. Here then was the final and arguably most pressing issue for the council, namely that the same mistakes as happened in WWI would not reoccur and leave the city in dire circumstances for decades after the war.

However, these concerns of the council do not appear to have been a priority for national government. In a written response to the town clerk on the 23 May 1939 the General Manager of the Daimler Company, writing on behalf of the Air Ministry, apologising for the handling of the factory extension. The second part of the following quote from Daimler's general manager confirms the view that local council concerns were low on the list of priorities;

> It was our desire that the whole of this scheme should be discussed with the corporation before matters had proceeded too far, but we were instructed by the representatives of the Air Ministry to leave all the matters relating to the acquisition of the land in their hands. (Herbert Archives, letters of correspondence)

The air Ministry later clarified that they left everything up to the local people and things had "fallen between two stools" (CCA/3/1/7601/1-4). The council were keenly aware of the problem, attributing oversights to sub-divisions within government departments failing to liaise with each other. This was not the only instance of imposition placed upon the local authorities by the concentration of manufacturing activities in Coventry in such a short period of time by poorly coordinated central government. The establishment of shadow factories in brown lane and

Broad Lane incurred costs of £14,850 to the council, of which the Air Ministry contributed £2500 (ibid., June 2).

On the 22 June the council received an outraged letter from the Browns Lane and District Ratepayers and Residents Association as the land occupied by the new factories had been earmarked for residential housing. This prompted a letter from the Town Clerk to the House of Commons bemoaning the lack of consultation with the Air Ministry. Despite reassurances from Walter Elliott, Minister of Health, that future consultation would occur, the relegation of Council issues by government departments became a recurring theme for the first year and a half of the war. This would reach a new level when it came to the issue of housing workers.

Local Authorities and the Implementation of the Shadow Factory Scheme(s) in Coventry

Among the key challenges when implementing the Shadow Factory Scheme(s) were the infrastructural changes required to house tens of thousands of new workers as well as the additional need for gas, water, electricity, and drainage. Coventry had already been undergoing significant expansion of the workforce before the war. Lancaster and Mason (1986) estimates that approximately 42,000 migrants arrived to the city between 1931 and 1939. The arrival of these semi-skilled migrants also created significant issues for local society (ibid., 1986). Coventry City was under pressure to provide housing and education even before the second wave of Shadow Factory Scheme(s) placed an enormous burden on council resources.

On 3 November John Black of Standard contacted the council inquiring as to the availability of housing. The council was unmoved without financial recompense, and instead encouraged Black to approach the Air Ministry. A fortnight later Billy Rootes contacted the council to complain about the suspension of building work for their 4000–5000 workers in need. When the council again refused to help, Alfred Herbert, a noted Coventry industrialist, was moved to intervene.

In the course of a letter strongly criticising the perceived truculence of the council, Herbert observed,

> When the war is over, whether we win it, or lose it, Coventry will have to go through a time of depressions of much greater severity than ever before, and many existing houses will be vacant and will probably fall into decay. (CCA/3/1/7601/1-4)

The most interesting aspect of this exchange was the willingness of Herbert to mortgage Coventry City's future for the war effort. The challenges of Coventry's post-war development can be located, partially, in the pre-war and wartime period of rearmament, with firms prioritising rapid weapons production over more carefully planned industrial expansion in parallel to measured town planning to support this growth. What is perhaps not always appreciated is how firm owners at least anticipated some of the subsequent structural problems that would accrue from such an approach that would be such a feature of post-war reconstruction.

On 25 November members of the Shadow Scheme committee sent a message to the Air Ministry stating that temporary housing should be sufficient for the new workers considering that there are already many houses vacant (since many young people had left for war). However, one of Coventry Council's representatives, Mr. Varley, contradicted this assessment by stating that these vacant houses were not fit for long-term occupation, as they were vacant only between tenancies, sometimes just for a week. In a bid to make clear the full challenge, the council sought the Shadow Scheme Committee to translate their concerns to the Air Ministry. Letters from Coventry's archive indicate that the Government in London was more responsive to local industrialists than to the Coventry Council. It is telling that a town clerk had to entreat the committee to rouse the Air Ministry since the Council had written five or six times to the Air Ministry and sent two wires, however, these efforts did not elicit a response. A certain frustration and defiance were reflected in the following statement from the town clerk to members of the committee,

> As a matter of fact, I do not believe that they have given the matter any consideration whatever to the problem of obtaining labour, and that they are now hoping, by delaying the matter, to get the local authority into the position of solving the problem somehow in their own way and at their own cost. The present city council, however, will, definitely, not tolerate this. (Coventry City Council, letters of correspondence, 30 November 1939)

These observations were not without basis. A scoping exercise undertaken by the council in early 1940 shows the estimated cost of the new phase of the scheme to local authorities in Coventry. New housing, land acquisition, roads and sewerage would require £2,725,000. New schooling was estimated at £340,450. Additional transport for workers, £112,000. However, these figures were the higher end of the cost spectrum and would be offset by wage expenditure and rates increases. Perhaps more telling was the anticipated costs of road and works improvements, including land purchases near the new shadow factories to help make production and transport of goods more effective. This expenditure was to be offset by government grants, but there was a notable distance between the anticipated costs, as shown in Table 3.1 (CCA/3/1/7601/1-4).

Again, it would seem that planning from central government was broad stroke in nature. In fact, much of the decision-making around locations and production methods were largely left to industrialists.[1] In turn, as noted above, industrialists were willing to make sacrifices to ensure the winning of the war, engaging in split production and rapid building to support this industrial system. Long-term development was not the priority, as demonstrated by Herbert's solution to accommodation which was to introduce 'hutments' or other such temporary accommodation, rather than by "slow, expensive and ultimately redundant building schemes" (A. Herbert, letter to the City Council, 25 November 1939, Letters of Correspondence, CCA/3/1/7601/1-4).

In the event, the problem of housing was resolved in a number of ways, using a combination of billeting, other temporary accommodation

[1]Author's conversation with Prof. T. Donnelly.

Table 3.1 Coventry Council estimated costs of road works for shadow factories

	Cost	Ministry of Transport Grant	Net cost
	£	£	£
Banner Lane	31,070		31,070
Broad Lane	5567	1875	3692
Broad Lane (West)	31,040	15,520	15,520
Tile Hill lane	22,400	10,000	12,400
Butt Lane	12,000		12,000
Town Planning road, Allesley	13,600		13,600
Windmill Hill	10,000		10,000
Road across Hearsall Common	42,000	21,000	21,000
Brownshill green road	25,000		25,000
Total	192,677	48,395	144,282

Source City of Coventry Town and planning committee, Minute book 4, 1939

and transporting of labour from surrounding towns. Furthermore, in March and April, agreements were reached with government officials to recompense the city council after the war. These promises, alongside the decision to raise rates, gave the council the necessary means to surmount the immediate challenges of investment costs. However, such solutions were ad hoc and transitory, in effect postponing dealing with the problems of rapid industrialisation until the war was finished.

For their part Coventry's captains of industry also faced significant pressure from various government departments to increase production for wartime needs. A letter of correspondence in early 1941 captured much of the frustration of Coventry's industrialists with the demands being made by the Air Ministry in particular, when it was noted in reference to the new shadow factories "We are getting all kinds of conflicting Departments interfering with the progress of our designs and it will be an awful job to get it going" (PA2567/4/202). Further aggravation arose from the perception that international rivals were already planning for post-war industrial competition with the UK while government officials were still focussed on arms production (PA2567/4/202). It was this backdrop of impatience and a general air of urgency that served to contextualise the relationship between Coventry labour and industry during the war years.

Coventry at War

The Second World War came as something of a surprise for many motor producers and led to puzzlement and difficulties for local authorities, as noted above (Thoms and Donnelly 1985). It also impacted on the natural operations of the market, for example, in 1939, Rootes could not deliver its vehicles to dealers, as the army made clear that these goods were now needed for the war effort. The government's instructions to produce aircrafts, armaments and fighting vehicles came fast and demanded quick adjustments of production patterns. Not all production was for the air force, for example 25,000 water pumps were built in the city, as well as generators for emergency lighting. Herbert's delivered 65,000 machine tools between 1939 and 1944. But the bulk of the productive effort went to aircraft production, with just one firm, BTH, producing 500,000 magnetos for planes (Richardson 1972).

Coventry's motor manufacturers had to cope with a range of difficulties such as a shortage of raw materials, lack of factory accommodation and a lack of skilled workers, which was further exacerbated by the army draft. Moreover, people outside of Coventry were less inclined to work in the city due to the lack of adequate housing and the danger of air raids, which could not be dismissed considering that there were around 40 air raids from 1940 to 1941 (Richardson 1972). Accordingly, by 1941, 60% of the employees in Coventry worked in the engineering industries while other sectors remained undeveloped and neglected. This "exaggerated overspecialisation" had been exacerbated by the expansion of the motor and aircraft sector while other, already underdeveloped sectors were shrinking (Thoms and Donnelly 1985). This 'occupational profile' continued to endure until 1945.

The concentration of workers in engineering was also fostered by improved wage bargaining. The outbreak of war had made competition for skilled labour acute. Migrant workers helped partially fill the demand gap. Recruitment of women was also used to address the labour shortage, however it proved difficult for engineering firms to attract female recruits, in particularly married women; consequently, the engineering sector in the Midlands suffered from labour shortages generally until 1944 (Donnelly and Thoms 1989). This was further aggravated by the management decision to increase working hours by 20% or more at the outbreak of the conflict, a strategy that would be maintained until the later stages of the war. Inducements were required to attract and retain labour and so, after government legislation restricted labour movement in the summer of 1940, a new agreement with labour was considered timely to renegotiate a higher level of pay.

The Coventry Tool Room Agreement of 1941 meant a clear break in the relationship between workers and management. Toolroom workers' pay rates were determined by a weighted average of the standard hourly earnings of the skilled workers in twenty to thirty establishments. These were then adopted, after a three-month lag, as the Coventry District Toolroom Rate (Knowles and Robinson 1969). The agreement was backed by all engineering companies in Coventry and protected the incomes of apprentice-trained craftsmen. It had major consequences for the entire engineering industry until its termination in 1971 and led to increased wages, as other groups of workers in associated sectors used it as a guide for their own wage negotiations (Flanders 1957; Knowles and Robinson 1969; Brown 1971).

This translated into a surge in wages, with standard hourly earnings of skilled production workers in Coventry rising from 3s 4d in 1941 to 5s in 1944 (Knowles and Robinson 1969). Alongside the growth in wages came the strengthening of the organisation of labour by unions in the war years. In particular the gang system became an integral part of production as management pragmatically ceded control of the work floor to shop stewards in particular, in a bid to increase productivity (Lancaster and Mason 1986; Richardson 1972). Tolliday's[2] discussion of Standard Motor's use of the gang system is revealing in terms of how the exigencies of wartime lead to a largely non-unionised firm being 80–90% organised by the war's end (Lancaster and Mason 1986). Mallier and Rosser (1982) conclude that this decision made sense during the conflict but was detrimental to progress thereafter. Senior management relied on elected gangers, who frequently doubled as shop

[2]This essay can be found in Lancaster's volume of Coventry inspired articles.

stewards. This made change difficult and frequently resisted. Ewart (2011) concurs with this assessment, describing the role of gangers as being quasi-managerial with stewards effectively controlling access to employment and having, by extension, a significant role in decision-making around output. While large scale disputes were few, they maintained the status quo and limited attempts at reform.

The Post-war Challenge

From an employers' perspective, high wages and powerful shop stewards were a necessity of wartime production. However, as the war increasingly entered its final phase, management and workers alike began to consider what the post-war Coventry world would look like. In 1944, workers anticipated the conflict was reaching a conclusion and feared large scale redundancies were planned. In some companies rumours seeped through that the management planned to cut personnel by up to 25% (Thoms 1989). Towards the end of the war motor manufacturers were uncertain about converting their premises back to peace time operations and were worried that the high wages would become a problem when facing international competition. Accordingly, different interests collided and the tone of the companies towards the workers became agitated, for example, Humber in 1945 (Thoms and Donnelly 1985). This unrest was not aided by a decline in wages, as during 1944–1945 earnings for skilled labour fell by up to a shilling per hour (Knowles and Robinson 1969).

The workers and the unions did not want to go back to pre-war salaries and the companies were not willing to keep the wage level high. Announced layoffs led to strikes. In 1945, for example, 5000 workers at Humber stopped working for nine days, which further worsened relations with the company. Workers reduced their productivity and companies reacted with mass redundancies. As a consequence, both sides agreed that there could be no return to the period of poor labour relations between the two world wars (Thoms and Donnelly 2000). Furthermore, as Donnelly and Thoms (1989) observe, the partnership between firms that had been the hallmark of the war years began to give way to companies, notably automotive manufacturers, acting independently once more, while trade unions continued to benefit from war time organisation. This left the Coventry labour force in a relatively strong position in terms of work negotiations after 1945.

Continued specialisation also influenced this situation. Measures between 1940 and 1945 contributed to developments that led to a deindustrialisation of the region. The strong focus on engineering industries in Coventry and the neglect of other sectors can be attributed to the concentration of shadow factories in the area during the time of the war. After 1945, many local manufacturers such as Massey Ferguson and Jaguar continued to use the premises of the former shadow factories. Accordingly, an industrial reorientation did not take place after the war and engine and automotive companies continued to dominate the local economy. Moreover, companies such as Singer, Daimler, and BSA survived the war years due to government contracts as opposed to being competitive in the market, which did not auger well for renewed trade (Thoms 1989).

These companies were not alone in being less than optimally prepared for post-war growth and expansion. The firm Jaguar can be named as an exception that, despite the pressure to produce military equipment, was able to invest in design and production, manufacturing its own drives and thus reducing its dependence on suppliers. However, auto manufacturers such as Rootes, faced with a shortage of raw materials and under pressure to exploit market opportunities, ended up relying on repurposed models such as the Hillman Minx and Humber cars (Donnelly et al. 2019). Manufacturers that produced aero engines and other supplies for the military had to constantly fight with inefficiencies caused by internal factors, for example, low productivity and fluctuating work motivation and external factors, such as the lack of supply of raw materials, changing product specifications, and the adaptation of production methods. These challenges made it difficult for regional vehicle manufacturers to adapt to the requirements of international markets after the war (Donnelly et al. 2019).

There are many factors that need to be mentioned when it comes to explaining the demise of the automotive industry in the West Midlands. Arguably many automotive manufacturers lacked competitiveness after the war. Moreover, Coventry's engineering industries were heavily interconnected and therefore even more vulnerable to potential economic weaknesses in the sector. Many automotive companies would ultimately show poor profitability and low productivity, not helped by structural problems such as physical space restrictions and a lack of economies of scale. Other issues were high labour cost and poor labour relations and conflicts with ever stronger trade unions. Low profitability also led to a lack of investments and innovations and the reliance on old models, which now had to compete with American, German and Japanese producers. Another factor that cannot be neglected was the role of the government, which had failed to provide incentives for the development of other sectors and, by handing over the shadow factories to the car companies, had rather reinforced the strong concentration of engineering industries.

Coventry's post war economic growth was based on a "very narrow industrial base" (Thoms and Donnelly 1985). A factor that explains why there was such a narrow economic base in Coventry is connected to the city's "failure to evolve as a regional centre" that would have provided important administrative infrastructure (Rosser and Mallier 1981). A city's development as a 'regional centre' is often connected to the widening of its economic base. "'Regional offices' of public utilities, major financial institutions and distribution organisations" (Rosser and Mallier 1981) would be examples of administrative infrastructure and could have attracted more firms from other industries, for example, service companies or vehicle component producers. The proximity to Birmingham may also be a factor that explains why fewer companies in other sectors located in Coventry.

Mallier and Rosser (1982) state that the public perception that Coventry was a 'car town' resulted from the fact that "many motor manufacturers have assembled their final product" in Coventry. However, the components used were bought from other companies based outside of Coventry, especially from suppliers in Birmingham and Wolverhampton (Thoms and Donnelly 1985). Coventry's motor industry was more vulnerable to market changes and changing demands due to the focus of Coventry's vehicle companies on the final assembly and not on the production of components. Component producers are less dependent on the production of a specific model, while assembly companies feel the direct impact of a declining demand. Therefore, the lack of the city's industrial diversification reflected in the high dependence on the motor industry was a significant factor that led to an unbalanced economy and to problems in the decades after the end of the Second World War.

However, after a difficult few years immediately after the war, by the 1950s the car industry was seen as being increasingly successful (Donnelly et al. 2001). Vehicle demand globally was on the rise after years of pent-up demand, while exports were encouraged by the UK government eager to see a steady stream of foreign currency into their coffers. Coventry vehicle manufacturers benefited from this environment and contributed largely to the development of the city. Jobs were created, wages continued to be above average and a new prosperity was in evidence across Coventry. Ultimately though this period of growth only served to paper over the cracks as firms focussed on profits and burgeoning demand. The problems that had been in evidence before, during and just after the war were never fully addressed.

In the situation of monopsony, the government was the only buyer and provided production targets, which needed to be fulfilled. Vehicle firms focused on output and produced as many aero engines and components as possible to contribute to the re-armament of the British army. The automotive manufacturers neglected the development of new car models and the preparation of the post-war time. Whitehall's priority was to win the war and there was not much place for concerns of the car manufacturers about their post-war future and appropriate measures to take during the wartime in order to be steeled for the time after. After the Second World War, the government's focus was on the new world order and the establishment of new ground rules. Coventry's motor companies had to adapt to a globalised and market-oriented economy and switch back to the production of cars and car components by relying on designs and expertise of the 1930s (Donnelly et al. 2017). The results were inflexibility regarding the production of models that would meet the requirements of foreign markets and a lack of domestic and international competitiveness. Notably too, Coventry car manufacturers began to lose ground against other UK manufacturers, with Coventry's share of UK's output declining after 1951 (Thoms and Donnelly 1985; Donnelly et al. 2017).

Concluding Remarks

This chapter provided insights into the narrowing of Coventry's industrial base in the 1930s and 1940s, illustrating the factors that lead to a focus on a few industrial areas, namely metal engineering, vehicle manufacture and aero component production. Coventry's failure to grow to a regional centre and develop its administrative infrastructure, and thereby widen its economic base can be seen as one of the factors that contributed to this overspecialisation by the mid-1930s. The shadow factories created a situation which involved motor companies shifting their focus from car production to the manufacture of aero engines and thereby intensified Coventry's focus on a few industries. In the course of the scheme, around 50,000 new workers entered the city and worked in the new factories. The involved automotive companies built additional factories, which they could borrow or buy after the end of the Second World War.

The introduction of new plant brought with its numerous challenges for industrialists and local authorities; logistical problems, construction costs, the sourcing of skilled labour and the infrastructural support required for a burgeoning population brought into operate machinery and transport goods and workers. The fact this expansion occurred in a very short period and at times under the spectre of war and aerial attacks only served to heighten the urgency and concern of those tasked with expanding production. In this hothouse atmosphere with national government pressing for results and industrialists, labourers and local authorities eager to contribute to the war effort, decision-making was not always optimal. In particular, planning for a post-war economy when it was clear the war was won was delayed and, arguably, never properly addressed.

Furthermore, the Shadow Factory Scheme(s) led to a state of near monopsony and the singular relationship that emerged between motor manufacturers and governmental authorities contributed to several issues. The companies had to cope with a lack of raw materials, constantly changing product requirements, and a lack of skilled labour. Moreover, until 1945, automotive manufacturers existed in a protected environment, first by tariffs, then by focusing on meeting the requirements of the government. In a situation where the motor companies did not have to face international competition and were able to accumulate profits might have engendered a certain degree of complacency that was ill-suited to the demands of the post-war period. Moreover, the government kept the pressure high to produce until the end of the Second World War, which might explain the lack of preparedness and strategic planning of some motor companies when the time came to switch back to the production of automobiles and face a market economy.

In particular what was lost during this period of conflict and production focussed output was not just entrepreneurial spirit. The suspension of the operations of market occurred in tandem with the suppression of research and development of new models of passenger car, in both volume and luxury markets. In the aftermath of the war, with pent up demand finally released, car manufacturers in Coventry returned to aging pre-war models and designs. Allied to an extended period without real competition in the market place, these firms were poorly equipped to respond to international rivalry when globalising forces brought increasing competition into then important domestic sphere. Consequently, the 1950s showed the first signs of declining productivity and the proportion of vehicles produced in Coventry decreased in national comparison. The automobile companies had to pay tribute for lack of productivity, low innovation and investment power, as well as lack of economies of scale.

References

Adeney, M. (1988). *The Motor Makers: The Turbulent History of Britain's Car Industry*. London: Robert Hale.

Begley, J., Donnelly, T., & Collis, C. (2019). The Rootes Group: From Growth to Takeover. *Business History*. In press.

Brown, W. (1971). Piecework Wage Determination in Coventry. *Scottish Journal of Political Economy, 18*(1), 1–30.

Carverhill, G. (2018). *Rootes Story: The Making of a Global Automotive Empire*. Ramsbury Marlborough: The Crowood Press.

Coventry History Centre, City of Coventry Town and Planning Committee, Minute Book (CCA/1/4/42/4).

Coventry History Centre, Coventry City Council, Letters of Correspondence (CCA/3/1/7601/1-4).

Coventry History Centre, Coventry City Council, Letters of Correspondence (PA2567/4/202).

Donnelly, T., Begley, J., & Collis, C. (2017). The West Midlands Automotive Industry: The Road Downhill. *Business History, 59*(1), 56–74.

Donnelly, T., & Thoms, D. (1989). Trade Unions, Management and the Search for Production in the Coventry Motor Car Industry, 1939–75. *Business History, 31*(2), 98–113.

Donnelly, T., Tully, J., & Morris, D. (2001). The Decline of the Coventry Car Industry 1945–68. *Midlands History, XXVI,* 198–211.

Dunnett, P. (1980). *The Decline of the British Motor Industry: The Effects of Government Policy, 1945–1979*. London: Croom Helm.

Ewart, H. (2011). 'Coventry Irish': Community, Class, Culture and Narrative in the Formation of a Migrant Identity, 1940–1970. *Midland History, 36*(2), 225–244.

Flanders, A. (1957). Wage Movements and Wage Policy in Postwar Britain. *The Annals of the American Academy of Political and Social Science, 310*(1), 87–98.

Forbes, N. (2015). *Business in the Age of Extremes: Essays in Modern German and Austrian Economic History* (pp. 1309–1310). Abingdon: Taylor-Francis.

Knowles, K. G. J. C., & Robinson, D. (1969). Wage Movements in Coventry. *Bulletin of the Oxford University Institute of Economics & Statistics, 31*(1), 1–21.

Lancaster, B., & Mason, T. (Eds.). (1986). *Life and Labour in a Twentieth Century City: The Experience of Coventry*. Coventry: Cryfield Press.

Little, Stephen E., & Grieco, M. (2011). Shadow Factories, Shallow Skills? An Analysis of Work Organisation in the Aircraft Industry in the Second World War. *Labour History, 52*(2), 193–216.

Mallier, A. T., & Rosser, M. J. (1982, January). *Industrial Declines in Perspective: The Car Industry in Coventry* (Staff Seminar Discussion Paper No. 47). Department of Economics, Coventry (Lanchaster) Polytechnic.

Maxcy, G., & Silberston, A. (1959). *Automobile Industry and Trade*. London: Allen & Unwin.

Richardson, K. (1972). *Twentieth Century Coventry*. Coventry: City of Coventry.

Robson, G. (2011). *The Book of the Standard Motor Company*. Dorchester: Veloce Publishing.

Rosser, M. J., & Mallier, A. T. (1981, May). *The Economic Base of Coventry*. Public Sector Economics Research Centre, University of Leicester, Leicester.

Shay, R. (1977). *British Rearmament in the Thirties: Politics and Profits* (p. 94). Princeton: Princeton University Press.

Stone, T. (2017). *Sustaining Air Power: Royal Air Force Logistics Since 1918*. Stroud: Fonthill Media.

Thoms, D. (1989). *War, Industry and Society: The Midlands 1939–1945*. London: Routledge.

Thoms, D., & Donnelly, T. (1985). *The Motor Car Industry in Coventry Since the 1890s*. London: Croom Helm.

Thoms, D., & Donnelly, T. (2000). *The Coventry Motor Industry: Birth to Renaissance*. Aldershot: Ashgate.

Whisler, T. (1999). *The British Motor Industry, 1945–94: A Case Study in Industrial Decline*. Oxford: Oxford University Press.

Wingrove, P. (2015). The Shells Scandal of 1915 [online]. *The Times*. Available at https://www.thetimes.co.uk/article/the-shells-scandal-of-1915-bf5sgblhh7h. Accessed 1 Mar 2019.

4

Coventry in the Long Boom 1950–1970

Michael Haynes

The Long Boom

The period between 1945 and the early 1970s were the years of 'the long boom'. For almost three decades, the British economy, like other advanced economies, grew steadily. Standards of living increased in ways that could not have been imagined in the past. In 1957, the Prime Minister Harold Macmillan, caught the mood of the time when he said 'most of our people have never had it so good.' There was one city that seemed to capture this spirit and that was Coventry. In the minds of contemporaries it rose from the ashes of the war—the embodiment of a brave new world. In 1959 an article in the *Times* described Coventry as a symbol for post-war recovery, an architectural adventure, a show-place for visiting delegations, 'a shop-window for the socialist ideal', 'a powerhouse of technical progress', 'an Eldorado for its workers', the first expression of a new Americanisation of industry, and 'to some

M. Haynes (✉)
University of Wolverhampton, Wolverhampton, UK

J. Begley et al. (eds.), *Revival of a City*, Palgrave Studies in Economic History,
https://doi.org/10.1007/978-3-030-22822-4_4

intellectuals a wilderness of vulgar materialisation'. The article continued that, 'with the highest average wages in the country, the city oozes prosperity' (*Times* 31 March 1959).

This was a time when the global links deepened. The export situation became an obsession of the day. A greater and wider variety of goods flowed in as foodstuffs, raw materials, intermediate and finished goods—some of them beginning to appear in greater numbers in the shops of the new retail centres in Coventry. Capital flowed more easily than it had done since before 1914. The boom sucked in migrants to the city. With good wages in the 1960s many Coventry workers were able to go aboard for the first time. Ideas moved too. Coventry became one of the most studied British towns of its size as commentators explored its achievements and problems. The city became an international symbol of reconstruction—drawing on some of the most advanced architectural ideas of the day. The erection of a new Cathedral with a striking design seemed to embody hopes of reconciliation and a better world. Even 'town' twinning took place on a larger scale than in most other towns.

But the boom was not to last. Although the pace and steadiness of growth in these years was historically remarkable, a number of other advanced economies seemed to grow faster still. This prompted concern that progress was not quick enough and the strengths and weaknesses of the car industry in a city like Coventry became a focal point of debate. When the boom faltered in the 1970s, the economy of Coventry was badly hit as the next chapter will show. The debate over what, if anything, was been wrong became politically sharper as new policies based on what some later called 'neo-liberalism' became the order of the day. But historical perspectives are always changing. Although in the next decades the economic base of Coventry shifted and in the long run incomes grew, the pattern has been much more uncertain and the distribution of gains and losses more unequal. The era from 1945 to the first years of the seventies has not been displaced as the period of relative 'good times' in the modern economic history both of Coventry and beyond.

Growth

The simplest measure of the expansion of Coventry in the boom is the rapid growth of its population. Coventry from 1950 to 1965 was the fastest growing city in Britain (CS 19 May 1966). The 1951 census showed that Coventry had a population of 238,242 making it the sixteenth largest city in England. In 1961 at was the ninth with a population of 305,060 and, helped by a 1964 boundary change, it then became the eighth largest. In 1971 the population was 335,400. Expansion was fastest in the 1950s. In 1961 the local newspaper said that if 'Coventry begins to rest on its laurels it will be a sign that it has passed its best' (CET 8 June 1961). Growth did began to slow in 1966 and in late 1971 the local paper noted that in the previous year Coventry's population had fallen for the first time for 32 years and asked was the 'boom over'? (CET 31 December 1971) But at this point this was because people were also attracted to satellite towns. Commuting was becoming ever more common and by the end of the 1960s it was estimated that some 40–50,000 of the workforce in the city travelled in from beyond its limits (CET 28 November 1968).

The long boom was defined by both sustained output growth and the lowest rates of unemployment in modern British peacetime economic history. Employment in Coventry in these years increased at three times the national average. In the 1950s and 1960s unemployment nationally averaged some 1.7% (Author's calculations from Denman and McDonald 1996). In Coventry unemployment hit its lowest point of 0.5% of the insured population in 1953. But the city did have an important peculiarity. The car industry, whose output was itself quite volatile in these years, had a tradition in Coventry of laying people off and using short time working to help smooth out variations in demand. Given that the city was so reliant on the industry this could lead to temporary increases in unemployment. In 1956–1957, for example, short term difficulties led to 10,000 workers losing their jobs with others on short time. 'All the commercial life of the city felt the pinch' and unemployment briefly rose to over 3% (*Times* 31 March 1959). The workers who lost their jobs had little choice but to wait for better times.

There were no real opportunities in the wider area, the city was an 'industrial island amid surrounding country' (*Times* 23 January 1957). But, after a short break, workers knew that would probably be taken back again on high wages. Later there were attempts to better manage demand but, even allowing for these fluctuations, the city still had unemployment rates much below those before or since. Long term unemployment remained at historically low levels even as labour force participation was increasing.

The Economic Structure

Britain was not only the first country to industrialise but its level of industrialisation rose in the post war years to one of the highest ever recorded only then to precipitously decline as the next chapters show. The share of the national labour force in manufacturing peaked in 1955 at 48% but Coventry was a manufacturing town on an even greater scale (F. 39). It seemed the exemplar of production prowess, the leading example of a city built around modern engineering. There were worries that its manufacturing base was too narrow but diversification proved hard and, so long as the prosperity continued, it did not seem to be a real problem. Indeed with the opening of the new motorway systems Coventry's central position seemed to make its role as a manufacturing centre the more important. Table 4.1 shows the basic structure of employment in the city and the overwhelming dominance of manufacturing in these years.

Table 4.1 The changing employment structure of Coventry 1952–1966 (Thoms and Donnelly 1985, p. 152)

	1952	%	1966	%	% change
Primary	3760	2.4	2067	1.0	−1.4
Manufacturing	113,267	72.1	135,837	66.4	−5.7
Construction	6717	4.2	9187	4.5	0.3
Utilities	6067	3.9	6307	3.1	−0.8
Services	27,429	17.5	51,110	25.0	7.5
Total	157,420		204,508		

There was a slight relative decline in the share of employment in manufacturing over time but in the late 1960s it was still running at quite an extraordinary level even as the share was falling faster elsewhere in the United Kingdom. Output measures show that roughly two thirds came from manufacturing in Coventry and one third services compared to a one third: two thirds ratio nationally. But it must be remembered that in these years the share of 'professional services' in the manufacturing labour force more than doubled and these was the more important in high technology industries like those in Coventry (Tomlinson 2006, p. 85).

Coventry was an engineering city. Car production was the biggest sector. Figure 4.1 shows the growth and fluctuations in national output and that of Coventry and its two largest mass car producers. The share of UK production from Coventry fell sharply in the early 1950s and then stabilised at ±20% in the late 1950s and 1960s. Output in the UK and the city alike peaked in 1964 in these decades. The Coventry

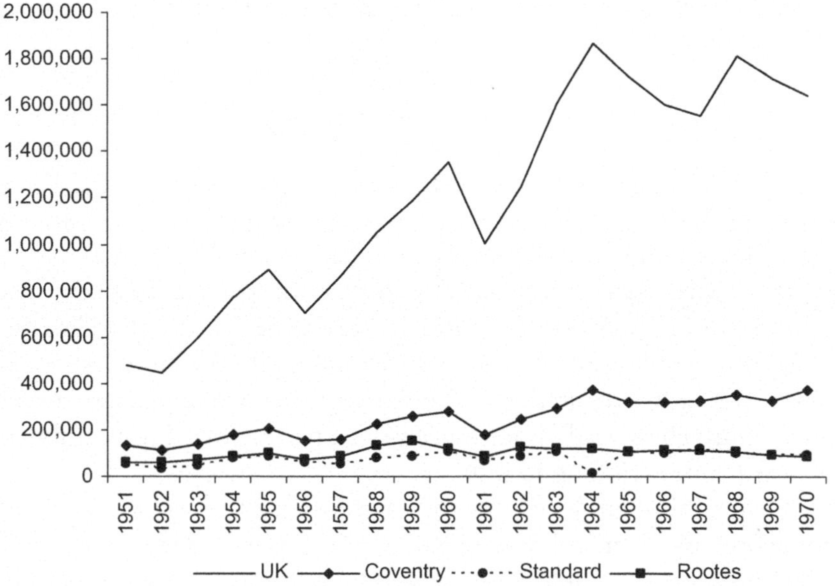

Fig. 4.1 The growth of UK and Coventry car production by Standard and Rootes 1951–1970

car industry employed between 30% and 40% of the city labour force depending on how the calculations are done. Employment in the car industry peaked later than in output in 1966 at 75,000 (Thoms and Donnelly 1985, p. 152).

The car industry in Coventry continued to be based on assembly drawing, at this point, largely on Midlands based supply chains. One part of the industry was high end where the most important company was Jaguar (which became part of BMC in 1966) but here there were 'too many firms and models, chasing too few customers' (Thoms and Donnelly 1985, p. 174). The mass producers were Standard and Rootes. With Vauxhall these were the smaller of the big 5 mass producers at the time (against BMC, created 1952, and Ford) and they suffered increasingly from a lack of economies of scale. 'Too small to survive' in the long run, their fortunes became the subject of various attempts at merger before Rootes was fully taken over by Chrysler in 1967 and Standard became fully part of the new British Leyland in 1968. The creation of Leyland as a consolidated firm briefly brought together 27,000 workers in the city under one management (Thoms and Donnelly 1985, p. 202).

As late as 1969 car imports made up only 10% of UK consumption although the share was to surge in the next years. Britain became a net importer of cars in 1975 and imports rose to almost 50% of consumption by 1977 (201–202). But before then exports were crucial to car producers. Writing of the Coventry car industry in 1959, one journalist said that it, 'stands or falls on its overseas earnings' (*Times* 31 March 1959). Exports were encouraged by the government but overseas marketing was not always concentrated to best advantage by the Coventry firms. High end products like the Triumph Spitfire and, especially, Jaguar had strong reputations. The story of the export of mass market cars is more chequered. Rootes even exported kit cars for assembly in overseas plants including to Iran.

Coventry also produced tractors and commercial vehicles. Tractor production by Standard was taken over by Massey Fergusson as the 1950s progressed. Dunlop was also an important employer but not so focused on the car industry. Defence and aeronautics were significant—split between the civilian and defence markets. Some defence production was undertaken by the car producers but other by firms like Armstrong Whitworth. But as in cars a degree of volume production was necessary. It depended on government support which was not always sustained. Times got worse in these sectors in the 1960s and the aircraft sector in the city lost 11,000 jobs between 1962 and 1967 (194). The other big employers in engineering were in machine tools with Alfred Herbert and electrical engineering which was growing in importance and particularly associated with GEC (Lloyd-Jones and Lewis 2006).

Beyond the manufacturing sector the city was alive with the noise of building and reconstruction. But the bigger non manufacturing employers were those related to utilities and services including public administration. All of these had to grow too, in some cases very fast, to accommodate the rapid population increase and the expansion in economic activity.

Schools and colleges were amongst the biggest beneficiaries of the long boom. Coventry was a city of younger people. The large number of young couples meant that it was a high birth rate city even though family size was falling. Only in the 1960s did the share of older people begin to gradually increase. In 1966 only 9% of the population were over 65 compared to an average nationally nearer to 14% (CS 14 November 1968; CET 8 November 1968, 22 August 1969).

By the mid 1950s national education spending had reached around 3% of GDP and it continued to grow to a peak of 6.4% in 1975–1976 (IFS 2011, p. 3). The school leaving age was raised to 15 in 1947 and then, after prolonged discussions, to 16 in 1972. Education was the more important in the city given the population bulge. School numbers rose from 26,645 in 1946 to 48,221 in 1956 and 59,554 in 1968 when 36,730 were in primary schools and 22,824 in secondary ones. There was demand for teachers, administrators and ancillary workers (Stephens 1969; CET 17 November 1969). New schools were built. Secondary schools became more important and controversial with the movement to comprehensive education against the divisions of the 11 plus. Urban areas like Coventry were more strongly pro comprehensive compared to county areas like Warwickshire and by 1964 the city already had eight comprehensive schools.

Education beyond 15 became important in terms of developing and maintaining a flow of skilled workers in the city. This was the task of the technical colleges and usually done on a part time day release basis. The role of higher education began to develop in the city. Schools needed teachers and a College of Education was created. Then in the 1960s the government began to develop higher education. Warwick University (the name was supposed to reflect a county base but Warwickshire thought too cumbersome) was approved in 1961 as part of a wave of new university creations. It took its first 450 undergraduates in 1965 on a new campus on the fringes of Coventry. It had been planned in part under the direction of the car magnate Lord Rootes. Rootes' death in 1964 prevented him being its first chancellor but in the first years his, and the wider government, aim of creating close ties between the new universities and industry seemed to be less controversial. But in the late 1960s, for its critics, 'Warwick University Ltd' became a symbol of an incipient narrowing of vision and commercialisation of higher education (Thompson 1970). A higher level College of Technology was created and this became the basis of the new Lanchester Polytechnic formed in 1968. Named after Frank Lanchester, a leading motor engineer, it would later become the University of Coventry.

As the welfare state developed following the reforms of the post-war Labour government a wider structure of social provision had also to be created including social welfare and health facilities with increased numbers of doctors and a bigger demand for hospital services. Given the high birth rate in the city there was initially a greater focus on maternity services than geriatric care. In 1967, 74% of local births took place in hospital (CET 14 May 1968). There were often labour shortages of everyone from school dentists to the police.

Tourism—both national and international—too should be mentioned not least in terms of the attraction of seeing the new Cathedral. Its foundation stone was laid in 1956 and it was consecrated to national headlines as 'a beacon to the generations' in 1962. It was a house, said the Archbishop of Canterbury, in which all the arts and the craftsmanship of the time had united: stone, wood, glass, metal, tapestry, the designer the builder, the painter, the sculptor (Campbell 1996). Days later Benjamin Britten's *War Requiem* was premiered there

(*Times* 26 May 1962). But many of those who came to admire in the next years also came to spend in the city's new shopping centre. Sluggish at first, the retail sector grew as redevelopment occurred with big new stores opening from the mid 1950s. In the 1960s the booming retail sector was a testament to the more secular interests of those with money in their pockets.

The High Wage Town

Engineering workers were some of the best paid workers in the country and the fact that there were so many of them in Coventry pulled up the average wage to levels far higher than in most over places. Coventry wages at the turn of the 1960s were said to be 30% higher than those in Dagenham (*Times* 31 March 1959). Engineering pay rates varied by district and workers in Coventry and the Midlands more generally benefited 'from the intense competition for the labour in which the motor and aircraft concerns have set a fast pace.' Rates then varied between jobs. They also varied depending on the extent to which they were time rates or piece rates and had additional payments. 'The great majority of piece workers earn far more than the fictional man of average ability in the industry,… in Coventry they have averaged 300% of the basic rate…', it was said in 1953 (*Times* 7 April 1953). There was an acute concern for differentials and the conditions of labour shortage created the basis for what was called wage drift in which workers could push up wages locally (Knowles and Robinson 1969; Brown 1971; Brown and Sisson 1975). If this allowed the employers to recruit they were not anxious, at least early on, to change the system. Estimating what Coventry workers actually earned in these years is difficult because of all this. But it was not only the skilled how benefited. In fact the labourer's rate in engineering was said to have risen from 64% of the craftsman's rate in 1914 to 87% in the early 1950s. Because of the difference between rates and actual pay the labourer in the 1950s probably took home 25% less for slightly more hours. But overall the movement of real wages for both the skilled and the unskilled was strongly up at this time.

There were left behind groups in Coventry as elsewhere. Living in substandard housing some struggled to make ends meet as their parents had. Contemporary studies showed that poverty was related to low pay (some 40% of the poor nationally had a family member working in 1970), family size, and unemployment and, in some instances, old age (Tomlinson 2006, p. 92). The 1966 sample census showed that of 29,000 over the age of 65 in Coventry some 5390 were still working (CS, 14 November 1968). But at the bottom wages councils (later abolished) offered some protection for some low paid. And for the insured population social security benefits were, in some respects, more generous in relative terms that they would be later. Unemployment benefit, for example, was connected to previous pay levels.

In the 1966 TV play *Cathy Come Home*, written by Jeremy Sandford and produced by Tiny Garrett and directed by Ken Loach, exposed the problem of those who fell out of the system to enormous national effect. But there was a degree of satisfaction that it did not seem to apply in Coventry. The city had some individual Cathy's but not a hostel population. "Cathy' has a place to call home', said an article in one local newspaper. This was, in part, it argued, because of the active policy of the local council but also because of the ability to house people temporarily in homes purchased for demolition (CS 9 February 1967).

Somewhat paradoxically, given the obsession with pay differentials, levels of wage and more general inequality in the UK were declining throughout this period and were much lower in this period than they would be later. Social mobility too was also higher with more 'room at the top' than there was before or since. As opportunities widened, Coventry was a place to which people came to 'get on', it was also a place in which they could 'get on'.

The Labour Force and Migration

Without new workers Coventry's economic boom would have faltered. A part of the new labour force came from those finishing school in the city but their numbers were far from sufficient and a small, growing minority were staying on after 15. Women workers provided a growing share of the labour force as old restrictions and attitudes began to crumble. The share of women in the national labour force rose from 31% in 1951 to 37% in 1971. The share of unmarried women peaked in the early 1960s at 77% before continuing education reduced this share. But the share of married women working surged from 24% in 1951 to 49% in 1971 (Lewis 1985, p. 3). In Coventry women were to be found not only in 'white blouse jobs' but also increasingly in the factories though not always on the shop floor. Already by the mid 1950s 22% of the workers in engineering were women. Machine tools had the lowest share of women at 10%, cars and aircraft had 13–15% and electrical engineering was already at 49%. Commentators struggled to make sense of this growing shift. In a 1957 article in the *Coventry Evening Telegraph* on the 'revolution on the factory floor', the author argued that the secret of women's rise in the labour force in Coventry, including in light engineering, was their willingness to work more efficiently than men for lower pay. 'Much of the work in modern light industry resembles nothing so much as knitting at which women are said to be a good deal better than men' (CET 12 December 1957). In the 1960s the issue became a question not only of employing more women but the demand for equal pay. The car industry in Coventry and elsewhere was often the centre of attention. At the turn of the 1970s the forthcoming Equal Pay Act was seen by some as an electoral ploy and by others as an unnecessary cost for business but a male backlash was not forthcoming. But when the newly formed Coventry branch of the National Women's Liberation Group tried to use a visit of the Queen to raise even wider demands for equality they were portrayed as 'Kitchen Sink Rebels' and met with some hostility from women on the day (CET 30 January 1970, 7 February 1970, 3 March 1970).

A stream of migrants too came to swell the size of the labour force. Most were from the UK, as they had been in the 1930s, attracted by the lure of better quality Coventry jobs and wages. In 1950 the UK had only 5.5% of its labour force in agriculture so internal migration mainly involved people moving from industrial areas in relative decline to areas where industry and services were growing (Feinstein 1999, p. 53). There was a regular stream from the Midlands coalfields, others came from the north east, Wales and Scotland. The 1971 census showed that 3% of the

Coventry population had been born in Wales. By this date nearly 20,000 had come from Ireland, north and south. There was also a significant Polish and Ukrainian community that had settled during and after the war.

Including those born in Southern Ireland, over 10% of Coventry's population had not been born in the UK in 1971. By this time the 'Irish' population had become more integrated and most attention was paid to the new Commonwealth migrants who came from the West Indies, India and Pakistan and to a lesser extent Africa in the 1950s and 1960s. At first largely male, they brought families over in secondary migration streams. In the 1950s West Indians were soon overtaken by migrants from India and Pakistan. The 1961 census included 3198 Indians, 708 Pakistanis and 1406 West Indians. A decade later the new Commonwealth percentage had increased to nearly 5% with 15,190 migrants. The Coventry Indian community numbered some 8600 and was said to be the fourth largest outside of London. There were 1570 Pakistanis, 1195 Kenyans and 1690 Jamaicans (CET 11 January 1968, 19 April 1974).

These workers experienced significant formal and informal discrimination. Those with high qualifications found that white collar jobs might not be open to them. There was discrimination too in recruitment in the factories and some factories segregated facilities. The bigger story of these years for the New Commonwealth community is therefore one of a struggle against racism and for basic equalities. It was led by organisations like the Coventry Indian Worker's Association, whose activities are only now being written up (Gill 2016). It also involved a subsidiary struggle against those within the immigrant community who sought to take advantage of their weaknesses either acting as labour brokers or in some cases, such as clothing, setting up their own concerns to employ wives and daughters.

Social Life

Coventry seemed to observers at this time to be a 'one class city', embodying the emerging narrative of an affluent society. 'With the highest average wage in the country' even people in higher white collar jobs took home no more than some car workers. But the texture of social and political life was also affected by the way that 'the motor car has enabled the executive classes of modern Coventry to make their homes in the pleasant towns and villages of Warwickshire'. Some thought the city the worse for this. 'We are a city in search of a soul' one journalist was told (CET 27 December 1951; *Times* 31 March 1959).

Coventry workers were getting more leisure time, saving more and spending more both on 'basics' (food rationing finally ended in 1954) and a widening range of consumer goods. 'Money and new ways to spend it are amongst [the population's] chief occupations…' (CET 25 July 1958; *Times* 31 March 1959). Two items of more conspicuous consumption grew in prominence. 'The cars parked on the council estates tell their own story', it was said in 1959, 'car ownership in the city of the motor car is twice the national average' (*Times* 31 March 1959). An even bigger surge came in the next decade and a half. In the 1960s car ownership nationally grew at 8% per year, creating new problems for the city's planners who began to talk of having 10,000 car parking spaces within the inner ring road (CET 28 February 1956, 2 April 1966). Then there was the summer holiday. High wages gave many Coventry workers wider opportunities earlier than in other parts of the UK. They continued to be taken until quite late on in Coventry Holiday Fortnight when the major plants shut down at the start of the summer school holidays.

The rich had always had the possibility of travelling further. In 1950 the Coventry City Architect, Donald Gibson, showed that continental travel could also be done cheaply when he astonished people by travelling 1100 miles in a two week European working holiday on a cycle fitted with a locally made Cyclemaster twin stroke engine. He even rode it down the Champs Elysee and through the Jura mountains to Switzerland (CET 21 October 1950). His example of 'Europe on the cheap' was not followed. Instead a later generation took advantage of the growing availability of air travel from nearby airports. In the late 1960s and early 1970s the special buses and trains were in decline as groups of Coventry workers began holidaying in Spain, Majorca, and the Mediterranean (CET 8 July 1975).

But the city had a social life too. Early on this was more submerged. Coventry 'lacks diversity of employment *and* social life', it was said in 1949 (*Times* 3 November 1949, my emphasis). Pubs and clubs were the main night out. In 1968 there were still 230 pubs and 40 working men's clubs in Coventry (CET 8 May 1968). But by this time these too were changing. The city centre ones were being taken over by young people and 'juke boxes and discotheques'—helped in part by the growing numbers of students. The cinema also thrived as a source of entertainment even though, along with better furniture and washing machines, black and white television and then the colour ones appeared quickly in Coventry households in the 1950s and 1960s.

The wider civic social life of Coventry was reflected in the opening of the Belgrade Theatre in 1958 with its own resident company. This was the first purpose built post-war civic theatre. Its name recalls the gift of wood that went into its construction from Belgrade. The theatre's 900 seats reflected ambition but performances were not always to full houses. In 1960 the Herbert Art Gallery and Museum was opened. But it was the new Coventry Cathedral that seemed too many people to be the most dramatic architectural, social and moral statement of the time.

Adjustment was not always easy for any newcomers. 'Official Coventry' prided itself on the city's cosmopolitanism but ruefully reflected that some people thought of 'foreigners' as anyone not born in Coventry. The local paper called such suggestions 'a display of more parochialism than we should have thought possible in a place like Coventry' (CET 5 December 1959). Integration was hardest for those whose skin colour was different. Various organisations took initiatives to try to create, in the words of the day, 'better understanding between the various races and creeds' (CS 22 July 1965). These included the Council, the Churches, the Citizens Advice Bureau, Community Relations Council etc. Migrant communities had their own organisations too. The first mosque was built in 1957. There were more political associations too like the West Indian National Association and the Indian Workers Association. Concentrated in older properties in the poorer parts of the city the local newspaper suggested that 'sometimes their [migrants] strange customs and habits cause trouble with neighbours' (CET 13 October 1964).

The paper supported immigration controls but nevertheless argued that 'the relationship between coloured people and the rest of the population falls short of anything that might be described as full integration. But at any rate it is tolerant, friendly and improving all the time'.

It is far from clear that those in migrant community saw things this way. One a measure of the gap that still existed is that when local amateur drastic society put on Showboat in 1968—a musical about American deep south—the issue was not whether or not white actors should 'black up' but whether the group would 'be sufficiently pioneering to use coloured actors' of whom, it was said, there were a number in the city (CS 22 August 1968). The young in particular faced not only more difficulties in education and work but also in their dealings with the authorities and not least the police. The first Asian and black councillors were only elected in the city in the 1980s and 1990s. It fell to the associations to try to direct and represent the concerns of the wider migrant communities and the young in particular. As the boom came to end Coventry was one of the places that the Select Committee on Immigration in 1971–1972 took evidence from about community relations though it was more concerned to reflect the narrative of the police than those felt that relations had broken down (BPP 1971–1972).

There was one thing that could bring people (or at least the white male population) together at this time on a larger scale and that was football. In the 1950s there was much grumbling about the fact that a city like that of Coventry should have such a low ranked team. This reached a peak in the 1957–1958 season when Coventry were relegated to the lowest (fourth) division. Even so attendance at the Highfield Road stadium was impressive. In the 1960s, with the team now managed by Jimmy Hill, fortunes changed. Highfield Road was partly redeveloped and the team began to climb the divisions playing in a new kit that led to the Sky Blues nickname. Hill's ambitions on the field were matched off it. With money in their pockets, Coventry fans could travel to watch away games too on specially laid on football trains. Attendance at Highfield Road peaked in 1967 in a game with nearby rivals Wolves at an official figure of 51,455. This was the season that saw Coventry promoted to the first division as division 2 champions. Thereafter, in the late 1960s, the average attendance was around 35,000.

Even allowing for away fans this was probably the biggest coming together of the population on a regular social basis other than through work in these years.

Local Politics and the Structuring the Townscape

In these years Coventry was the town which seemed to embody the ideas of a post-war progressive and outward looking municipal socialism. The local 'Labourist' internationalism of the day can be seen in the enthusiasm for the town twinning of Coventry as 'a city of peace and reconciliation'. Table 4.2 shows the twinning of the time and the evocative names of many of the places involved. There were gestures too in the twinning towards the areas from which Coventry's international migrants were coming.

In parliamentary terms Coventry had three constituencies between 1950 and 1974—North, East and South. With the exception of Coventry South (1959–1964) these were all Labour seats. Richard Crossman, who would achieve fame as Labour Cabinet minister in the 1960s, represented Coventry East and Maurice Edelman, a prominent backbencher represented Coventry North. In Coventry South Elaine

Table 4.2 Coventry town twinning 1944–1970

	West	East
1944		Volgograd (USSR)
1947		Kiel (GDR) Lidice, Ostrava (Czechoslovakia)
1955	St. Etienne (France)	
1957	Caen (France)	Sarajevo, Belgrade (Yugoslavia) Warsaw (Poland)
1958	Arnhem (Holland) Cork (Ireland)	
1959		Dresden (GDR)
1960	Bologna (Italy)	
1962	Kingston (Jamaica)	Dunaujvaros, Kecskemet (Hungary) Galati (Romania)
1962	Coventry (USA)	
1963	Cornwall, Granby, Windsor (Canada)	

Burton and Bill Wilson were the Labour MPs and for one parliament, Philip Hocking the Tory. But in each seat there was always a very large Tory minority vote. This made them good places to try out rising stars (including from the right of the party) and several defeated candidates went on to be elected elsewhere and achieve high office including Michael Heseltine and Ian Gow. After the 1950 liberalism all but disappeared in the city as a parliamentary force save in Coventry East where a Liberal candidate occasionally stood as did a Communist. The majority of contests were two horse races. Turnout declined from the mid to high 80s in 1950 to the low to mid 70s in 1970. In the 1950s too the Labour majority over the Conservatives in the three constituencies fell from 20% of votes cast in 1950 to 7% in 1959. This decline, along with the temporary loss of Coventry South in 1959, form an important part of Tiratsoo's analysis of the impact of affluence on politics in Coventry. But, with extended hindsight, what might seem more remarkable is the resilience of the Labour vote in the 1960s. The Labour share of votes cast over those for the Conservatives in the three constituencies rose to 20% again in 1966 and was still over 12% in the 1970 election. The problem is to know the extent to which this had become more vote based on instrumentalist concerns rather than one based on a more gut class instinct.

In local government, the council had become Labour in 1937 and Labour continued to dominate it through the long boom. As might be expected the Labour vote for the council was weakest in the leafier suburbs—wards like Bablake, Cheylesmore, Sherbourne and Whoberley. The Labour vote was strongest in Charterhouse and Binley, Foleshill, Longford, Radford, St. Michaels, and Westwood. In the other wards the vote was divided more equally. Yet even in the wards where Labour was strongest there was always a solid minority Conservative vote. But, despite the inevitable ups and downs of local politics, it was as a Labour Council that Coventry stood out in these years. Coventry's council with a team of far seeing technocratic planners was ambitious. Tiratsoo calls it 'a bastion of Labour progressivism' (Tiratsoo 1990, p. 2).

The needs of reconstruction and the rapid expansion of Coventry created the possibility of planned development in a way that had never occurred before (Tiratsoo 2000). Both Labour and Conservative governments looked more positively, if inconsistently, on local planning and the idea of national direction. Some frictions aside, both had support from local industry though those in the county areas around the city were less enamoured as Coventry expansion trespassed on what they saw as their interests. 'Coventry has', said the *Economist* in the 1960s, 'many people agree, the most enlightened system of professional city government, yet seen in Britain' (*The Economist* 2 April 1966).

To succeed the politicians and the planners had to build support locally and nationally. Local commercial interests worried about the impact of adventurous redevelopment on local business had to be brought on board. Private lands had to be bought out or compromised with. Money was not always available to the extent that they hoped. Some local rate payers complained about costs and local 'taxes'. In the mid 1960s half of the householders paid rates. 'A young man in his twenties may be driving a car in rates-maintained roads, playing games in rates' provided parks, seeing plays in the rates subsidized Belgrade theatre and even living in a rates-subsidized council house.' it was said, 'But he pays no rates' (CS 10 March 1966).

Then the planners had then to decide with what to do. Above the ground there was the problem of housing, city centre development and, initially underestimated, the impact of car ownership. Below there were sewage, water, electricity, gas systems etc. to be put in. At the forefront of the city's development was the architects department led initially by Donald Gibson (1938–1954), then Arthur Ling (1955–1964) and Terrance Gregory (1964–1973). It conceived of a boldly modernist city reflecting the perceived needs of the people with culture and arts near its centre. Heliports appeared on some early plans and a trip was made to Japan to learn about the possibilities of a monorail (Couperus 2016; Fischer and Larkham 2018). In the event it was under Gibson's successors that the plans for remodelling much of the city were delivered. But they remained sufficiently striking and advanced for the city became a magnate for planners and architects the world over.

The demand for housing was immense. After the war the city still had its slums and the new problem of tens of thousands of war damaged buildings. Additional and replacement housing was needed to meet the growth that followed (including later student demand).

'If there has been anything good to come out of the Blitz, it is that so many new houses have had to be built' said one local politician, looking back in the mid 1960s. The balance of council and private building remained a source of contention. By that the mid 1960s 17,000 council houses had been built but private building overtook building by the council from the late 1950s on. The new housing developments took the form of new estates around the city with some high rise development. Today much of the housing of this time is still prized compared to that built later. The waiting list for council was 6000 in 1966 but was said to be less than in many other cities. To get on the list a family had to be resident for three years. Allocation depended on a merit based points system whose form varied from between towns and cities. It was made more complex by transfers and fact that 99% of people on the list specified an area where they wanted to live (CS 11 August 1966). Unfortunately financial constraints as well as pioneering technical and commercial practices meant that some of the housing was not without problems. But here too perspectives change.

In the city centre the planners had to work out what parts of the old could and should be kept and how the new was to be configured. Gibson conceived of what, for the time, was an adventurously planned pedestrianised city centre with shops, civic areas and amenities, squares and bold statues—the most famous or infamous being that of Lady Godiva. Later the demands from the car led to the inner ring road being added. The city centre became 'the steel and concrete jungle' of Coventry (CET 21 August 1970). But, though some dispute this, it was a 'steel and concrete jungle' that seemed to have popular support and appreciation at the time, attracting visitors from well beyond the city well as regulars from within.

Coventry and the Debate on British Economic Performance

Much of the story of Britain since 1945, indeed on some accounts since the late nineteenth century has been written terms of decline. Once Britain had been able to impose its *Pax Britannica* on the world though its empire and its global reach. But its relative power has more and more diminished. Given its smaller size, relative decline much of this relative decline was inevitable once other powers began to develop. But the legacy of bigger ambitions and the idea that Britain should be able to, and needed to, punch above its weight fed into growing anxiety from the 1950s onwards that the economy was not doing better than it was. This was magnified by the political debates of the day in which each side charged the other with 'economic failure'. Coventry's position as a powerful manufacturing centre—a symbol of the structural shift away from the old staple industries of coal, iron and steel and textiles towards engineering and cars and then the shift towards a 'post industrial' Britain—has meant that we find the city appearing in the big national debates and these big debates in turn help to mould our understanding of the city's development.

Today historians tend to argue that 'historical declinism has significantly distorted our understanding of modern Britain' (Tomlinson 2009, p. 229). The statistics do not show a major problem in the UK in our period especially when account is taken of the fact that the UK was already highly developed in 1950. Labour productivity in manufacturing, for example, grew by an average of some 4.4% per year in the years 1951–1973 compared with 4.9% in West Germany. The differences are marginal given the different starting points of the two economies and the gap was only slightly smaller in the 1960s than the 1950s. It was only after 1973 that sharp differences appeared—to the advantage of West Germany in the 1970s and the UK in the 1980s (Broadberry and Crafts 2003; Booth 2006). Once the choices that were made are seen in terms of what was possible they appear more rational. And a focus on sectors and cities that were declining needs to be offset by an understanding of the sectors and cities that were doing well given the inevitability of long run structural change. But the stories of decline remain powerful. They focus on the same three issues—workers, employers and the state but left and right interpret their roles in different ways (Donnelly and Thoms 1989). We need therefore to conclude by reviewing how such arguments play out in the analysis of the story of Coventry in our period. Good though the times seem to have been in the 1950s and 1960s, might they have been better still had it not been for the influences of bad workers, bad bosses or the bad state?

In the 1950s and 60s the view developed on the right that what two contemporaries called 'the cussedness of the workers' was holding the British economy back. Coventry was a union stronghold not only in the workplace but through the Labour Party in the city as a whole. In 1955 there were said to be 75,000 trades unionists in the city. To their opponents unions were said to be imposing overmanning, restrictive practices and striking too easily. These ideas captured the political imagination too through the 1959 film 'I'm All Right Jack'. Set in a defence factory, it satirised the clash between a management focusing on profit and a union on protecting its own. A writer in the local Coventry paper said 'it is all the more brilliantly done because nobody can really be offended' (CET 20 October 1959). Later some left wing historians and commentators flipped the argument and analysed workplace practices as examples of 'worker resistance'. Andrew Friedman used Coventry and its car industry in the 1950s and 1960s as a case of a wider process of struggle in the workplace (Friedman 1977). A key aspect of bargaining at this point was that much of it took place at the shop floor level through local stewards. Coventry was 'a piece work city' and resisted measured day working in part because it enabled workers both to get high wages and to get back some of the wages lost in bad times (CET 14 May 1968). Yet constructive proposals also came forward from below some of which were taken on board. In fact some later historians are sceptical that the problem was anything like it was portrayed at the time or that social relations at work in the UK were so different from elsewhere (Tiratsoo and Tomlinson 1994). Ironically Coventry itself was seen at different points as a model for progressive labour relations. 'The Coventry conception of high wages tied to productivity rather than individual skill, and of an identity of interest between labour and capital, so that the system is kept going at all cost, has much in common with American practice', the Times wrote in 1959 (*Times* 31 March 1959).

There were equally complaints about the poor quality of UK management. Critics of employers and managers accused then of being amateurs with few managerial or technical skills. Their perspectives were too short termist. Too many had a public school background and when they did not (if they were self made, for example), they wanted one for their children who themselves might aspire more to a life in finance, if not a life of leisure. Coventry certainly had its own managers and executives who rose from the shop floor (Morewood 1990). One was Sir George Harriman who started as a Morris apprentice in the 1920s and became chairman of BMC in 1961. At the time there was much local praise for its 'bosses'. 'In the final resort [Coventry] owes its wealth to brilliant direction of industry' said the CET in 08 June 1961. The difficulty was that many of the problems that existed were structural and therefore beyond the capacity of any individual or even a group of them to solve. The car industry leaders, for example, did not have the capacity to realise the economies of scale that were becoming ever more important in that industry. That was one of the reason why the state was involved in encouraging change (Thoms and Donnelly 1985; Donnelly et al. 2017).

But there was considerable criticism too of state policy. Some critics argued that there was too much 'planning' and interference. In 1950 it was disparagingly said that more than a dozen government ministries had an input into what was going on in Coventry. For others the argument was that the state was mismanaging because of mistaken policies linked to the influence the City-Treasury nexus on policy making. One manifestation of this, already noted, was so called 'stop' and 'go'. Hire purchase regulations were said to have been changed 17 times between 1952 and 1970 (Thoms and Donnelly 1985, pp. 151, 177). Given that cars were a major item bought on credit this had an inevitable impact in a city like Coventry but though this generated much argument at the time it is to clear it was a major issue. 'Cycles in the British economy induced by stop-go were no greater than in the European countries held out as models of good economic performance' (Tomlinson 2009, p. 243). There was also much criticism of attempts to plan the location of industry. Declining areas were renamed 'development areas' and development certificates soon required for new units of more than 5000 square feet. At one point the Chairman of the Chamber of Commerce said that the Board of Trade had 'the power of life and death in this city' (Tiratsoo 1990, pp. 70–71). But in the long run this made little difference to the expansion of Coventry's core industries as the benefits of spill-over were well understood. In any case, export drives in which Coventry's engineering output played a key role trumped relocation objectives. Complaints were continually made, however, that it limited the diversification of the City and the ability to attract new businesses. But even here account has to be taken of the ways in which high wages in the city might have been a disincentive to new sectors starting there.

Beyond these issues there is also an important global dimension to any argument about the UK's economic performance in these years and the story of a city like Coventry. Britain's political leaders continued to see themselves as being at the head of a weaker but still great imperial power. It was the era of the Cold War and Britain was second only to the US in the NATO alliance. And, even as decolonization speeded up, 'Empire' still mattered. There was a British global mission. Even at the level of sport we see signs of this. One of the heights of achievement for a Coventry athlete—often from the Godiva Harriers club—was participation in the British *Empire* Games. In 1966 in Jamaica, Coventry's contingent was said to be 'a magnificent seven'—'six proud men' and one 'lone female athlete' who, reflecting the pull of the town, the paper noted had been born in Wales (CS 28 July 1966). Only in 1970 did it become the games become the *Commonwealth* Games.

The result was what critics at the time and later saw as imperial or great power over commitment (Geiger 2017). Military expenditure peaked at 9.8% of output in 1953 but averaged just fewer than 8% in the 1950s and just fewer than 6% in the 1960s (Author's calculations from SIPRI database). This expenditure helped the long boom and it directly benefitted the arms factories in Coventry that sat alongside the car plants. Not the least of these was Armstrong Whitworth with defence contracts related to the Seahawk, Hunter, Javelin and Avro Vulcan planes and firms contributing to the production of guided missiles. But the commitment also held overall investment down, especially the civilian sectors. It constrained choices.

During the war those involved in reconstruction planning had been told that they should not think of costs. The unlimited mobilization for war seemed to open up the possibility of an unlimited mobilisation for peace. But it was not to be. In the 1950s and 1960s private interests were reasserted, Cold War demands diverted resources elsewhere. If there was more done in the 1950s and 1960s than people had once imagined possible less was also achieved than needed to be. But it was easier to point to real or imagined partial weaknesses than to question the bigger ways in the realisation of the more grandiose hopes of the time were being limited in the long boom.

Bibliography

CET: Coventry Evening Telegraph.

CS: Coventry Sentinel.

Booth, A. (2006). *The Management of Technical Change Automation in the UK and USA Since 1950*. Houndmills: Macmillan.

BPP (British Parliamentary Papers). (1971–1972). *Select Committee on Race Relations and Immigration*, Session 1971–72. *Police/Immigrant Relations.* Volume 3. *Evidence, Documents and Index*. London: House of Commons.

Broadberry, S., & Crafts, N. (2003). UK Productivity Performance from 1950 to 1979: A Restatement of the Broadberry-Crafts View. *The Economic History Review, 56*(4), 718–735.

Brown, W. (1971). Piecework and Wage Determination in Coventry. *Scottish Journal of Political Economy, 18*(1), 1–30.

Brown, W., & Sisson, K. (1975). The Use of Piecework Comparisons in Workplace Wage Determination. *British Journal of Industrial Relations, 13*(1), 23–53.

Campbell, L. (1996). *Coventry Cathedral: Art and Architecture in Post-war Britain* (Vol. Clarendon Studies in the History of Art). Oxford: Clarendon Press.

Couperus, S. (2016). Rethinking the "Blueprint for Living Together": Community Planning and Sociology in Coventry, 1940–55. In S. Couperus & H. Ka (Eds.), *(Re)Constructing Communities in Europe, 1918–1968* (pp. 57–76). London: Routledge.

Denman, J., & McDonald, P. (1996, January). Unemployment Statistics from 1881 to the Present Day. *Labour Market Trends, 104*(1), 5–18.

Donnelly, T., Begley, J., & Collis, C. (2017). The West Midlands Automotive Industry: The Road Downhill. *Business History, 59*(1), 56–74.

Donnelly, T., & Thoms, D. (1989). Trade Unions, Management and the Search for Production in the Coventry Motor Car Industry, 1939–75. *Business History, 31*(2), 98–113.

Feinstein, C. (1999). Structural Change in the Developed Countries During the Twentieth Century. *Oxford Review of Economic Policy, 15*(4), 35–55.

Fischer, K. F., & Larkham, P. (2018). Coventry: A Model of Modernist Reconstruction. In K. F. Fischer & U. Altrock (Eds.), *Windows Upon Planning History*. London: Routledge.

Friedman, A. (1977). *Industry and Labour: Class Struggle at Work and Monopoly Capitalism*. London: Macmillan.

Geiger, T. (2017). *Britain and the Economic Problem of the Cold War: The Political Economy and the Economic Impact of the British Defence Effort, 1945–1955*. London: Routledge.

Gill, T. (2016). The Indian Workers Association Coventry 1938–1990: Political and Social Action. In V. Kalra & S. Sharma (Eds.), *State of Subversion: Radical Politics in Punjab in the 20th Century* (pp. 156–187). London: Routledge.

IFS (Institute for Fiscal Studies). (2011). *Trends in Education and Schools Spending* (Briefing Note BN 121).

Knowles, K., & Robinson, D. (1969). Wage Movements in Coventry. *Bulletin of the Oxford University Institute of Economics & Statistics, 31*(1), 1–21.

Lewis, J. (1985). Women and Society: Continuity and Change Since 1870. *Refresh, 1*(Autumn), 1–4.

Lloyd-Jones, R., & Lewis, M. J. (2006). *Alfred Herbert and the British Machine Tool Industry, 1887–1983*. Aldershot: Ashgate.

Morewood, S. (1990). *Pioneers and Inheritors: Top Management in the Coventry Motor Industry, 1896–1972*. Coventry: Centre for Business History, Coventry Polytechnic.

SIPRI. (Under review). Stockholm International Peace Research Institute database. www.sipri.org/.

Stephens, W. B. (Ed.). (1969). The City of Coventry: Public Education. In *Victoria History of the Counties of England: A History of the County of Warwick: Volume 8, the City of Coventry and Borough of Warwick* (pp. 299–315). London: Oxford University Press.

Thompson, E. P. (Ed.). (1970). *Warwick University Ltd: Industry, Management and the Universities*. Harmondsworth: Penguin.

Thoms, D., & Donnelly, T. (1985). *The Motor Car Industry in Coventry Since the 1890's: Origins. Development, Structure*. London: Croom Helm.

Tiratsoo, N. (1990). *Reconstruction, Affluence, and Labour Politics: Coventry, 1945–1960*. London: Routledge.

Tiratsoo, N. (2000). The Reconstruction of Blitzed British Cities, 1945–55: Myths and Reality. *Contemporary British History, 14*(1), 27–44.

Tiratsoo, N., & Tomlinson, J. (1994). Restrictive Practices on the Shopfloor in Britain, 1945–60: Myth and Reality. *Business History, 36*(2), 65–82.

Tomlinson, J. (2006). De-industrialisation, Not Decline: A Meta Narrative for Post-war British History. *Twentieth Century British History, 27*(1), 76–99.

Tomlinson, J. (2009). Thrice Denied: 'Declinism' as a Recurrent Theme in British History in the Long Twentieth Century. *Twentieth Century British History, 20*(2), 227–251.

5
Recession and Relative Recovery

Clive Collis

There was a rapid decline in the economic performance of Coventry during the 1970s and early 1980s which mirrored that of the British economy over this period. Deteriorating national economic conditions in the early 1970s were associated with the 1973/1974 international oil crisis, followed between 1978 and 1982 by a severe recession and then a recovery phase in the remainder of the 1980s. Compared to Britain as a whole, Coventry lost a higher proportion of its employment during the recession but the city gained relatively more employment in the recovery phase during the rest of the 1980s. This change in Coventry's relative employment performance has been taken by Healey and Dunham (1994) as indicating a change from relative competitive disadvantage to relative competitive advantage.

This chapter examines in detail the changes in Coventry's economic performance during the period 1971–1990. As a context, the chapter begins with a brief regional overview followed by a synoptic history of the Coventry local economy.

C. Collis (✉)
Coventry University, Coventry, UK

J. Begley et al. (eds.), *Revival of a City*, Palgrave Studies in Economic History,
https://doi.org/10.1007/978-3-030-22822-4_5

The West Midlands Regional Context for Coventry's Local Economy

Green and Berkeley (2006) described the regional context as one, where during the long post war boom from 1945, the West Midlands emerged as one of the most prosperous regions in England with rapid population and employment growth. Collis and Mallier (1985) pointed out that in this period of full employment and rising real incomes the West Midlands was a region which benefitted from a growing level of prosperity flowing from its manufacturing base. In 1971 the region was second only to the South East in its level of Gross Domestic Product (GDP) per head. However, in the 1970s the era of prosperity rapidly eroded when the West Midlands had the lowest growth rate of any of Britain's regions and by the end of the decade its GDP ranking had fallen to the third lowest of the UK's eleven regions . Between 1980 and 1983 the West Midlands had the highest increase in the unemployment rate, the worst long term unemployment and the greatest contraction of the employment base. It is generally agreed that the process of economic change which culminated in the crisis of the early 1980s in the West Midlands had begun in the mid-1960s (Collis and Roberts 1992). Green and Berkeley had suggested that the region's over-reliance on manufacturing, particularly car production, had left the region exposed to external foreign competition. Others have looked internally within the region for an explanation citing the strategies of the large manufacturing firms who dominated employment in the region as responsible for the process of change from prosperity to crisis. For example, Gaffikin and Nickson (1984, p. 6) argued that, 'through cutting back production in Britain and expanding overseas the transnational corporations traditionally located in the West Midlands bear a major part of the blame for the economic crisis of the region.' These included Dunlop and the General Electric Company (GEC), two of Coventry's largest employers at the time.

However, in 1984 the West Midlands Industrial Development Association, later renamed the West Midlands Development Agency, was set up to coordinate the marketing of the region to foreign-owned companies. During the 1980s the West Midlands became a major regional recipient of inward Foreign Direct Investment (FDI) flows to the UK joining Wales and Scotland at the top end of the league table as a host region for flows of FDI projects and jobs (Collis 1992, 1995; Collis et al. 1998). The main areas of origin of both the stock and new flows of FDI were North America and the European Community (Collis et al. 1994). The most important industries in which FDI took place were Distribution, and Metals, Engineering and Vehicles, the latter group being the region's major industries. The main factors which attracted foreign-owned companies to choose the West Midlands as a location were national and regional communications and local accessibility. International accessibility via Birmingham Airport was also a factor. Whilst outward investment from the region by transnational corporations may have previously weakened the West Midlands region, appropriate policies successfully attracted inward FDI and contributed to regional resurgence (Collis and Noon 1994; Collis and Peck 1996). Benefits included jobs safeguarded and created. An estimated 100,000 jobs were provided by foreign-owned firms located in the West Midlands in 1989. Many of the foreign-owned companies exported final products from the region; purchased some of their capital equipment locally; contributed to the region's skills base through workforce training; and made use local services (Collis and Roberts 1992).

A Brief History of Coventry's Local Economy

By the 1800s the weaving of silk and ribbons was the main industry in Coventry's prosperous local economy. However, faced with strong international competition the industry declined during the 1860s and the local economy went into decline. Other industries developed and the local economy prospered. These industries included watch and clock making, sewing machine manufacturing, bicycle and motorcycle manufacturing and, by the late 1930s, motor car manufacturing. Coventry became the centre of the British motor vehicle industry. A number of industries related to cycle and motor car manufacture grew up in Coventry, notably mechanical and electrical engineering. Aero engine manufacturing also developed and in the 1940s was a major activity which continued thereafter although many of the car firms who had switched to aircraft activities in war time returned to car production. The changing structure of industry in Coventry over time resulted from the interplay of a number of factors. These were the effects of international competition as globalisation impacted on the city; the entrepreneurship of local business leaders; and the accumulated industrial skills of a versatile local workforce.

Coventry's Local Economy in the 1970s

Collis and Mallier (1985) have provided an analysis of the local economy for the 1970s. In 1971 employment in Coventry totalled 192,400 but by 1981 it had declined to 181,600. Thus over the period the net loss of jobs amounted to 10,800, a 6% decline in employment. During the same period national employment grew by 3%. The major job losses in Coventry occurred in the Secondary Sector where employment fell from 121,000 to 100,900, a 17% decline, representing 20,300 jobs lost. This loss was only partly offset by a gain in the period of 14% in the Tertiary Sector where employment rose to 79,000. Thus the main feature of the local industrial structure was a Secondary sector, dominated by manufacturing, in which job losses were concentrated. Coventry's economic difficulties in general, and for the car industry in particular, arose in the context of Britain's de-industrialisation and the increasing internationalisation and globalisation of trade.

In the 1970s manufacturing employment in Coventry accounted for two thirds of total employment in the city almost twice the GB figure, a dependence which persisted (Collis et al. 2001). Manufacturing employment was concentrated in a relatively small number of large firms, many externally owned. The main firms in the 1970s were British Leyland, Peugeot-Talbot, GEC, Rolls Royce, Massey-Ferguson, Dunlop, Courtaulds and Alfred Herbert.

Employment was also concentrated in a limited number of broad industrial sectors: Vehicles, Electrical Engineering and Mechanical

Engineering. In 1971 over a third of all employment in the city was concentrated in the Vehicle industry, a concentration of employment in a single industrial grouping which gave to Coventry an employer base narrower than any other comparative sized city in Britain. The employment concentration in these particular manufacturing industries, rather than services, produced a further unique feature, namely a male bias in employment. Some 50% of those employed in the Coventry in 1971 were males in manufacturing, whilst nationally the comparable figure was 25%.

The high employment concentration in manufacturing industries was accompanied by a relatively smaller service sector than might have been anticipated for a city the size of Coventry. Within the service sector, a third of the service sector employment was in Public Administration, Education and Medical Services, the remaining two thirds of service sector employment was in All Service provision. Employment in Public Administration was primarily generated by the local City Council plus limited counter services provided by central government agencies. Similarly in Distribution, Banking, and Insurance the employment in Coventry was primarily in the provision of counter services, with the regional offices and associated employment being located elsewhere.

However, these microeconomic factors should be seen in the context of the macroeconomic environment and government policy actions. For example, Fothergill and Gudgin (1982) have argued that the most obvious way in which the national economic context in Britain affected manufacturing is the fact that the declining fortunes of the economy have led to fewer jobs everywhere. Mallier and Rosser (1982) have argued that government macroeconomic policy measures, particularly the control of hire purchase and credit facilities, affected the motor industry in Coventry harder than the rest of the industry elsewhere in the country. The motor vehicle industry in Coventry was also affected adversely by regional policy, particularly through Industrial Development Certificate (IDC) refusals but also through the incentives available in the Assisted Areas located outside Coventry.

Employment Change in Coventry 1971–1978: A Shift-Share Analysis

The importance of a local economy's industrial structure to its changes in employment may be seen through the use of shift-share analysis which, despite its critics, has been shown to be robust. In this technique the share indicates the employment change which would have occurred in an area if its total employment had grown at the national rate. The shift is made up of a structural component and a differential component. The structural component measures the effect of variations between local and national industrial structures and the main aim of the technique is to measure the influence of an area's mix of industries on its employment change. The differential component represents the effects of variations between local and national industry growth rates and is equal to the difference between actual and expected employment change. The influence of both the mix of industries and their national growth rates are reflected in the expected employment change which is the sum of the structural and share components. The difference between actual and expected local employment change reflects the influence of local factors on an area's growth.

A refinement of the technique, which is of relevance to Coventry, is to sub-divide the differential component into a competitive effect and an allocative effect. The competitive effect measures the effect on employment change in a local economy of the differences between local and national industry growth rates. The allocative effect indicates the extent to which the local economy exhibits differential growth in its specialist industries.

Shift-share analysis can be carried out using data for different bases and different levels of industrial disaggregation. In its most general form the base for comparison between the local and national economy is the total national economy (total employment). However, if the local economy is dominated by manufacturing as in the case of Coventry, the appropriate base for comparison can be the national manufacturing economy (national manufacturing employment). Not only can the base economy be disaggregated so can the industries used.

Thus, the analysis can be undertaken at the level of industry order such as Vehicles or Electrical Engineering or at the level of specific industries within groups, e.g. motor vehicle manufacturing within Vehicles or telephone and telegraph apparatus within Electrical Engineering.

In the analysis presented below, Collis and Mallier employed the versatility of the shift-share technique to present results for Coventry using alternative bases and different levels of disaggregation. The first results were for a shift-share analysis for order groups and total employment for 1971–1981. Since order groups can be aggregated into sectors the results are also provided for primary, secondary and tertiary sectors. Secondly, with a national base (total employment) results are presented at a more specific level of industrial disaggregation. Thirdly, the base economy is disaggregated so that the base economy used for comparison is the national manufacturing economy. The latter results are presented using two levels of industrial disaggregation, for order groups and specific industries within them.

A shift-share analysis for total employment at the broad industry group level for Coventry for the period 1971–1978 showed that the 10,800 jobs lost resulted from a negative shift consisting of both an adverse industrial structure, which accounted for 43% of the employment shift, and adverse differential factors which accounted for 57%. When the analysis was conducted at a more disaggregated level, for more narrowly defined industries, the negative structural component accounted for 52% of the shift and the adverse differential factors accounted for 48%. It was apparent that the dominant Secondary Sector was both the major source of the local economy's overall structural weakness but also the sector in which the adverse differential factors were concentrated.

Given the dominance of the manufacturing sector in the Coventry local economy, an important comparison to make is between the local and national manufacturing economies. A comparison of the two manufacturing economies using order group data showed that the expected decline in manufacturing employment in Coventry between 1971 and 1978 was 10,307 with the dominant factor in expected decline being the decline in national employment shown by a negative share of 11,821 jobs. However, since the actual decline in Coventry was 20,300 manufacturing jobs, nearly half of the actual decline was the result of differential factors. Analysis using specific industry level data also showed the importance of differential factors.

In order to investigate the nature of these differential factors it was necessary to establish which particular industries performed worse in Coventry than nationally. Within the three dominant manufacturing industry groups there were four specific industries in which employment was concentrated. Two of these industries were in the Vehicles group, firstly, motor vehicle manufacturing and, secondly, aerospace equipment manufacturing and repairing. Within the Mechanical Engineering industry group was the specific industry of metal working machine tools and within the Electrical Engineering industry group was telephone and telegraph apparatus and equipment. These four industries were not only the major secondary sector employing industries in Coventry during the period but were also the ones in which job losses were concentrated. It is apparent that industries which were previously the cause of Coventry's prosperity were in steep decline in the in the 1970s. A striking aspect, however, is that both the motor vehicle manufacturing industry and the telephone and telegraph apparatus and equipment industry declined much more in Coventry than in Great Britain as a whole.

A disaggregation of the negative differential components for both the Electrical Engineering and Vehicles industries indicated that the nature of the differential effect on Coventry's local economy was mainly of the allocative kind showing a large negative differential employment change in its specialist industries which declined more in Coventry than in the country as a whole. The competitive effects were also negative showing that Coventry was an unattractive location for these industries over the 1971–1978 period.

A number of conclusions arise from the shift-share analysis for Coventry for 1971–1978. A comparison of the Coventry economy with the national economy revealed that the problems of the local economy between 1971 and 1978 were in roughly equal proportions, an adverse industrial structure and a set of unpropitious differential factors. The adverse industrial structure stemmed from the dominance of manufacturing in the Coventry economy which specialised in Vehicles,

Electrical and Mechanical Engineering. However, when comparing the local and national manufacturing economies, Coventry's decline was seen to be the result of both national decline and adverse differential factors. Fothergill and Gudgin (1982) have shown that urbanised areas with an adverse industrial structure, a high proportion of the labour force in large factories and which was located outside the regional policy Assisted Areas were likely to have a poor performance in manufacturing employment. Coventry between 1971 and 1978 contained most of these adverse characteristics. Like other urban areas Coventry suffered from physical location constraints which led to investment in capital equipment replacing labour from existing floor space, thus reducing employment. Being outside the regional policy Assisted Areas, Coventry was at a disadvantage when companies sought to take advantage of government incentives and invested elsewhere. The size structure of Coventry's factories was large and, given the association between size structure and the rate of new firm formation, the size structure of factories was a local factor which undoubtedly contributed to Coventry's employment performance. Indeed, as Fothergill and Gudgin (1982) pointed out, the estimated differences in new firm formation rates between Coventry and its neighbour city, Leicester, represented a loss of above 1000 jobs a year to the Coventry area. This is an important factor when, major local industries were in decline. In addition, there were particular local conditions which were conducive to external ownership being a factor in Coventry's manufacturing employment decline. Given high unit labour costs, labour relations problems and the marginal nature of many of Coventry's plants to external owners, corporate status was a factor contributing to Coventry's manufacturing decline between 1971 and 1978.

Industrial Decline in Coventry 1974–1982

In their 1984 article, Healey and Clark also presented the results of a shift-share analysis using data for manufacturing employment and specific industries. These results may be compared with those presented by Collis and Mallier for the same base economy and level of industrial

Table 5.1 Shift-share analysis for manufacturing employment in Coventry, 1971–1978

Actual change	Share	Structural component	Differential component
−20,300	−11,821	−376	−8115

Source Adapted from Collis and Mallier (1985), p. 67

Table 5.2 Shift-share analysis for manufacturing employment in Coventry, 1974–1982

Actual change	Share	Structural component	Differential component
−52,908	−31,484	−4577	−16,847

Source Adapted from Healey and Clark (1984), p. 309

disaggregation. The results for 1971–1978 and 1974–1982 are shown, repectively, in Tables 5.1 and 5.2.

Tables 5.1 and 5.2 show, that in both studies, the share component represented the major factor in manufacturing employment change and that the differential component was more important than the structural component. However, whilst the ranking of the shift-share components remained the same in the two overlapping time periods, in the 1974–1982 period the relative importance of the adverse structural component was greater. Thus the industrial composition of Coventry's manufacturing sector became somewhat more unfavourable over time.

Healey and Clark (1984, 1985) updated the story of the development of the local economy. On the evidence of its 1974 unemployment level of 5300 Coventry's economy was near the start of a two year recession. In 1978 the unemployment level at 12,600 was well above the 1974 level. Coventry's economy went into deep recession in 1979 with the unemployment level reaching 32,000 in 1982. Unemployment rates of less than 1% were common in Coventry up to 1966. The 5% barrier was not reached until 1975. The 10% rate was reached in 1981 and the 15% rate was reached in 1982. Relative to GB the Coventry situation gradually worsened and after 1974 the total employment rate in Coventry was consistently above the GB average.

With respect to employment change in Coventry's main sector, manufacturing, the decline in employment had accelerated in the late

1970s and early 1980s. Total manufacturing employment in Coventry was 115,300 in 1974, and 100,700 in 1978 but fell to 62,400 in 1982. Thus, between 1974 and 1982 Coventry lost almost 53,000 jobs from its manufacturing workforce. This represented a fall of 46% compared to a fall of 32% in the West Midlands as a whole and 27% nationally. Three quarters of these lost jobs occurred after 1978.

Of the industries within manufacturing, it was in Vehicles that manufacturing employment fell the most, from nearly 60,000 to just over 26,600 with its share of manufacturing employment falling from 52% in 1974 to 43% in 1982. Mechanical engineering shed 9900 jobs and Electrical Engineering shed 3100 jobs. Nevertheless, by 1982 four fifths of manufacturing jobs were still in these three industrial groups.

On the other hand, 9200 jobs were added to the service sector in Coventry between 1971 and 1981. Of this most of the job growth occurred before 1976 with less than 1000 additional service sector jobs created in Coventry between 1976 and 1981.

As well as the continued dominance of manufacturing in the local economy there continued to be a dominance of a few large firms, many externally owned. The top 7 firms contributed nearly three quarters of the decline in manufacturing employment. There was also a dominance by a few large plants. In 1974 twenty two plants, each employing more than one thousand workers accounted for 70% of manufacturing employment, some 81,300 jobs. Between 1974 and 1982 the large plants had shed over 44,000 jobs, their total employment falling to 37,200.

Many of the jobs lost were in establishments owned by firms based outside Coventry. Employment in the externally owned group declined by 48% between 1974 and 1982. Of the externally owned sector it was the foreign based sector which shed the highest proportion of jobs, a 53% decline. In comparison there was a 39% decline by companies based in the rest of the West Midlands and a 47% decline in those based elsewhere in the UK. Even after these job losses the externally owned establishments still made an important contribution to employment in Coventry. By 1982, three fifths of manufacturing jobs in Coventry were in establishments of UK companies based outside the West Midlands region and one sixth of these jobs were in foreign owned firms.

As a result of the dominance of large externally owned enterprises in Coventry most of the city's manufacturing jobs were in establishments which belonged to multi-plant firms which accounted for over 90% of manufacturing employment in 1974. It was subsidiary companies which dominated employment in Coventry rather than independent firms. In establishments belonging to multi-plant enterprises and those operated by subsidiary companies the fall in employment was nearly 50% between 1974 and 1982.

There is evidence that in general the employment performance of a plant can be affected by the age of the buildings in which manufacturing takes place. In fact in Coventry specifically in 1982 over three quarters of manufacturing employment was in plants built before 1946 and in these plants the number of jobs fell by 50% between 1974 and 1982.

The dominant large firms in Coventry were the same seven companies in 1974, 1978 and 1982. These top seven firms accounted for three quarters of the decline in Coventry's manufacturing employment between 1974 and 1982. One company alone, BL at Canley which had employed 11,000 people in 1974 accounted for one quarter of the net job losses in Coventry in this period. Alfred Herbert, machine tool manufacturer, was just outside the top seven in 1978 with 2300 employees in Coventry but the company closed in 1983 when the workforce numbered only 400.

More broadly, in 1974 the largest fifteen companies employed 94,000 people or 82% of the manufacturing workforce in Coventry. By 1982 these companies employed 45,000 people, less than half as many as in 1974. Between 1974 and 1982 the largest fifteen companies contributed 93% of the net loss of manufacturing jobs in Coventry but still accounted for 72% of all manufacturing jobs in Coventry.

There is general evidence that the larger is a plant size, the more the propensity it has to shed jobs, rather than close completely. The high degree of employment concentration in a few large firms and plants in Coventry therefore helps to explain why most of the job losses in the city between 1974 and 1982 were in situ contractions by surviving firms. Complete closures of plants by large firms took place later, at the beginning of the twenty-first century, following earlier contractions. It was at this time that the risk of closures by foreign investors became a reality.

Coventry's economic problems should be seen against the background of a weakening national economy and a declining level of international competiveness. However, since these factors are common to all local economies, a key questions is why Coventry's rate of decline was so much more severe than in many other areas. Fothergill and Gudgin (1982) have suggested that the uneven spatial employment change in manufacturing in the United Kingdom can mostly be accounted for by four factors: industrial structure, urban structure, size structure of factories and regional policy. Healey and Clark (1984) applied this framework to Coventry for the period 1974–1982. With respect to industrial structure the conclusion was that, given Coventry's dependence on the manufacturing sector and Vehicles in particular the local economy fared well during the 1950s and early 1960s but thereafter this overspecialisation made the city vulnerable. Their shift-share analysis showed that of the net 53,000 jobs lost in manufacturing, the largest component was the share or national component, giving a loss of 31,500, next was the differential component, giving a loss of 17,000 and then the structural component which contributed a loss of 4500. Thus, although an adverse industrial structure contributed to the decline of Coventry's manufacturing sector during this period, the major influence was national deindustrialisation. However, the size of the negative differential factor suggests that other factors were at work.

With respect to Coventry's urban structure, the evidence suggests that, at least until the late 1970s, firms in the City suffered from constrained locations. Operating in outmoded factories in built up spaces with no room for expansion, firms were unable to invest in new space-demanding flow-line production methods of production and became uncompetitive. However, the impact of firm's shedding jobs leading to underused factory space and some plants being closed, leading to empty factories, meant that the constrained location argument was less applicable in Coventry, particularly given that the City Council relaxed planning constraints on industrial development in its built-up areas and opened up new industrial development land.

The size structure of factories can influence a city's economic well-being. There is evidence to suggest that a dominance of large plants in a local urban economy inhibits new firm formation because large plants seem not to provide the environment for entrepreneurship. The dominance of large plants in Coventry may have meant that the size structure of factories may have been an adverse factor in its economic fortune. To their examination of the role of large plants Healey and Clark (1985) added a discussion of the effects of the size and ownership characteristics of the large firms which operated these plants. Coventry's largest firms made big cut backs, for example, BL, the largest employer in 1974 reduced its workforce by 21,000 which represented a 71% reduction. Peugeot-Talbot, another motor car assembler, shed the next largest number of employees, losing 8000 workers. Rolls Royce, Massey-Ferguson and Alfred Herbert each shed between 2000 and 3000 jobs. This job shedding by Coventry's large firms has been attributed to their external ownership and the marginality of the Coventry plants to their overall corporate activities.

Government regional policy had sought to reduce inequalities between regions through diverting investment from prosperous to poor regions. In the 1960s, the then prosperous West Midlands, including Coventry, were seen as a source region and city from which new investment could be diverted. The stick in this policy was the IDC which had to be obtained for new industrial development. When Rootes wished to expand in Coventry an IDC was refused and at the government's behest the investment was diverted in 1963 to Linwood in Scotland, which necessitated the purchase of land there but leaving land in Coventry unutilised. By 1972 there were 8000 employed at the Linwood plant, jobs which might have been in Coventry. It is generally believed that UK government regional policy had a detrimental effect on donor areas both through its effects on industrial movement as a result of the stick of IDC's and the carrot of financial incentives given for investment in disadvantaged regions. The effects of this policy appear to have been adverse to Coventry, directly in the early 1960s through IDC refusal, and indirectly, over a longer period through constraining the process of industrial movement into the city.

Healey and Clark (1985) as did Collis and Mallier (1985), argued that Coventry's labour market structure may have also contributed to the decline in the city's manufacturing employment. In the past Coventry workers had collectively negotiated high wage levels and increases, so that, for example, in 1959 the Coventry car workers were paid 20% more than their counterparts elsewhere in the UK although their advantage had been eroded away by the 1970s. In addition to Coventry male workers in Vehicles and Engineering being highly paid, they were also militant workers with the highest rate of work stoppages of all local areas in the late 1960s and early 1970s. The reputation of Coventry workers for industrial dispute and the high cost of their labour may have deterred new investment and thereby have constrained growth of the local economy.

In order to throw more light on the processes accounting for the net loss of 53,000 jobs in manufacturing between 1974 and 1982 in Coventry, Healey and Clark (1984, 1985) analysed the components of change. This approach decomposes changes in the number of establishments and associated jobs into entries, such as new enterprises and branch openings, and exits such as transfers out of the city and complete closures. In situ expansion is when a firm who has survived in the city expands its workforce and in situ contraction is when a survivor sheds jobs.

The results of the components of change analysis for Coventry were as follows. Overall there was stability in the total number of plants. Despite Coventry's industrial decline there were only 18 fewer plants operating in 1982 when there were 648 establishments than in 1974 when there were 666. However, of the 666 establishments present in the city in 1974, only 300 survived throughout the period but these survivors had experienced major in situ job losses. Table 5.3 presents a summary of the components of net job losses.

Table 5.3 Total net job losses, Coventry, 1974–1982

All gains			All losses			Net change
Entry gains	In situ expansions	Total	Exit losses	In situ contractions	Total	Net loss
5547	3720	9267	−16,399	−45,778	−62,175	−52,908

Source Adapted from Healey and Clark (1985), p. 1359

The main conclusion to come from this components of change analysis was that despite the high turnover of plants, with less than half of the establishments in 1982 still operated by the same firms as in 1974, it was the loss of 45,778 jobs from the surviving plants which contracted that contributed most towards the 46% decline in manufacturing employment in Coventry which had fallen from 115,317 to 62,409 jobs between 1974 and 1982. Most of the job losses occurred in the large externally owned and controlled firms in Coventry's main industries, namely Vehicles, Mechanical and Electrical Engineering which drastically reduced job levels in their branch plants in Coventry over the period. This had knock-on effects on local supplying and related industries. Healey and Clark (1985) concluded that Coventry's local economy collapsed largely as a result of disinvestment decisions taken by corporate head offices located externally outside Coventry and who saw the plants there as marginal to their overall operations.

Studies carried out for other places have indicated that exits through plant closures were the main cause of employment decline. However, compared to other areas in Great Britain for which components of change analyses have been carried out, a number of features of Coventry's experience stand out: greater industrial decline, the importance of job losses in surviving establishments, fairly low rates of job loss due to exits, and a low rate of job gains through entries. These differences between Coventry where in situ contractions were the main component of job losses and other places, where the main culprit was exits through plant closures, reflected the fact that Coventry at the time was outside the government's regional policy assisted areas and was dominated by large firms, often externally owned, operating in a few major industries with large-sized Coventry branch plants many of which operated in old buildings.

The details of the importance of Coventry's large firms and the extent of external ownership are worthy of further analysis. All of the top 15 firms shed jobs between 1974 and 1982. In 1974 the largest 15 companies in Coventry employed 94,000 people, just over 80% of the city's manufacturing workforce. But by 1982 they only employed 45,000 which was less than half as many as in 1974 but still more than 70% of all manufacturing jobs. With respect to external ownership, in 1982 foreign owned firms controlled 1 in 6 jobs in Coventry and 3 in 5 jobs were in establishments by UK companies located outside the West Midlands region so that less than one quarter of manufacturing jobs in the city were in locally owned establishments. With respect to marginality, the fact is that most of the top 7 companies, the same firms in 1978 and still in 1982, were marginal to their external owners. In 1978, for example, in 3 of these 7 companies the Coventry proportion of their UK workforce was less than 10% and a further 2 had less than 15%. In Peugeot-Talbot the proportion was higher but being a foreign owned company with plans outside the UK the Coventry workforce was a small proportion of the company's total international employment. From this evidence it is clear that the major plants in Coventry were not only externally owned but also marginal to the activities of their external owners. This combination of external ownership and marginality provides a major explanation for Coventry's manufacturing job losses between 1974 and 1982. It is not surprising that after this period of job contraction the next stage was for the external owners to close plants completely. The closure of BL's plant at Canley and the closure by Rolls Royce of one of its two Coventry plants which had both occurred during the 1974–1982 period, were forerunners of other closures which took place later on. Alfred Herbert, the machine tool manufacturer, was closed in 1983. The Massey Ferguson tractor factory in Banner Lane was closed in 2002. In 2005 Jaguar's Browns Lane plant was closed. Then in 2007 Peugeot's Ryton plant was closed and in the same year so was the Little Heath plant of Courtaulds. Thus whilst the in situ contraction of surviving establishments was the major component of manufacturing decline in Coventry between 1974 and 1982, subsequently plant closures by the major Coventry companies became more important than before.

Coventry's Changing Competitive Advantage 1971–1990

Healey and Dunham (1994) applied Michael Porter's concept of the Competitive Advantage of Nations to Coventry's local economy over the period 1971–1990. Porter (1990) suggested that nations gain competitive advantage through four main determinants: factor conditions; demand conditions; firm strategy, structure and rivalry; and related and supporting industries. Two other factors, government and chance, were influences on the four main determinants. Porter illustrated this as a diamond which depicted a dynamic system in which interactions between the determinants reinforce competitive advantage or disadvantage. In this dynamic system it is possible for there to be a reversal of competitive advantage or disadvantage.

In applying Porter's concept to localities the determinants may be viewed as interacting to engender a set of competitive advantages or disadvantages which vary from place to place and over time in any particular locality. Porter used data on trade flows as an indicator of national competitiveness but, because such data is not available at local level in Britain, employment has been used as a surrogate measure. Thus, Healey and Dunham used changes in employment levels as their indicator of Coventry's changing competitive advantage.

Porter (1986) argued that one important factor which affects the local impact of national and international changes in demand is industrial structure. Accordingly, Healey and Dunham included industrial structure as an important factor in their discussion of demand conditions. Using shift-share analysis they calculated expected employment change which takes combined account of national changes and the local industrial structure. They then compared the expected employment change in Coventry with the actual change in total employment which took place in the City. The difference between the actual change and the expected change leaves a residual, the differential shift. This differential component is used to illustrate the competitive advantage of Coventry's local economy compared with other areas. In order to show change in competitive advantage over two consecutive time periods, they compared 1971–1981 with 1981–1989. They produced evidence to show that Coventry's local economy as a whole performed much worse than expected in the 1970s but performed slightly better than expected in the 1980s.

As Table 5.4 shows between 1971 and 1981 total employment in Coventry fell by 46,100, a loss of nearly a quarter of the local economy's jobs. Adding the share component to the structural component gave an

Table 5.4 Shift-share analysis of total employment in Coventry 1971–1981 and 1981–1989

Years	Total change	Share component	Structural component	Expected change	Differential component
1971–1981	−46,103	−4855	−22,775	−27,630	−18,473
1981–1989	−6000	+6164	−16432	−10,268	+4245

Source Adapted from Healey and Dunham (1994), p. 1288

expected fall of just over 27,600 jobs. Thus, the actual fall in employment of just over 46,100 was almost 18,500 more than expected. In the subsequent period, 1981–1989, employment fell by just 6000 when the expected fall was well over 10,000, the differential shift being just over 4200. In both periods Coventry's unfavourable industrial structure stood out.

In order to indicate which industry groups contributed most to the change from relative competitive disadvantage to relative competitive advantage the differential component for each group in the 1971–1981 period was subtracted from that in the 1981–1989 period. The results of this exercise showed an improvement in the size of the differential component for the city's economy as a whole of nearly 23,000 jobs. This was mainly due to the Metal goods, Vehicles and Engineering group of industries which experienced an improvement of 13,771 jobs, equivalent to 60% of the total improvement. Notable, but smaller, improvements occurred in Other Services of nearly 5800, and in Transport and Communications of 3250.

In conclusion, the shift-share analysis indicated that Coventry's local economy turned from a position of relative competitive disadvantage in the 1970s to one of relative competitive advantage in the 1980s mainly as a result of the performance of the Metal goods, Vehicles and Engineering industry group. Within this group the performance of two firms made a significant contribution to Coventry's changing relative competitive advantage, namely Jaguar and Peugeot-Talbot. Accordingly it is the role of Coventry's firms in the diamond that requires examination.

Coventry's firm structure, notably the dominance of a few large firms, had relevance to the employment change which took place. These changes were influenced by the corporate strategies of these large firms, over half of these being transnational companies. In the period 1974–1982 all of the top eight firms shed jobs. Rover shed the most jobs, followed by Peugeot-Talbot, these two shedding a combined total of 12,000 jobs in the eight year period. By contrast, in the 1982–1990 period Jaguar took on 4000 more workers and Peugeot-Talbot an additional 1000. Courtaulds marginally increased its employment.

With the low value of the pound in relation to the dollar, and the importance of the USA as a market, Jaguar expanded production to benefit from the favourable exchange rate. Jaguar's production was increased from 13,000 cars in 1980 to 52,000 cars in 1988.

Given that high wages and work stoppages in Coventry were things of the past, ameliorated by the recession of the 1970s, Peugeot, faced with militant workers at its Poissy factory near Paris, allocated the Peugeot 309 and 405 models to Coventry's Ryton plant for assembly. Output of assembled cars at Ryton was increased from 20,000 cars in 1984 to 117,000 in 1990. A night-shift was reinstated at the factory in 1988 for the first time in 15 years. However, the success of Peugeot-Talbot in Coventry in the 1980s was not sustained in the longer term. Being a 'screwdriver' plant assembling cars from parts imported from France, Coventry's Ryton was vulnerable to the corporate decisions made by its foreign owners.

In addition to firm strategy, structure and rivalry, another interconnected influential factor in the diamond is related and supporting industries. In Coventry, whilst the Vehicles industry has been dominated by motor car assemblers, almost half of the 42,000 workers employed in the industry in the sub-region in the late 1980s worked in the supply sector of supporting firms. The revival of Jaguar and, to a lesser extent Peugeot-Talbot had beneficial impacts on local suppliers and sub-contractors. Jaguar sought to source from within the Coventry area wherever possible. In the mid-1980s an estimated 4000 jobs in the components industry in the West Midlands was dependent on Jaguar. Porter (1998) described the geographical concentration of interconnected companies as a 'cluster' and the vehicle assembly and supporting industries meets this definition.

Two other clusters which developed in Coventry in the 1980s were the clothing industry cluster and a high technology cluster. Both of these clusters of activities contributed to Coventry's changing relative competitive advantage. The clothing cluster has a number of interesting characteristics: it was one of the few manufacturing sectors in Coventry which grew in this period, it was located in the inner city, and it reflected the entrepreneurship of the Asian community. By 1989 the 93 clothing firms provided 2300 jobs, a fivefold increase in the number of firms and employees in eleven years. Further jobs were provided for local businesses supplying the clothing manufacturers and for home-workers so that in total the cluster provided jobs for 3000 Coventry people.

Porter (1998) suggested that many clusters include institutions such as universities. On the outskirts of Coventry a cluster of high technology activities has grown up at the University of Warwick Science Park. Since its formation in 1984 this Park grew rapidly and by 1991 housed 65 companies employing 1150 people. The Park has become renowned for companies involved in automation, computer-aided design and related computer technologies particularly relevant to the needs of the local manufacturing economy. The Warwick University Science Park was another contributor to the relative competitive revival of the Coventry economy in the 1980s.

With respect to factor conditions, the remaining feature of the diamond left to discuss, Healey and Dunham suggested that numerous changes in the cost and availability of land, labour and capital may have contributed to the turnaround in the city's economic fortunes in the 1980s. They assessed the impact of these by examining their effect on inward investment.

Being located in a built-up area, Coventry's businesses may have suffered from operating in 'constrained locations' which adversely affected their performance. However, the recession led to a number of sites being available for redevelopment. These, together with the release of greenfield sites, meant that there was a steady flow of land for development. The largest of these developments, at the University of Warwick Science Park and the City Council's Westwood Business Park, attracted a number of inward investing firms. The office sector, long under-represented in Coventry, saw a number of projects come into the city in the late 1980s. Between 1980 and 1989, the Land Registry, Barclays Bank and the National Grid all decided to relocate to Coventry together contributing 3000 jobs to the local economy. High rents in London and Birmingham and lower rents in Coventry had made Coventry a more competitive location for offices.

Changes in the availability of capital may also have attracted a flow of inward investment into the city. Towards the end of 1984 Assisted Area status was granted as part of government regional policy and this enabled mobile firms to take advantage of capital grants to locate in the area. After designation 128 inward investment decisions to come to the city were made between 1986 and 1990 bringing with them a planned 9000 jobs. Assisted Area status also enabled Coventry City Council to obtain capital from the European Regional Development Fund for infrastructure investment particularly for new roads in Coventry.

Healey and Dunham concluded that, taken together, these changes in factor conditions made a contribution to the turnaround in Coventry's economic fortune during the 1980s. However, as well as the traditional factor conditions discussed by Healey and Dunham it could be suggested that entrepreneurship might have been added as a factor condition, rather than as an example of a cluster, given that the recent growth of the clothing industry in Coventry owed much to local Asian entrepreneurs.

With respect to Healey and Dunham's analysis supportive comments are in order. Firstly, their application of Porter's framework to Coventry's local economy was innovatory. Secondly, given that Porter (1986, p. 40) has argued that the 'final potential benefit of local demand conditions is a base load of demand for product varieties that will be sought after in international markets' it was appropriate to have examined the role of Coventry's industrial structure when discussing the demand factors of Porters diamond. Thirdly, the importance given to the shift-share differential component in their analysis of Coventry's competitive advantage was appropriate given the importance given to the differential in other studies, for example in regional policy analysis.

However, a number of critically constructive comments may be made. Healey and Dunham assert, rather than demonstrate, that the differential component reflects 'factor conditions; firm strategy and structure;

and related and supporting industries' although they did admit that there may have been other influences at work. They referred to inward investment in their discussion of 'factor conditions', and discussed Jaguar, British-owned until acquired by Ford in 1989, and French-owned Peugeot-Talbot under 'firm strategy'. However, they did not discuss the influence of inward FDI specifically as a possible separate influence on the differential component in its own right. Research by Collis and Roberts (1992) showed that for the West Midlands as a whole foreign-owned firms contributed to the region's recovery from the recession of the early 1980s both from new inflows and from the stock of older established foreign-owned firms who substantially increased their employment. It is possible, that in the case of Coventry, foreign-owned companies could have made an overall contribution of 8000 jobs in 1987 on the basis of the city's share of jobs created by them in the region, enough to make them a further separate factor in the differential component. Also, given the importance they had given to the differential component it would have been helpful had Healey and Dunham sub-divided it into an allocative effect and a competitive effect for both the sub-periods they analysed. For example Collis and Mallier (1985) sub-divided the differential for Coventry's main industries for the period 1971–1978. Another improvement to Healey and Dunham's analysis would have been to have given more attention to the two factors which affect the four main determinants, namely the roles of chance and government.

In retrospect it is easy to suggest improvements to the analysis of Healey and Dunham but at the time the study was innovative and shed new light on Coventry's changing competitive advantage.

Globalisation, FDI and Coventry's Vehicle-Making Firms

Globalisation "is the closer integration of the countries and peoples of the world which has been brought about by the enormous reductions of costs of transportation and communication, and the breaking down of artificial barriers to flows of goods, services, capital, knowledge, and (to a lesser extent) people across borders" (Stiglitz 2002).

Increased globalisation is measured by greater trade flows between countries and, in terms of the spatial extension of production, by FDI. The latter is a key component of globalisation. It is the interplay of ownership advantages, internalisation factors and location factors which determine FDI—why, how and where it takes place (Dunning 1993). FDI occurs when Multinational Enterprises (MNEs) build production facilities in countries other than their own country; expand or reinvest in such facilities; engage in cross-border mergers and acquisitions (M&As); or establish joint-equity ventures (JVs) with companies from a different country. The benefits that FDI can bring to a local host economy include investment, jobs created or safeguarded and exports. However, there are also risks to the host economy that external owners may decide to reduce employment before closing local factories completely and relocating production elsewhere.

The impact of globalisation and the role of FDI can be illustrated by the automotive industry. It is an industry of mainly very large corporations, a consolidation which resulted from a succession of mergers and acquisitions, within and across national borders. Gomes et al. (2010) have provided an overview of mergers and acquisitions as strategic methods of business development in the industry. Bailey et al. (2008) cited a number of developments in the vehicles industry which have been occurring, mostly as a result of trade barriers coming down and FDI spreading. These developments have been a consequence of structural changes in the industry. Firstly, because of rapid technological change, the costs of new model development have risen and this has put more pressure on firms to recover costs. Car firms have sought to generate funds for new model development through large scale production over different models and brands using shared platforms. Secondly, there has been increased international sourcing of components. Thirdly, there has been a shift of labour-intensive vehicle assembly operations towards lower cost locations in Central and Eastern Europe, southern states of the USA and countries in South America. These developments have had serious consequences for the vehicles industry in Coventry and the wider West Midlands region. Bailey et al. cited as examples the closures of Jaguar's Browns Lane plant in Coventry in 2005, of the former Rootes plant at Ryton in Coventry in 2007 and of MG Rover and the Longbridge plant in nearby Birmingham in 2005. A contributing domestic structural factor in the demise of these car firms was the long standing problem of engineering skills shortages (Begley et al. 2015).

Coventry was once a major location for the automotive industry within the West Midlands region of the UK. In 1914 one third of all British automobile production came from Coventry. In the 1920s and 1930s, Coventry companies Standard and Rootes were major players in the UK volume automobile industry and Jaguar was a prominent producer of luxury cars. Up until the 1960s 'Coventry was considered the classic car town with strong inward migration and high incomes and with factories such as Standard's Canley plant being known as the Klondike' (Donnelly et al. 2001, p. 199).

However, the story of the Standard Triumph factory at Canley in Coventry provided one of the many examples of the car industry's decline in Coventry after the 1960s. Car production at Canley ended in 1980 as part of a rationalisation by British Leyland. Then followed a period when FDI occurred first through a strategic alliance and subsequently through acquisitions. The company formed an alliance with Honda of Japan, producing the Triumph Acclaim at Longbridge in Birmingham in 1981. Jaguar, a constituent part of British Leyland, was bought by Ford of the USA in 1989 thus stripping out the luxury carmaker from British Leyland which had been renamed the Austin Rover Group in 1982. Rover was sold firstly to British Aerospace in 1988 and then sold on to BMW of Germany in 1994. BMW thus acquired Land Rover which was one of the world's leading producers of four-wheel drive sports utility vehicles. In 2000 BMW broke up the company. BMW kept the Mini plant in Oxford and the Hams Hall engine factory in Birmingham. Land Rover was acquired by Ford in 2000 after a fuller evaluation process than when it acquired Jaguar (Gomes et al. 2007). The rest of Rover, with its Longbridge factory, was sold by BMW to the Phoenix Consortium which renamed the firm MG Rover. In April 2005 Rover was forced into administration and the Longbridge factory was closed and 6000 workers lost their jobs. Nanjing Autos purchased the residue of the company but Nanjing produced virtually nothing at the Longbridge site and instead proposed to make the MG sports car in Oklahoma, USA. There have been numerous explanations of the demise of Rover (Bailey et al. 2008; Berkeley et al. 2005; Donnelly et al. 2017): lack of investment on plant, new model development, and workforce skills; low productivity related to over manning and too low a level of capacity utilisation; and poor labour relations. As well as internal managerial failure, external factors included the decisions of external owners, exchange rate volatility and deficiencies of government policy. Coffey argued that: 'if a single consistent theme runs through the history of the last major British car firm, it is the progressively dissipating effects on its fortunes of the internationalisation of the sector' (2009, p. 376).

In 2008, another foreign owned company, TATA of India, purchased Jaguar and Land Rover (JLR). The Jaguar plant at Browns Lane in Coventry had been closed by Ford in 2005. To date JLR has exemplified positive aspects of FDI: investment, jobs safeguarded and jobs created, and exports. New model development has included the Range Rover Evoque, the Jaguar F-Pace and the XE small saloon. Whilst car making is no longer currently undertaken in Coventry, JLR's headquarters are located at Whitley in Coventry. Plans for the site and its surrounding area include the expansion of advanced engineering and design activities, power-train development, a location for JLR suppliers and the development of a new generation of electric vehicles. Along with this a number of other developments in Coventry have put the city at the forefront of vehicle design and electric vehicle development. These include Coventry University's investment in vehicle design, Warwick University's work through WMG on automotive innovation and battery development along with government funding of electric vehicle battery development in Coventry.

Rootes/Chrysler/Peugeot provides a further example of the effects of globalisation and FDI on the Coventry motor vehicles industry. During the years of World War Two the Ryton plant in Coventry made aeroplane engines for military aircraft. In 1946 the Rootes group converted the Ryton site to car production. Output rose to a height of 150,000 cars in 1959 but then fell slowly during the next decade as Rootes suffered from weak model development and low profitability. The UK government directed investment from Ryton to Linwood in Scotland as part of government regional policy in the 1960s. Chrysler of the USA was seeking to gain a foothold in Europe and acquired Rootes over which it had full control by 1967. Chrysler invested in a new track at Ryton and new equipment was installed at the nearby engine plant in Coventry. However, Chrysler introduced only one new model in Coventry, the Avenger. After its launch in 1970 this vehicle was a success but was soon overtaken by new and revamped models produced by Ford and Vauxhall and Chrysler's market share fell. By 1975, with losses mounting, Chrysler made it clear to the UK government that it might have to close its UK factories and exit the country. The government rescued Chrysler with a 162 million pound package in return for a commitment to remain so saving the Coventry Ryton and Coventry Stoke plants from closure. However, Chrysler's problems were not confined to its British operations as the corporation was also losing market share in its home market in the USA. In 1978 Chrysler announced that it had agreed to sell its British plants in Coventry and Linwood to Peugeot of France. Peugeot gave a commitment to continue production at the Ryton and Stoke plants in Coventry whilst closing the Linwood factory in Scotland.

In the 1980s Peugeot 309 and 406 models were produced at Ryton. The production of the 206 began in 1998 and in 2004 the one millionth Peugeot 206 rolled off the production line at Ryton. However, Ryton had limited production capacity compared to Peugeot's main production sites in France and Spain. Also Peugeot was preparing production facilities in Eastern Europe. Peugeot decided not to assemble the new 207 model at Ryton where car production ceased in December 2006, Coventry's Ryton plant was closed in July 2007 with the loss of the remaining 2400 jobs, the total jobs lost at Ryton between 1975 and 2007 having been 16,000. The story of Rootes/Chrysler/Peugeot in Coventry illustrates the vulnerability of local industry to the decisions of foreign external owners pursuing their global corporate strategies.

LTI Ltd., the London Taxi Company, produced its first ever black cab in Coventry in 1948. Since then more than a 100,000 cabs have rolled off the production line, it being the last motor vehicles company producing cars in Coventry. Manganese Bronze had purchased the company from Carbodies in 1973. In 2012 Manganese went into administration, not having made a profit since 2012. Geely of China, who had previously entered a joint-venture with Manganese with a 20% share ownership, purchased the company's remaining assets in 2013, The business was saved along with 300 jobs as taxi production continued at the Holyhead plant in Coventry. Whilst Holyhead Road continued to produce the last of the TX4 diesel taxis, in 2017 Geely opened a new plant at nearby Ansty. Geely spent £55 million on the plant and £195 million developing a new electric hybrid cab, the TX5. The company is seeking actively to develop international markets in Europe, the USA and China.

Massey-Ferguson in Banner Lane is also an interesting example of the effects of globalisation and FDI. Between 1946 and 1956 more than 500,000 Ferguson tractors had been produced by the Standard Motor Company at the Banner Lane factory in Coventry. At the height of production over 6000 people were employed there. All of Standard's tractor assets were sold to Massey-Ferguson in 1959. Banner Lane became Massey-Ferguson's base for tractor-building operations and by the year 2000 tractor output was in excess of 70,000 per annum, the majority for export. However, the Coventry factory was closed in 2002 with a loss of the remaining 1000 jobs.

The context for the demise of the Banner Lane factory was the development of the company as a large transnational corporation. In the 1970s Massey-Ferguson had become the largest manufacturer of tractors in the western world. At its peak it employed 68,000 people worldwide and had 50 manufacturing plants in 12 countries. In 1994 Massey Ferguson became part of global corporation AGCO of the USA, with Banner Lane the headquarters of the European, Middle East and Far East business. As new models began to be launched elsewhere, such as Beauvais in France and Canoas in Brazil, the company started looking for factories from its global operation to close and chose Banner Lane where costs of production were higher than in competitor locations.

It is evident that FDI in Coventry's major vehicle manufacturers has brought with it many of the benefits at different points in time. For example, investment in new track by Chrysler at Ryton and the production of new models there by Peugeot; jobs safeguarded by Geely at LTI and the investment in a new plant and development of an electric hybrid cab; and TATA's investment in the West Midlands with jobs safeguarded and created and new models developed and exported along with a number of new developments at its Whitley site in Coventry. However, the risks of FDI to the local economy were exemplified by instances of in situ job reductions and factory closures. Examples included the 16,000 jobs lost between 1975 and 2007 at Ryton under the ownership of Chrysler and Peugeot before the latter finally closed the factory and the reduction of 5000 jobs at the Banner Lane factory of Massey-Ferguson before its closure in 2002 with the loss of the remaining 1000 jobs. In these cases FDI proved costly to Coventry as external owners closed Coventry factories as they relocated production to lower costs locations elsewhere in the world as part of the process of globalisation.

References

Bailey, D., Kobayashi, S., & MacNeil, S. (2008). Rover and Out? Globalisation, the West Midlands Auto Cluster and the End of MG Rover. *Policy Studies, 29*(3), 267–279.

Begley, J., Collis, C., & Donnelly, T. (2015). Skills Shortages: A Brake on the British Car Industry? *Local Economy, 30*(6), 593–608.

Berkeley, N., Donnelly, T., Morris, D., & Donnelly, M. (2005). Industrial Restructuring and the State: The Case of MG Rover. *Local Economy, 20*(4), 360–371.

Coffey, D. (2009). Production Counterfeits and Policy Collisions: The Rover Trajectory—A Salutary Tale. In M. Freyssenet (Ed.), *The New Auto Mobile World in the 21st Century*. Basingstoke and New York: Palgrave Macmillan.

Collis, C. (1992). Overseas Inward Investment in the UK Regions. In P. Townroe & R. Martin (Eds.), *Regional Development in the 1990s: The British Isles in Transition*. London: Jessica Kingsley and the Regional Studies Association.

Collis, C. (1995). Foreign Direct Investment in the UK: An Overview and Three Regional Case Studies. In P. Stonham & K. Redhead (Eds.), *European Casebook on Finance*. Hemel Hempstead: Prentice Hall.

Collis, C., Berkeley, N., & Botchway, Q. (2001). Coventry, West Midlands, UK. In *OECD Territorial Review, Bergamo, Italy*. Paris, France: OECD.

Collis, C., & Mallier, T. (1985). Employment Change in Coventry, 1971–78: A Shift-Share Approach. *British Review of Economic Issues, 7*(17), 51–85.

Collis, C., & Noon, D. (1994). Foreign Direct Investment in the UK Regions: Past Trends and Policy Issues. *Regional Studies, 28,* 843–848.

Collis, C., Noon, D., & Berkeley, N. (1994). Direct Investment from the EC: Recent Trends in the West Midlands Region and Their Implications for Regional Development and Policy. *European Business Review, 94*(2), 14–19.

Collis, C., Noon, D., & Edwards, T. (1998). Overseas Inward Investment in Regional Development: The Case of the West Midlands. In S. Hill & B. Morgan (Eds.), *Inward Investment, Business Finance and Regional Development.* London: Macmillan Business.

Collis, C., & Peck, F. (Eds.). (1996). *Industrial Restructuring: FDI and Regional Development.* London: Regional Studies Association.

Collis, C., & Roberts, P. (1992). Foreign Direct Investment in the West Midlands: An Analysis and Evaluation. *Local Economy, 7*(2), 114–130.

Donnelly, T., Begley, J., & Collis, C. (2017). The West Midlands Automotive Industry: The Road Downhill. *Business History, 59*(1), 56–74.

Donnelly, T., Tully, J., & Morris, D. (2001). The Decline of the Coventry Car Industry 1945–68. *Midlands History, XXVI,* 198–211.

Dunning, J. (1993). *Multinational Enterprises and the Global Economy.* London: Addison-Wesley Publishing Company.

Fothergill, S., & Gudgin, G. (1982). *Unequal Growth: Urban and Regional Employment Change in the UK.* London: Heinemann.

Gaffikin, F., & Nickson, A. (1984). *Jobs Crisis and the Multinationals: De-industrialisation in the West Midlands: A Birmingham Trade Union Group for World Development Study in Co-operation with the Birmingham Trade Union Resource Centre.* Birmingham Trade Union Resource Centre.

Gomes, E., Donnelly, T., Collis, C., & Morris, D. (2010). *Mergers and Acquisitions as Strategic Methods of Business Development in the Global Automobile Industry.* Lewiston, Queenston and Lampeter: The Edwin Mellen Press.

Gomes, E., Donnelly, T., Morris, D., & Collis, C. (2007). Improving Merger Process Management Skills Over Time: A Comparison Between the Acquisition Processes of Jaguar and of Land Rover by Ford. *The Irish Journal of Management, 28*(1), 31–57.

Green, A., & Berkeley, N. (2006). The West Midlands: The Hinge in the Middle. In I. Hardill, P. Benneworth, M. Baker, & L. Budd (Eds.), *The Rise of the English Regions?* London: Routledge.

Healey, M., & Clark, D. (1984). Industrial Decline and Government Response in the WM: The Case of Coventry. *Regional Studies, 18*(4), 303–318.

Healey, M., & Clark, D. (1985). Industrial Decline in a Local Economy: The Case of Coventry. *Environment and Planning A, 17,* 1351–1367.

Healey, M., & Dunham, P. (1994). Changing Competitive Advantage in a Local Economy: The Case of Coventry 1971–90. *Urban Studies, 31*(8), 1279–1301.

Mallier, T., & Rosser, M. (1982). The Decline and Fall of the Coventry Car Industry. *The Business Economist, 13,* 12–29.

Porter, M. (1986). Competition in Global Industries: A Conceptual Framework. In M. Porter (Ed.), *Competition in Global Industries.* Boston: Harvard Business School Press.

Porter, M. (1990). *The Competitive Advantage of Nations.* New York: Free Press.

Porter, M. E. (1998). Clusters and the New Economics of Competition. *Harvard Business Review, 76*(6), 77–90. Boston.

Stiglitz, J. (2002). *Globalisation and Its Discontents.* London: Penguin.

6

Affective Regeneration in Coventry

Jonathan Kershaw

Introduction

The post-war reconstruction of bombed British cities such as Coventry, Birmingham and Plymouth has been documented (e.g. Hubbard et al. 2003a, b; Adams 2011; Essex and Brayshay 2007), wherein much focus has been on the challenges of creating a Modernist urban 'utopia', one promising contemporary notions of progress and better living. Such visions, facilitated by a post-war 'blank canvas', necessarily impacted upon how these cities that had grown organically, authentically, prior to hostilities would in future be experienced, as they were replaced by rational, utilitarian projects.

However, the setting, the place, and the history of a city theoretically suggests a unique regeneration that warrants exploration, in terms of conception, perception, and experience. In Coventry, for example, it is perhaps remarkable that, despite being the birthplace of the country's car industry—Britain's 'motor city'—much of the city's

J. Kershaw (✉)
Coventry University, Coventry, UK

J. Begley et al. (eds.), *Revival of a City*, Palgrave Studies in Economic History,
https://doi.org/10.1007/978-3-030-22822-4_6

medieval origins remained intact prior to the blitz of November 1940. These two factors of history and industry may have well impelled an extant need for urban redevelopment in Coventry yet, however hastened, the dominance of such an industry in such a setting necessarily predicates a unique regeneration. To what extent did Coventry's history and automotive industry—perhaps key to the city's innate character or 'essence'—drive its redevelopment? Was the rationale behind Coventry's regeneration also influenced by a national post-war regeneration mood in a world that was also opening up to a nascent globalisation?

Analysis of previous interviews will permit insights into how Coventry's regeneration was perceived and experienced that, following Anderson (2015), will permit the exploration of contemporaneous atmospheres and affects that influenced and drove a unique regeneration. A Coventrian regeneration.

Boom Town

Coventry in the late 1930s was a city of relative prosperity. Unemployment rates in single-digit figures were a stark contrast to areas such as the North East whose unemployment reached 25% (Walters 2013). In 1937, the city headed the then-new 'Purchasing Power Index', and boasted private-car ownership rates that wouldn't be matched nationwide until the 1960s (ibid.).

Yet Coventry was still akin to a medieval city. From ribbons to clocks, from bicycles to cars, the city had always adapted to changes in economic fortunes, and yet despite much rebuilding during the eighteenth and nineteenth centuries, the city had retained its medieval plan or layout (Gould and Gould 2016). This meant that much of the city's historic infrastructure remained intact. In the 1920s, a journalist from the London Illustrated News is quoted as describing Coventry as "arguably the best preserved medieval city in Europe" (Walters 2013, p. 214). Whilst the city's extant infrastructure obviously contributed to an innate authenticity, it is perhaps remarkable that the birthplace of the country's car industry—Britain's 'motor city', first coined 'Britain's Detroit' in the Times in 1916 (Walters 2013)—arose within such historic surroundings.

Coventry grew rapidly in the first part of the twentieth century and, though picturesque, it's facilities and infrastructure didn't keep pace with the needs of a burgeoning population. The city expanded administratively from 1678 hectares in 1919 to 10,521 hectares in 1939, its population rising from 70,000 in 1901 to 230,000 in 1938 (Gould and Gould 2016). So as to meet the needs of this rising population, house-building steadily increased during the 1930s, resulting in over 25,000 houses being built over the decade (ibid.; Coventry Environmental Education Project 1985).

Plans were made in the 1930s to redevelop the city centre. As an example of what was planned to come, the ancient thoroughfare of Butcher Row was razed to make way for the more car-friendly Trinity Street. To avoid the false regenerative dawns of the previous decade, the Labour council elected in 1937 made the decision to form a 'City Architect's Department', appointing Donald Gibson, whose ideas would transform the city, to the post in 1938 (Turner 1962). Coventry was the fastest growing city in the country at the time (Rigby-Childs and Boyne 1953), and Gibson confirmed that Coventry's burgeoning population had led to plans for the city's development (Gibson 1962).

Architectural Affectus

While changes to, and the development of, Coventry were planned before the outbreak of World War 2, the blitz of November 14, 1940, along with later attacks until April 1941, irrevocably changed the city. It not only hastened the need for redevelopment, but also lent a different *nature* to it. It can be argued that no longer were old buildings in various states of decay merely being removed and replaced with something more in keeping with more modern times, standards and/or vision. Instead, the city had had its heart ripped out by enemy forces, and a new city would rise from the ashes.

Not only would councillors, engineers, architects drive Coventry's regeneration, but so too would its citizens, as exhibitions were held to gauge public opinion. But how would citizens see Coventry's future?

How did they see the 'old' Coventry—the unique, organic hodge-podge that had remained somehow locked into to its medieval origins, despite being Britain's 'motor-city'? How did they 'feel' the city, old and new, before and after? How was a Coventrian post-war regeneration not only effected, but '*affected*'?

In a book with a predominately economic mien, this is an interesting proposition to explore, to bring more of a 'people-focus' to proceedings. But how can we, in the early twenty-first century, begin to assess such contemporaneous feelings from 70, 80, even 90 years ago? The only way, perhaps, is to garner opinions and thoughts from those who lived the profound changes to the city at the time and, following Anderson (2015), try to 'cast back', to "retrospectively reconstruct something of now residual atmospheres" (ibid., p. 9), atmospheres that may live on and be felt as they are recalled and named (ibid.).

To this end, we are indebted to the authors of a previous paper exploring Coventry's regeneration (Hubbard et al. 2003a), who were kind enough to allow access to transcripts of interviews conducted in 2001. In reading these transcripts of Coventry pre- and post-war memories, along with contemporary newspaper reports/letters, texts and artefacts, it may be possible to elicit a contemporary 'feel' for the city and, following Anderson (2009, 2015), to explore contemporaneous atmospheres and affects that influenced and drove a unique, Coventrian regeneration.

Feeling the City

As a non-Coventrian and semi-regular visitor to the city during the course of my Ph.D., Coventry's architecture always prompted reflection. A product of the blitz and the motor industry, with medieval survivors and the modernist visions side-by-side, one really couldn't be anywhere else. Such a mix of architecture, together with the reasons behind it, lends Coventry a unique atmosphere.

To explore if and how such an atmosphere is manifest among Coventry's citizens and the impact it may have had upon the city's regeneration, it is useful invoke the notion of 'affects', originally posited in the seventeenth century by Baruch de Spinoza in his posthumously-published book '*Ethics*' (1996 [1677]), and subsequent academic interpretations thereon, in an attempt to explore contemporary atmospheres that may have impacted such feelings.

Metaphysically, Spinoza says that God is Nature, something that is purely in and of itself. This 'Nature' is something of which we are possessed; it is an essence that is innate and authentic to us, that is 'us', and from which affect stems. Therefore, our 'Nature' determines how external 'causes'—that is, encounters with other people or objects or things—'affect' us, thus resulting in an increase in happiness, what Spinoza called a 'greater perfection', or in sadness, leading to 'lesser perfection'. As such, affect may be defined as the "ability to affect or be affected", with affection as "each state of this affect between the affected and affecting bodies" (Deleuze et al. 2004, p. vxii). Such affection is associated with an innate 'flow' between affecting and affected bodies (Stewart 2007) that is wrought by encounter, and borne of knowledges and Nature which, because affect is "synesthetic, implying a participation of the senses in each other … [an] … ability to transform the effects of one sensory mode into another" (Massumi 2002, p. 35), results in intangible feelings; in everyday, ordinary intimacies, that are nonetheless real.

Affect can also be said to be possessed of four components. Firstly, it is "a set of embodied practices that produce visible conduct as an outer lining" (Thrift 2004, p. 60), with our actions manifest as an "expressive/aesthetic feeling-cum-behaviour of continual becoming" (ibid.), in which any context will inevitably influence how we act. Secondly, it is the Id and the Unconscious contriving an "affect in process" (ibid., pp. 60, 61) resulting in a psychological 'drive', something that ties in with Spinoza's observation of our 'essence', or our true meaning or self. Thirdly, echoing Stewart (2007), it is "the property of the active outcome of an encounter" (Thrift 2004, p. 61), manifest as mind and body acting together thereon. Lastly, it is Darwinian, not only in that emotion evolves from affect "as a means of preparing an organism for action" (ibid., p. 63), but also in that while some basic emotions are common to all cultures, how they are communicated is necessarily influenced socially in different ways.

Anderson describes affective atmospheres as subjectivities that are at once non-cognitive and pre-cognitive, that transcend "human and non-human materialities" (2009, p. 78), making them "the shared ground from which subjective states and their attendant feelings and emotions emerge" (ibid.). Following Anderson (2009), a city's residents will be similarly 'affected', as from our encounters, a capacity to both affect and to be affected arises, with and by positive and negative sources that stem from what is innate, authentic and essential to us individually, and from shared encounters, atmospheres arise. The reflection I noted earlier, invoked as I make my way around Coventry, is an example of this, stemming from my own Nature and knowledges, producing my own 'take' on the city. Similarly, what follows is an individual retrospection of public atmospheres and individual affects, in the mien of Anderson (2015). A word of caution, however: Hubbard et al. (2003b) noted that the multiple readings of public art mean that its retrospective interpretation has its difficulties. The same is true here.

Pre-war Memories and Wartime Accounts

A contemporary feel for pre-war Coventry can be garnered by perusing artefacts such as old postcards and photographs (e.g. Cremin 2001; Coventry City Council 1988; Douglas et al. 1987), which provide an idea of how, despite a pervasive historicity, Coventry has perhaps always been a 'work in progress' as the city has evolved to meet its changing fortunes, industries and subsequent growth. Though young at the time, some of the interviewees of Hubbard et al. (2003a) recounted the organic nature of pre-war Coventry, with note made of its haphazardness—described by one as 'olde worlde', and another as 'higgledy-piggledy'—and of an apparent 'smallness' of the majority of retail establishments. While such places may have resonated a 'quaintness' that some felt were authentic of the old Coventry, several interviewees spoke highly of the then-new Owen Owen department store which opened on Broadgate between Cross Cheaping and the newly-instated Trinity Street in 1937, describing it as an 'up-town' thing and marvelling at the novelty of escalators, a feature new to the city. The building didn't last long however as, badly damaged in the blitz of November 1940, it was later demolished as part of the city's redevelopment.

The night of November 14, 1940, after which only 31 buildings out of 975 remained intact (Barratt 1962), and its aftermath has been well documented. While later publications provide photographs and contemporary reports (e.g. Chalmers and Williams 1990; Douglas et al. 2003) which provide an indication of the horror and aftermath of the blitz, a perhaps more authentic commentary is provided by a first-hand account by the then vicar of Holy Trinity of the attacks in the build-up to the blitz, their efforts to protect the church, and their dismay at the destruction of the nearby cathedral (Clitheroe 1942). A small book of 64 pages, it is in itself a contemporaneous artefact, evocative even, that provides the reader with a real 'feel' for the events of that fateful night, and an insight into feelings of courage, of gloom, and of defiance of Coventry, on the night of the blitz and the days after.

The BBC documentary series 'Timewatch' (BBC 2009) also spoke to people who had lived through the blitz, with one recounting that Coventrians had a lively, prosperous town one moment and the next nothing, and another saying that, after the shock, the reaction was that "we're not going to let the buggers get away with it!" (ibid.). Though some were young at the time, most of the interviewees of Hubbard et al. (2003a) recounted experiences of the night of the blitz, and of the condition of the city afterwards, lacking gas, electricity and water. One noted how disorientating going into the city was, noting the Council House, unscathed in the attacks, as a focus point for location. While utilities were quickly reconnected and food aid coming from outside, and with 80% of workers back in employment within a fortnight of the attack, morale was high as the city initially recovered and civic life was restored (Clitheroe 1942; Walters 2013).

The Phoenix Rises

As noted earlier, while plans to develop and modernise the city were already in train, the blitz not only impelled their necessity, but also their nature, their driving force; city architect Donald Gibson later noted that "in consequence of devastation through bombing, opportunities for new thinking were presented" (Gibson 1962). The city council moved to begin the regeneration of the city in December 1940, with competing plans drawn up by early the following year. In 1945, the 'Coventry of the Future' exhibition was attended by over 30,000 people, with 20,000 copies of a brochure entitled '*The Future Coventry*' (The Corporation of Coventry 1945) containing proposals for roads, industry, housing, amenities, and the central redevelopment of the city, printed to complement this. In this brochure, acknowledgement was made as to the problems posed by a burgeoning population that had grown threefold in the first four decades of the twentieth century, coupled with the medieval foundations of the city, noted as "incongruous in one of the main car producing centres of Britain" (ibid., p. 9), issues that were exacerbated by the war years.

Reaction to the plans was mixed, as illustrated by letters to the Coventry Evening Telegraph at the time. One letter from 'C.S.P.' printed on the 13th of October 1945 critiqued the plans, saying that "the concept of the scheme is not in keeping with the characteristics of the Coventry people, who would not feel at home in it … what is wanted is the old Coventry, restored with a new Sunday dress, but the old Coventry nevertheless" (Coventry Evening Telegraph 1945a). This view was contradicted on the 22nd of October by a reader signed 'S.B.' who said that "those with whom I've discussed the new scheme are full of praise for the courageous ideas now envisaged" (Coventry Evening Telegraph 1945b).

One interviewee of Hubbard et al. (2003a) stated that, immediately post-war, people were tired and run down after the war years, another that Coventry was a 'drab old place', both a corollary of the city still largely being in ruins, with another saying that nothing really happened until the early 1950s. Although work to rebuild the city in earnest began in 1951 (Walters 2013), Coventry's redevelopment in fact began on the 8th of June 1946, with the unveiling of the Levelling Stone, an artefact both symbolic in depiction of a phoenix rising from the flames—thus constituting the first post-war public art in the city—and also practical, as it served as a fixed, co-ordinated point from which surveyors and engineers could 'ground' and 'locate' the city's reconstruction (Hubbard et al. 2003b).

The futuristic mien of the plans was evident to two interviewees of Hubbard et al. (2003a), who invoked the sci-fi spirit of Flash Gordon and Buck Rogers respectively in reaction to the raised highways posited in the plans they saw as youths as part of the Coventry of the Future exhibition. A feeling of modernity was also duly experienced by several others of those interviewed, with one saying that the pedestrianised precincts made Coventry feel 'different', and a modern city, and that they were proud of it. Another who expressed pride in the 'exciting' new Coventry claimed that the city's pioneering pedestrianisation even attracted visitors to observe this new experience. The dual levels of the precinct were initially well regarded, with one interviewee saying they were redolent of The Rows in Chester, although it later transpired that few shoppers were incline to visit the upper levels, and the units soon became empty. An intriguing observation is that the Upper Precinct was somehow regarded more favourably than was the Lower Precinct, with most mention of the Lower Precinct made with positive regard to the circular café. One of the interviewees of Hubbard et al. (2003a) recounted their experience of the new city, in that while they came to appreciate the ability to wander around, they initially felt 'lost'. Another similarly affected said that they tried to counteract their disorientation by relating everything to the position of the cathedral.

The new cathedral was widely praised, and the way that the old and new cathedrals connected and intertwined was widely regarded positively. An interesting and important aspect of the cathedral wasn't so much its contemporary architecture, which drew mixed reaction, but its symbolism and its spirit. One interviewee felt that the new cathedral encapsulated the spirit of Coventry—a spirit of reconciliation, of a civic moral stand, the symbolism of which inside the cathedral was declared as 'beautiful'. Some interviewees acknowledged that while the old cathedral couldn't be saved—and even that any restoration may have destroyed it—its preservation as a memorial was important.

Recalled by one interviewee of Hubbard et al. (2003a) as a cobbled street prior to its regeneration, one aspect that attracted much praise was Broadgate, at least in its original 'new' form. With a statue of Lady Godiva, surrounded by grass and other greenery, at its centre the traffic island in the centre of Broadgate was described almost as an oasis those interviewed by Hubbard et al. (2003a), and was universally applauded. The original incarnation of the island was noted as a striking contrast to the immediate post-war ruined drabness of Coventry, and was lauded as a 'lovely garden' and a 'garden island', replete with benches providing somewhere to sit. Broadgate was regarded as a focal point too, described by one interviewee as the 'centre' of Coventry, with the poled elephant at the junction of Broadgate and the Upper Precinct frequently cited as a meeting point.

With the National and Provincial (now NatWest) bank at the junction of Broadgate and Hertford Street as a focal point, Figs. 6.1 and 6.2

Fig. 6.1 Old Broadgate, looking south (1931 postcard—author's collection)

Fig. 6.2 New Broadgate, looking south (1950s postcard—author's collection)

provide a useful illustration of how much Broadgate had changed from a bustling retail thoroughfare to the more open 'oasis' alluded to above.

The two depictions concerning Coventry folk heroine Lady Godiva brought contrasting comment from interviewees, with the almost universal regard for the statue of Godiva which has variously faced south or west on Broadgate over the years contrasting with the very mixed views of the clock depicting Godiva and Peeping Tom, whose figures appear on the hour. Opinions of the clock ranged from it being a novelty and a bit of fun, to being grotesque, crude, vulgar, even a travesty, although it was noted how tourists and children liked it.

Not everyone saw the city's redevelopment as positive, with one interviewee of Hubbard et al. (2003a) feeling that 'ugly' concrete blocks were being thrown up at the expense of 'beautiful' half-timbered buildings, saying how such actions had pained him, and describing modern flat-glass-fronted shops as "un-Coventry". This same respondent also noted an inauthenticity to Spon Street, in that some of its medieval buildings aren't original, having instead been relocated from elsewhere in the city—for example from Little Park Street—during the 1970s and 1980s, describing it as 'a joke'. Other interviewees, though, acknowledged that at least the buildings' relocation had actually preserved them. Despite an initial enthusiasm for the futuristic plans they had seen as a youth, one respondent declared that he actually wasn't impressed by the 1950s architecture of the new city, while another in hindsight wished that more of Coventry's older buildings could have been kept, instead of just building 'boxes'.

Time lends an affect in itself, in terms of itself and of its passage. For all the initial notions of modernity and futurism, in practice and over time, some interviewees said that their initial enthusiasm for their new city had waned, and that they didn't like a much now as they once had. To some, the new city centre had become a place to 'do', not to linger or to 'be'. Others bemoaned the lack of investment in maintenance, saying concrete discolours, and that the city doesn't look as 'clean' as it once did as a result. Even Broadgate wasn't as regarded as it was, though that was due more to recent developments, such as Cathedral Lanes, the Upper Precinct escalators, and the canopy covering the Godiva statue at the time of the interviews, all of which attracted widespread opprobrium.

Discussion

The texts and artefacts collated in forming this chapter have indeed permitted an insight into the atmospheres of Coventry past. Books such as those by Cremin (2001), Coventry City Council (1988) and Douglas et al. (1987) are fascinating, and permit an insight of Coventry years and/or decades before WWII, as well as afterwards. Meanwhile, the first-hand account of the blitz (Clitheroe 1942) is extremely evocative, both in terms of its writing and of the book itself, with the result that atmospheres surrounding the event may be readily imagined. The publication *The Future Coventry*, issued by the local authority to accompany the exhibition and consultation of the city's future is a similarly evocative tome. With its forward-looking mien and positing of innovative proposals to infrastructure and housing, it is easy to understand the sense of wonder noted by some respondents, especially considering the conditions under which Coventry's citizens were living.

Reading the interviews conducted by Hubbard et al. (2003a), while an affection for the 'old' Coventry is evident, the overwhelming impression is that, despite the occasional dissenting voice, the new Coventry was anticipated and greeted with real optimism. The Darwinism identified by Thrift (2004) as a component of affect, as a non-cognitive preparation to act in this brave new world, is in evidence here. This impression is augmented by interviewees' feelings of pride and of a modernity, as a subconscious reaction to the 'flow' (Stewart 2007) concomitant with encounter (Thrift 2004); likewise, the disdain expressed by those less enamoured of the direction and form of the new city. Even so, it can be suggested that a population that was exhausted by years of war can't fail to have been lifted by the promise of a brighter future, exemplified by their city rising in the way it did, especially as it would be the young who would drive this. The hope symbolised by the Levelling Stone and the interior of the new cathedral, the depiction of folk history that was both regarded as both beautiful (the Godiva statue) and almost profane (the Godiva/Peeping Tom clock) looked both back and forth. For Coventrians, the new city brought with it new ways of performing everyday life in their city, of experiencing their city, of *feeling* their city.

How might this 'architectural affectus' fit with the globalisation theme of this book? Massey noted that globalisation is "a product of society—a political and economic project" (2003, p. 3) that requires large corporations and financial institutions and to drive it (ibid.) and, certainly, many think of globalisation as a business construct. Yet it is more than that. Amin suggests that globalisation concerns "the spatiality of contemporary social organisation, about meanings of place and space associated with intensified world-level forces … and raised global connectivity" (2002, p. 305), which ties in with the 'Darwinian' aspect of Thrift's fourth definition of affect (2004) in how the communication of culturally-common emotions are variously socially influenced. Coventry was no exception to effects concomitant with reaching out. Echoing an interviewee's observation of the city's 'new' attraction, Gould and Gould (2016) note that Coventry's new renown for progressive planning and architecture did indeed attract visitors from around the world, and that the city had both influenced and *was* influenced by contemporary developments across the continent. A tacit connection which Coventrians had to their city changed, as the new Coventry rose from the ruins. A Coventrian regeneration, of rebirth, optimism, even reconciliation, was reaching out beyond national borders.

A 'Coventry' Automotive Affectus

Many interesting memories and opinions emerged from the interviews of Hubbard et al. (2003a), but one in particular perhaps hints at the impact of the car industry upon the city, as a driver of its growth and its post-war recovery. As noted earlier, Coventry is regarded as Britain's 'Motor City'. From the beginning, over a hundred car companies had started and either failed or were taken over by larger firms, with 15 firms remaining by 1931 (Coventry Environmental Education Project 1985). Nonetheless, the importance of the car industry to the city is illustrated in that almost 40% of the city's 100,000+ workforce was so employed by 1939 (Thoms and Donnelly 2000), rising to 63,000 in 1952, and over 74,000 by the mid-1960s (ibid.).

An interesting outcome of this is something that subconsciously indicates an importance of the car to Coventry. Just as the car industry was key to the city's growth before WWII, so it would be again afterwards. The difference this time was that while the industry had previously focussed on the domestic market, post-war production was aimed primarily on international sales, prompted by the Government's directive to make at least half of automotive production for export, so as to drive economic recovery (Thoms and Donnelly 2000). Although pre-war production wasn't matched until 1949, growth in output continued until well into the 1960s, as companies took various approaches to expand markets and sales globally (ibid.). In the interviews, several interviewees mentioned that their parents worked in the car industry. Yet what is interesting is that the city's car companies weren't simply referred to as Standard, or Humber, or Maudsley, or Daimler—rather, these companies were referred to as *the* Standard, or *the* Humber, or *the* Maudsley, or *the* Daimler. So prefixed, reference to these companies suggests something about their existence that is special to Coventry and to Coventrians, fostering a kind of reverence, fondness or ownership, even though their presence has mostly long gone.

It can be suggested that there are parallels between the industry that brought much pre-war prosperity to Coventry, also doing much to impel its post-war recovery and prospects of its citizens, and of the regenerated city itself. Both the city and its industry were seen to be at the forefront of technology and progress, in terms of automobility and architecture—the latter perhaps graphically illustrated not by a car, but by the hoisting up of the fleche atop the new cathedral by an RAF Chinook helicopter—but also of hope. Both the city and its historic, primary industry were sources of pride among Coventrians, and were forward-looking. An atmosphere of optimism, of looking forward, is retrospectively tangible.

Conclusion

Originally by design, but ultimately out of dreadful necessity, the fabric of Coventry changed dramatically over the twentieth century. As such, the nature, the authenticity, the essence, of the city also changed and, as a result of the affectual flow from encounter, borne of innate natures and knowledges, this will have 'affected' Coventrians in myriad ways. This, in turn, will have had an impact upon how the city and its citizens recovered from the ravages of war as the world 'opened up'. The starkness of the modernist architecture of Coventry city centre has perhaps softened over the years (and may be regarded more favourably than more recent developments), but is resolutely 'of its time'. It is emblematic of a city reaching out in the name of hope, of progress, and of reconciliation; its key industry also reaching out to global markets. One can look back with fondness or horror, and look forward with hope or dread. The profound changes that were wrought upon Coventry will no doubt have invoked all of these feelings. To some extent, they still do.

References

Adams, D. (2011). Everyday Experiences of the Modern City: Remembering the Post-war Reconstruction of Birmingham. *Planning Perspectives, 26*(2), 237–260.

Amin, A. (2002). Spatialities of Globalisation. *Environment and Planning A: Economy and Space, 34*(3), 385–399.

Anderson, B. (2009). Affective Atmospheres. *Emotion, Space and Society, 2*, 77–81.

Anderson, B. (2015). Neoliberal Affects. *Progress in Human Geography, 40*(6), 734–753.

Barratt, C. (1962, July 10). Phoenix City Arises—With Garden as First Great Act of Faith. *The Birmingham Post.*

BBC. (2009). *Timewatch—Blitz: The Bombing of Coventry.* https://www.youtube.com/watch?v=PHknZf4AXKc. Accessed 14 May 19.

Chalmers, D., & Williams, S. (1990). *Coventry's Blitz.* Coventry: Coventry Newspapers Ltd.

Clitheroe, G. W. (1942). *Coventry Under Fire: An Impression of the Great Raids on Coventry in 1940 and 1941.* Gloucester: The British Publishing Company.

Coventry City Council. (1988). *Coventry Between the Wars: Photographs by Arnold Stringer, 1893–1988.* Coventry: Coventry City Council.

Coventry Environmental Education Project. (1985). *The Coventry Car Industry.* Coventry City Council.

Coventry Evening Telegraph. (1945a, October 13). *Letter to the Editor.*

Coventry Evening Telegraph. (1945b, October 22). *Letter to the Editor.*

Cremin, M. (2001). *Coventry on Old Picture Postcards.* Nottingham: Reflections of a Bygone Age.

Deleuze, G., Guattari, P. F., & Pérez, J. V. (2004). *A Thousand Plateaus.* London: Continuum.

Douglas, A., Moore, D., & Douglas, J. (1987). *Memories of Coventry: A Pictorial Record.* Coventry: Coventry Newspapers Ltd.

Douglas, A., Stretch, G., Hardy, C., & Douglas, J. (2003). *Coventry at War.* Studley: Brewin Books.

Essex, S., & Brayshay, M. (2007). Vision, Vested Interest and Pragmatism: Who Re-made Britain's Blitzed Cities? *Planning Perspectives, 22*(4), 417–441.

Gibson, D. (1962, July 10). Birth of the Precinct Idea. *The Birmingham Post.*

Gould, J., & Gould, C. (2016). *Coventry: The Making of a Modern City*. Swindon: Historic England.

Hubbard, P., Faire, L., & Lilley, K. (2003a). Contesting the Modern City: Reconstruction and Everyday Life in Post-war Coventry. *Planning Perspectives, 18*(4), 377–397.

Hubbard, P., Faire, L., & Lilley, K. (2003b). Memorials to Modernity? Public Art in the 'City of the Future'. *Landscape Research, 28*(2), 147–169.

Massey, D. (2003). Globalisation: What Does It Mean for Geography? *The Development Education Journal, 9*(2), 3–5.

Massumi, B. (2002). *Parables for the Virtual: Movement, Affect, Sensation*. Durham, NC: Duke University Press.

Rigby-Childs, D., & Boyne, D. A. C. A. (1953). A Survey by D. Rigby-Childs and D.A.C.A Boyne of Coventry. *The Architects Journal, 118*, 428–447.

Spinoza, B. (1996 [1677]). *Ethics*. London: Penguin Books.

Stewart, K. (2007). *Ordinary Affects*. Durham: Duke University Press.

The Corporation of Coventry. (1945). *The Future Coventry*. Coventry: The Corporation of Coventry.

Thoms, D., & Donnelly, T. (2000). *The Coventry Motor Industry: Birth to Renaissance*. Aldershot: Ashgate.

Thrift, N. (2004). Intensities of Feeling: Towards a Spatial Politics of Affect. *Geografiska Annaler B, 86*, 57–78.

Turner, K. B. (1962, July 10). Blueprint for New Coventry Began Two Years Before Blitz. *The Birmingham Post*.

Walters, P. (2013). *The Story of Coventry*. Stroud: The History Press.

7

Population, Migration and Commuting Patterns in a Changing City

Paul Sissons

Introduction

This chapter focuses on the evolution of population trends and patterns of spatial mobility through commuting and migration. Industrial change and wider economic and social trends have re-worked Coventry's relationship with the surrounding area and created new spatial interdependencies. Coventry's story has not been one of precipitous population decline and adjustment; although the population of the city did contract in response to the loss of industrial jobs it has subsequently grown significantly. Instead, it is primarily a story of change within place, and one of adjusting relationships to economic activities within the city and beyond.

P. Sissons (✉)
Coventry University, Coventry, UK
e-mail: Paul.Sissons@coventry.ac.uk

J. Begley et al. (eds.), *Revival of a City*, Palgrave Studies in Economic History,
https://doi.org/10.1007/978-3-030-22822-4_7

The chapter is structured as follows. Part 2 examines mobility responses to job losses in the 1980s, showing that out-migration was a significant short-term response to deindustrialisation; with expanded commuting patterns also playing a role in off-setting the impact of employment decline within the city. Part 3 develops the analysis of population change and mobility, demonstrating that the population decline which impacted the city in the 1980s, and right through to the early and mid-2000s, was subsequently turned around through a decade of sustained population growth. Part 4 builds on the discussion of commuting patterns and explores the extent to which the city has become less self-contained as a labour market overtime. Part 5 provides concluding thoughts.

The patterns of change described in this chapter are a re-working of Coventry's relationship both regionally, nationally but also more broadly internationally. Industrial growth altered Coventry's relationships through trade and drove changing patterns of inward migration, both inter-regionally and internationally. Conversely, one response to the city's industrial decline was through higher rates of out-migration from the city. More recently, migration patterns have been linked to Coventry's partial recovery but also to the growth of important sectors in the city, particularly education (a sector which is embedded in international networks). Growth of the student base of the city also reflects a new phase of openness and diversity for Coventry, but the student population has a high rate of churn and graduate retention is low. Changes associated with globalisation, such as the increasing importance of international networks in higher education and knowledge industries continue to re-shape the city's economy, but are balanced with changes of a more regional nature, and in particular the importance of commuting flows between the city and the surrounding area. There are particularly significant commuting flows to managerial and professional jobs in the city. These are linked in part to the intersection of labour and housing markets, and are partly explained by the nature of Coventry's comparative 'housing offer'. However, there is also a more prosaic and self-contained story of Coventry's evolution, with many workers both living and working in the city but being more highly concentrated in comparatively low-paid occupations. The city is at one time both internationally orientated and locally rooted.

The changes described in this chapter are systemically linked the wider cycle of growth, decline and the regeneration of the city, but also to historic patterns of housing development, the drawing of administrative boundaries and the relationships between Coventry and its surrounding local authorities. As Mackie (Chapter 9) describes, the economic base has radically shifted away from manufacturing (with the exception of some advanced manufacturing, particularly associated with JLR) towards education, health and the public sector. These shifts have reworked Coventry's relationship to the global, national and regional economy in multiple ways.

Industrial Decline and Mobility Responses to Job Loss

Coventry suffered significantly and disproportionately from national and regional deindustrialisation as a result of its industrial structure, the characteristics of local plants and firms, factors associated with the Coventry labour market, and the nature of regional policy (Healey and Clark 1984). Prior to the onset of industrial decline, at the beginning of the 1970s, two-thirds of Coventry's employment was in manufacturing, double the proportion of any other similar-sized UK city (Healey and Dunham 1994). A third of city's jobs were lost between 1975 and 1984, before a partial recovery in the mid to late 1980s based on service sector growth rather than manufacturing employment, as the city's labour market was transformed (Healey and Dunham 1994).

The loss of industrial jobs necessitated the absorption of manufacturing workers who had lost employment through other adjustments in the local labour market. One way of assessing the nature of mobility based responses to the type of industrial shifts and economic decline which Coventry has been experienced is through a framework of Labour Market Accounts (LMAs). LMAs are a method of interrogating the allocation of an economic shock, in Coventry's case the decline of manufacturing, into a range of labour market adjustments. These adjustments include permanent out-migration from the area, increased commuting to other labour market areas, and the withdrawal of discouraged workers into economic inactivity. Research on labour market restructuring in the UK coalfields found the loss of industrial jobs was associated with a large increase in, first male economic inactivity as a direct result of job losses (Beatty and Fothergill 1996), and then later a rise in female economic activity linked to complex patterns of local employment demand, health and labour market competition (Beatty et al. 2009). Other adjustments in the LMA framework are made for population growth (or decline) and the growth (or decline) of those 'working' in government schemes. The LMA components should be arithmetically related and the balance then equates to the growth (or decline) of unemployment; however the estimates suffer from some residual inaccuracies due to under enumeration in the 1991 Census. Table 7.1 presents LMA estimates for Coventry for men and Table 7.2 for women. The estimates are from the work of Turok and Edge (1999); they cover the period 1981–1991, and the working-age definitions are 16–64 for men and 16–59 for women.

Turning first to the LMAs for men, there was a significant employment loss during the 1980s, equating to 17.4% of economically active working-age men in 1981. As discussed by Mackie (Chapter 9), these job losses were concentrated in the manufacturing sector. Population trends meant the workforce would expand by 3.3% over the decade. There was a notable response through out-migration, equating to 13% of economically active men in 1981. There was also a more modest, but

Table 7.1 Male LMAs for Coventry, 1981–1991 (as a % of economically active men of working age in 1981)

		%
	Loss of employment	17.4
PLUS	Natural increase in workforce	3.3
MINUS	Net out-migration	13
MINUS	Change in net out-commuting	6.5
MINUS	Decline in economically active	5.5
MINUS	Number on government schemes	1.1
EQUALS	Change in unemployment	−6.5

Source Turok and Edge (1999)

Table 7.2 Female LMAs for Coventry, 1981–1991 (as a % of economically active women of working age in 1981)

		%
	Loss of employment	3.4
PLUS	Natural increase in workforce	3.2
MINUS	Net out-migration	10.3
MINUS	Change in net out-commuting	3.4
MINUS	Decline in economically active	−5.2
MINUS	Number on government schemes	1.7
EQUALS	Change in unemployment	−1.7

Source Turok and Edge (1999)

still significant, increase in the proportion of men commuting elsewhere for work (6.5%). There was a small increase in employment on government schemes and a larger increase in economic inactivity (something which as discussed has been noted in other areas experiencing rapid industrial change). Forms of mobility, either through permanent migration or through regular commuting, therefore played an important role in the initial adjustment of the City's labour market to job losses.

Turning now to the LMAs for women there are some similarities as well as important differences. The loss of female jobs was clearly much less pronounced (at 3.4% of economically active women in 1981). The level of out-migration was however still significant, although slightly lower than for men (at 10.3%). Changes in commuting were also less pronounced for women but still notable (3.4%); while in common with overall national trends, economic activity among women grew strongly over this period (by 5.2%).

Population Change and Migration

The LMAs suggest that one important component of adjustment to industrial job losses was through out-migration from the city (although in total population terms this was partially balanced against projected natural population growth). To further integrate these patterns, and to bring them up to the present, Fig. 7.1 presents data on Coventry's total population between 1981 and 2017. Coventry's population declined

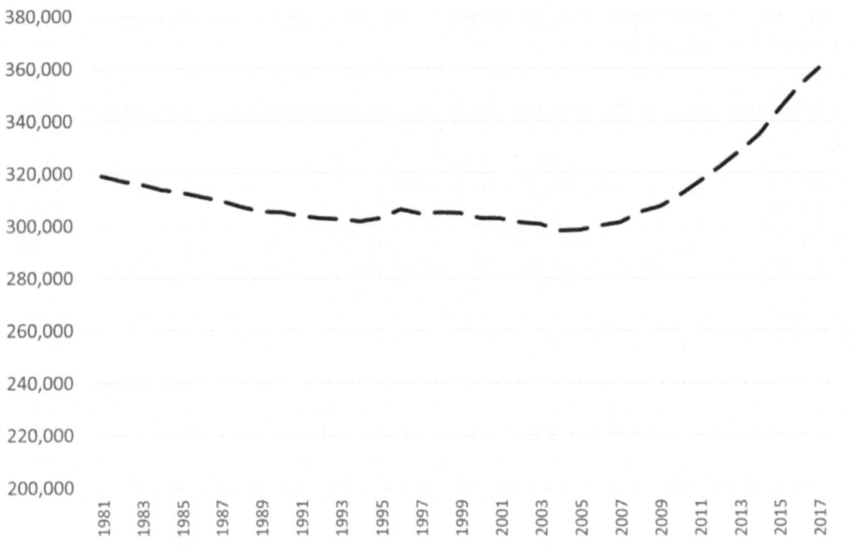

Fig. 7.1 Coventry's total population (1981–2017) (*Source* Office for National Statistics, local authority population estimates)

somewhat between the early 1980s and early 1990s, as suggested by the LMAs. With the city losing just over 15,000 residents between 1981 and 1991. After a period of relative stability in the 1990s and early 2000s, population growth accelerated markedly from the late-2000s onwards, rising to 360,100 in 2017. In the decade since 2007, the city's population had grown by 58,700, and was some 41,100 higher than in 1981.

Population growth can be driven by both demographic trends within a place and by patterns of migration inflows and outflows (and the relative balance between the two). Figure 7.2 provides details of inflows and outflows to Coventry stemming from internal migration over the past decade (i.e. migration to and from other places within the UK). Throughout the past decade the city has maintained a net outflow to other parts of the UK, with flows out of the city exceeding inflows for each year. However the difference between outflows and inflows has narrowed over time (particularly between 2012 and 2016). Both inflows and outflows have increased in volume over the period. Overall then, Coventry has a net balance of domestic outflows (albeit a relatively small one).

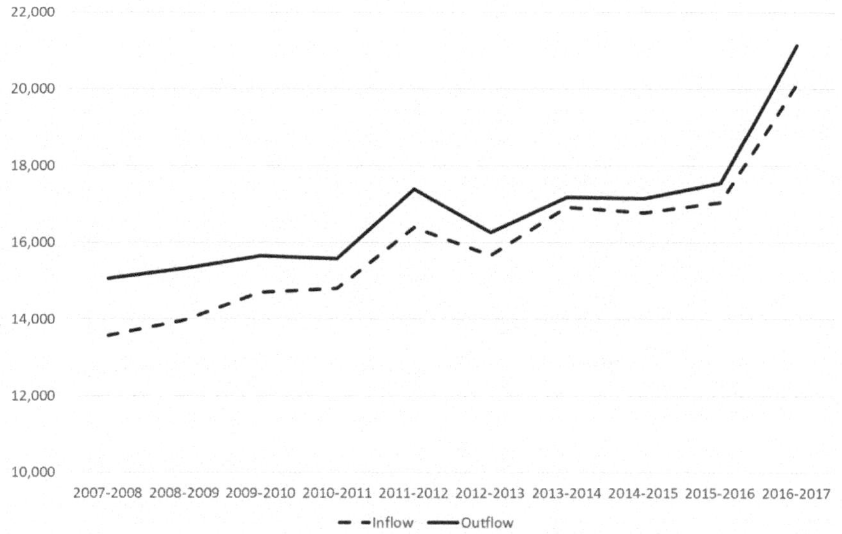

Fig. 7.2 Internal migration—Coventry inflows and outflows, 2007–2017 (*Source* Office for National Statistics, Migration Indicators Suite)

Coventry has a long history of international migration and population growth linked to its economic development and manufacturing base (Shenfield and Florence 1944; Thoms and Donnelly 1985). Successive waves of migration associated with the buoyancy of demand for labour in manufacturing have attracted migration particularly from Ireland (King et al. 1989) and from the Commonwealth countries—notably from India, Pakistan, and the West Indies (Stephens 1969). These patterns of migration were also associated with historical patterns of residential settlement for some groups within the city (the ward of Foleshill in particular still has a large proportion of residents who are Asian/Asian British [at around 50% in 2011]).[1] Migration was associated with a process of integration but also maintenance of different and distinct ethnic identifies, although these often altered over time (Ewart 2011). Lancaster (1971) however describes how post-war

[1]http://www.coventry.gov.uk/info/195/facts_about_coventry/2435/population_and_demographics/5.

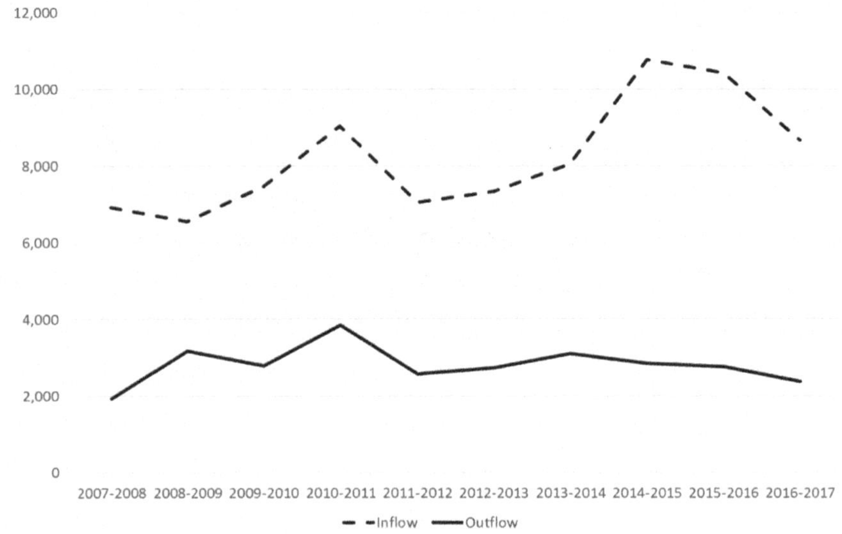

Fig. 7.3 International migration—Coventry inflows and outflows, 2007–2017 (*Source* Office for National Statistics, Migration Indicators Suite)

migrant communities also suffered from racial prejudice in the city (cited in Ewart 2011).

The patterns for recent international migration are presented in Fig. 7.3. There has been a comparatively large net inflow from international migration to Coventry over the past decade; with outflows exceeding inflows by a range between double in the closest years and 3.8 times in the years with the largest disparities. Inflows dipped notably in the year 2016–2017, this could potentially reflect the effect of the 'Brexit' vote (although flows had been gradually declining since 2012–2013). However, international migration continues to make a positive net contribution to Coventry's population and is an important part of the story of Coventry's recent population growth.

Figure 7.4 extends the discussion to look at the size of the population of the city's residents who were born overseas. In absolute terms the number has grown by around 31,000 between 2008 and the peak in 2015. The numbers were stable between 2015 and 2016 and then fell slightly in 2017 to 85,000 (although the figures are estimates and

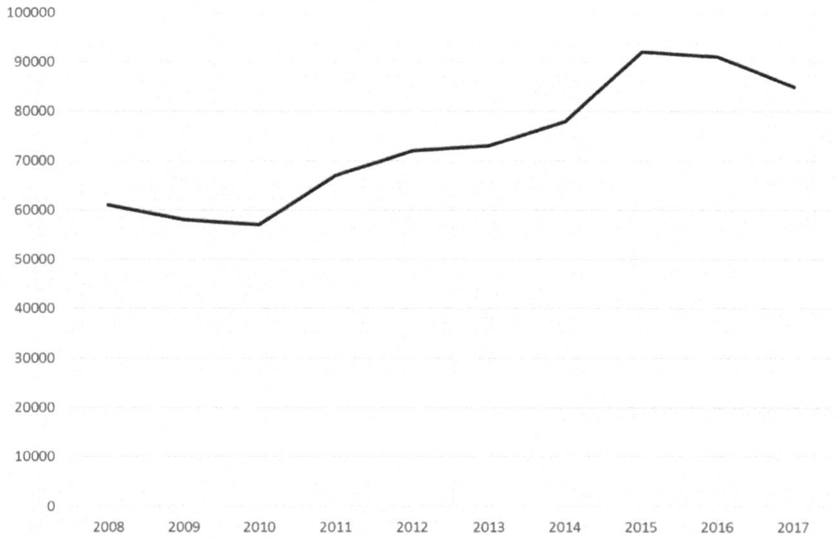

Fig. 7.4 Coventry population who were born overseas (*Source* Office for National Statistics, Migration Indicators Suite)

the size of this fall is within the confidence interval of the estimate). Residents who were born overseas now make up just under a quarter of the city's population. Of course an element of this growth will reflect the wider growth of the student population in the city, including the growth of overseas students studying at the city's two universities (as well as the international nature of staff recruitment in higher education).

One driver of population growth in the city has been higher education expansion, and particularly the growth of Coventry University. Table 7.3 shows the growth of student enrolments at Coventry University, and at the University of Warwick, which is on the outskirts of the city boundary. Coventry University's annual enrolments were in excess of 6500 higher in 2017/2018 than they were in 2014/2015, Warwick's were more than 2000 higher. A relatively large share of the city's student population come from overseas, some 31% in 2014/2015 (Centre for Cities 2017). Coventry however has a comparatively low graduate retention rate, being just 15% in 2014/2015; while 29% of the city's graduates moved to London and 16% to Birmingham (Centre

Table 7.3 Student enrolments by year and HE institution, 2014–2018

Year	Coventry University	University of Warwick
2017/2018	34,125	25,705
2016/2017	31,690	25,045
2015/2016	29,430	24,665
2014/2015	27,600	23,685

Source HESA

for Cities 2017). The city therefore experiences considerable mobility and population churn associated with higher education expansion.

Diversity in the City

Migration and demographic trends mean that Coventry has a relatively diverse population. As described previously, Coventry has a longstanding history of international migration into the city across a number of waves. The ethnic diversity of the city continues to grow, driven in part by trends linked to the growth of higher education in the city, but also an improvement in the local economy. However, Coventry's ethnic minority groups have historically suffered from higher unemployment and been located disproportionately in deprived neighbourhoods (Owen 1995). The recent changes in ethnic diversity in the city are presented in Table 7.4 which compares 1991 and 2011. The city's Asian/Asian British population has continued to grow, reaching 16.3% of the total population in 2011. The Black/African/Caribbean/Black British has also grown significantly, albeit from a lower base. Table 7.5 provides a more detailed picture of ethnicity in the city in 2011. Coventry's non-UK born white population stood at 15,385. A large part of this is attributable to comparatively newer migration flows from Europe. At the 2011 Census there were 4206 Coventry residents from the 'old' EU15 countries and 10,573 from the 'Accession states' of mainly central and eastern Europe. Coventry has a relatively large population of Asian/Asian British: Indian identity, reflecting migration patterns into the city over a long-period. There are smaller but significant numbers of residents from a wide-range of other different ethnic groups.

Table 7.4 Ethnic group of Coventry residents in 1991 and 2011

	1991	%	2011	%
White	259,513	88.2	234,029	73.8
Asian/Asian British	28,448	9.7	51,598	16.3
Black/African/Caribbean/Black British	4822	1.6	17,764	5.6
Mixed/multiple ethnic groups and other	1604	0.5	13,569	4.3
Total	294,387	100	316,960	100

Source Census, Office for National Statistics—accessed via NOMIS. *Note* Ethnics groups are combined because of differences in reporting between 1991 and 2011

Table 7.5 Ethnic group of Coventry residents, 2011

Ethnic group	Population
All usual residents	*316,960*
White	234,029
White: English/Welsh/Scottish/Northern Irish/British	211,188
White: Irish	7305
White: Gypsy or Irish Traveller	151
White: Other White	15,385
Mixed/multiple ethnic groups	8230
Mixed/multiple ethnic groups: White and Black Caribbean	3672
Mixed/multiple ethnic groups: White and Black African	943
Mixed/multiple ethnic groups: White and Asian	2388
Mixed/multiple ethnic groups: Other Mixed	1227
Asian/Asian British	51,598
Asian/Asian British: Indian	27,751
Asian/Asian British: Pakistani	9510
Asian/Asian British: Bangladeshi	2951
Asian/Asian British: Chinese	3728
Asian/Asian British: Other Asian	7658
Black/African/Caribbean/Black British	17,764
Black/African/Caribbean/Black British: African	12,836
Black/African/Caribbean/Black British: Caribbean	3317
Black/African/Caribbean/Black British: Other Black	1611
Other ethnic group	5339
Other ethnic group: Arab	2020
Other ethnic group: Any other ethnic group	3319

Source Census, Office for National Statistics—accessed via NOMIS

Patterns of Commuting

The LMAs for the 1980s also show that commuting was an important response to the loss of industrial jobs. Commuting flow figures can provide a good sense of the isolation or integration of Coventry's labour market with the wider sub-regional or regional labour market. As a Travel-to-Work Area (TTWA), the Coventry TTWA includes the city itself as well as small parts of Warwickshire to the South and Solihull to the West and North West, Nuneaton and Bedworth to the North, and Atherstone town at the northern boundary. Between 2001 and 2011, the Coventry TTWA was extended to include the neighbouring town of Rugby (approximately 13 miles to the east); indicating the size, and orientation, of Coventry TTWA has shifted somewhat.

Table 7.6 presents the dominant commuting flows from Coventry local authority to other local authority areas in 2001 and 2011 respectively (as well as those remaining in the city to work). The first obvious observation is that by 2011 a smaller proportion of Coventry residents both lived and worked in the city. Three-quarters of employed residents worked in the city in 2001, by 2011 this was down to two-thirds. There is a less clear picture about the out-flows which explain this change. There is a modest increase in flows to Warwick (of 2.1 percentage points) as well smaller increases in flows to many of the surrounding areas (with Birmingham becoming the second largest destination of

Table 7.6 Commuting out-flows Coventry local authority area, 2001 and 2011 (ranked by size of flow in 2001)

	2001		2011	
Destination	%	Total	%	Total
Coventry	74.9	93,949	66.5	78,767
Warwick	5.7	7200	7.8	9249
Rugby	3.8	4746	3.2	3805
Nuneaton and Bedworth	3.4	4220	4.1	4878
Birmingham	3.1	3882	3.8	4472
Solihull	2.1	2608	2.6	3072
Stratford-on-Avon	0.9	1068	1.7	1976
North Warwickshire	0.6	709	1.0	1134
Daventry	0.4	530	1.0	1196

Source Census, Office for National Statistics accessed via WICID

Table 7.7 Commuting in-flows to Coventry from surrounding districts, 2011

Origin	Number	As % of inflows
Nuneaton and Bedworth	11,392	22.5
Warwick	7903	15.6
Rugby	4909	9.7
Birmingham	4596	9.1
Solihull	3654	7.2
Stratford-on-Avon	1854	3.7
Hinckley and Bosworth	1840	3.6
North Warwickshire	1614	3.2

Source Census, Office for National Statistics accessed via WICID

out-flows). The out-flow increases are however relatively widely dispersed, being representative of a more mobile labour force generally. One other notable trend is that commuting flows from Coventry to London doubled over this period, although this was from a small base.

In 2011, there were in excess of 50,000 workers commuting into Coventry for employment, a considerable proportion of the city's labour force. Table 7.7 considers the origin of these flows. Some 22.5% of inflows came from Nuneaton and Bedworth local authority which is adjacent to the north of the city. Large numbers of in-commuters also come into the city to work from Warwick (7903), Rugby (4909) and Birmingham (4596). The net balance of flows into Coventry is most significant from Nuneaton and Bedworth, whereas flows out from Coventry to Warwick exceed flows in the other direction.

So far the analysis has considered simply aggregate flows of commuters to and from the city. However longer commuting patterns also tend to be associated more with some types of jobs than with others. Commuting patterns and commuting spaces tend to differ significantly by employment characteristics, with more highly skilled workers generally having wider travel-to-work patterns (Benito and Oswald 2000). National estimates of commuting spaces find that higher qualified workers are effectively 'contained'[2] within 262 TTWAs in the UK; for lower skilled workers the number of effective TTWAS is

[2]Using the standard threshold definition of TTWAs.

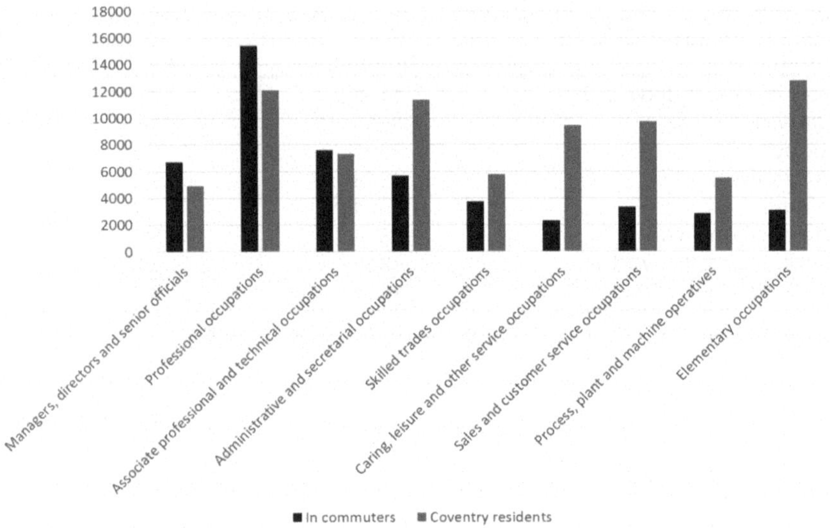

Fig. 7.5 Jobs filled in Coventry by Standard Occupation Classification and whether Coventry resident or in-commuters (*Source* Census, Office for National Statistics accessed via WICID)

416 (Coombes, undated). This demonstrates the more spatially constrained commuting space for lower qualified workers who are therefore more dependent on the conditions of more localised labour markets (Green 2009).

Figure 7.5 considers the nature of in-commuting flows alongside the patterns of workers who both live and work in the city; this shows the distribution of jobs within the city in terms of whether they are filled by residents or commuters. The figures are separated into occupational groups. Roughly speaking the three occupational groups towards the left of graph—Managers, directors and senior officials; Professional occupations; Associate professional and technical occupations—are considered to be higher-skilled.[3] Managers, directors and senior officials, and Professional occupations, are also the highest paid occupational groups; earning more than double the hourly rate at the median

[3]In the employment flows data the Office for National Statistics….

of workers in Caring, leisure and other services, Sales and customer services, and Elementary occupations (ONS 2018).[4] The figures provide a very clear picture of the significance of workers in highly-skilled occupations commuting into the city for employment. Of all the almost 40,000 managerial and professional occupation jobs within the city, in excess of half (56%) are filled by in-commuters. In professional occupations, in-commuters represent more than 15,000 of the city's workforce, for managerial occupations the figure is just over 6700. The city's more highly skilled sectors, such as parts of advanced manufacturing, education (the universities) and heath, are heavily reliant on highly skilled commuting into the city; drawing in workers from elsewhere in the TTWA and from further afield. The patterns for Associate professional and technical occupations are more evenly split between Coventry residents and in-commuters.

When looking specifically at the origin of highly-skilled commuters into Coventry the data demonstrate the importance of comparatively local links within the sub-regional area, and the relative economic integration within the sub-regional around commuting patterns. There are comparatively large flows of highly-skilled workers into Coventry from Warwick, with around 4500 Managers, directors and senior officials and workers in Professional occupations commuting to the city for employment. There are also relatively large and important flows of highly skilled workers from parts of Nuneaton and Bedworth, Rugby, Birmingham, Solihull, Stratford-on-Avon. Of course there are also flows of highly skilled residents out of Coventry to employment opportunities elsewhere.

The picture is very different for other occupations, with a predominance of local residents filling jobs. In both Caring, leisure and other service occupations and in Elementary occupations, 80% of workers are city residents. In Sales and customer service occupations, three-quarters of workers are city residents. The figures for Administrative and

[4]Figures from the Annual Survey of Hours and Earnings, 2018 (provisional figures). The data are available a https://www.ons.gov.uk/employmentandlabourmarket/peopleinwork/earningsandworkinghours/datasets/occupation2digitsocashetable2.

secretarial occupations and Process, plant and machine operatives are both around a two-thirds for local residents. As described previously from national analysis, Coventry bears out the different commuting patterns of different groups of workers, and the different relative integration of different occupations across wider or narrower geographical areas. Large numbers of local residents are therefore reliant on the availability (and quality) of work within the city in comparatively low-paid sectors such as Caring, leisure and other service occupations, Sales and customer service occupations, and Elementary occupations.

In summary, different parts of the Coventry economy are clearly linked in different ways to surrounding area, and to the wider region, in terms of commuting patterns. The more highly skilled occupational labour markets operate across the sub-region level and beyond. Across other occupations the commuting fields tend to be more localised for workers within the city. Of course, these patterns partly reflect the generally wider nature of professional labour markets which are known to operate over larger distances, but they do demonstrate important differences in the relationships with the surrounding region for different groups of residents. Many of those in-commuting to work in parts of economy such as the universities and advanced manufacturing are working at organisations which are globally-facing in terms of knowledge-flows and economic relationships—highlighting the multifarious nature of contemporary Coventry which is simultaneously embedded in international networks, reliant on wider sub-regional relationships, and at the same time partly locally and inwardly-focused.

There is significant overlap between the extended Coventry labour market and the scope of the 'sub-regional housing market' which is centered on the city but expands to include Warwick, Leamington Spa, and Southam to the south; Rugby to the east, and Nuneaton and Bedworth to the north of the city (Hill 2010; Coventry City Council 2012). Within the city itself there are also distinct patterns of housing, with more affluent housing areas to the south of city extending towards the University of Warwick, but with lower cost and less affluent neighbourhoods extending north from the city centre; these northern neighbourhoods contain higher incidence of disadvantage and unemployment, they also have larger BAME populations (ibid.). Coventry's 'housing offer' is therefore particularly oriented to lower value housing, with higher-value and larger housing located more in parts of Rugby and Warwick district; the limited nature of higher value housing in the city is linked to commuting patterns observed and the influx of professional commuters from outside the city, with a higher value 'housing offer' having the potential to support economic development in the city (ibid.). Although the city is tightly bounded so opportunities for large-scale development are constrained (Healey and Dunham 1994).

Housing has been an important issue in the city for the past hundred years. The rapid population growth as a result of migration into the city in the 1920s and 1930s placed considerable pressure on an already poor housing stock (Campbell 2007). The large-scale redevelopment of the city centre after the devastation of the city in the Second World War had been preceded by slum clearances in the 1930s (Gould and Gould 2009). During the reconstruction, the city centre was configured to support access by private car, with the development a new ring road which physically separated the city centre from the surrounding neighbourhoods. The post-ward period saw a mass programme of public housing development in city, particularly in the out-lying areas (but also in places located closer to the city centre), with more than twenty new mixed development estates built; this was followed by the development of large private estates from the mid-1950s onwards (Stephens 1969).

The sub-regional housing market has evolved differently across local authority areas over the last two decades. Figure 7.6 presents data for median house prices in Coventry and surrounding districts covering the period 1995–2018. House prices in Warwick and Rugby where higher than those in Coventry at the start of the period but have also grown more quickly. In nominal terms house prices in Warwick were 4.8 larger in 2018 than 1995, in Rugby they were five times larger; for Coventry the comparative change was 4.2. The differences in median house prices between Warwick (an important source of professional commuting flows) and Coventry are very significant; with median house prices in Warwick of £300,000 in 2018, comparing to £175,000 in Coventry. Rugby sits in-between the two (at £239,995), while prices in the areas to the north of the city are comparable to those within Coventry.

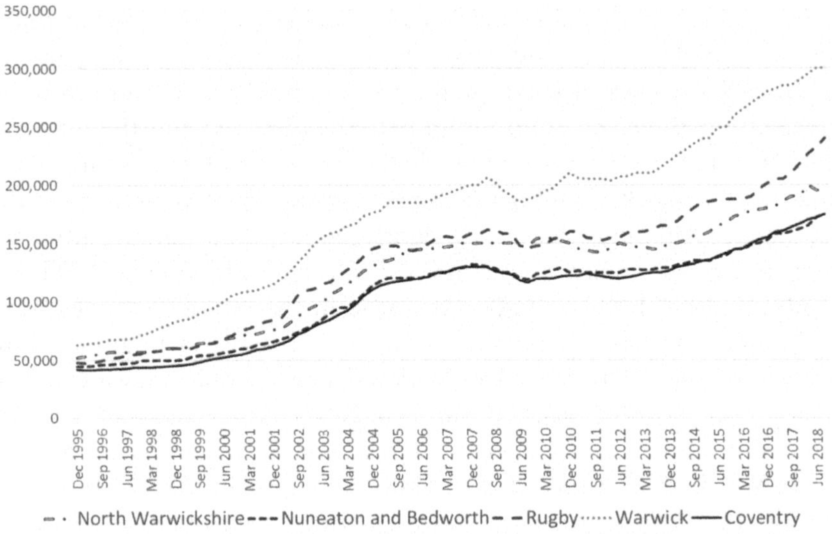

Fig. 7.6 Median house prices (nominal) in Coventry and surrounding districts, 1995–2018 (*Source* Land Registry, Office for National Statistics)

Conclusions

This chapter has focused on mobility and the way this relates to Coventry's evolution, and to its changing position in relation to the global, national and local. Coventry has long been a city associated with inward migration. International migration, fuelled by demand for labour in the growing manufacturing sector, created a more diverse city, with growing populations in particular from Ireland and parts of the Commonwealth. However, Coventry suffered disproportionately from national and regional deindustrialisation, changes which have left a lasting legacy on the city. In the immediate aftermath forms of mobility were important adjustments to job losses. Rates of commuting to employment outside the city increased and there was a relatively large out-migration of population from the city in response to industrial job losses. Economic inactivity among men also increased, a phenomenon which has been apparent in other old industrial areas. In total population terms, the city lost around 15,000 residents during the 1980s.

From the mid-2000s however this trend went into reverse and the population has grown rapidly, with 58,700 additional residents added in the decade from 2007. This population growth was though of a different nature, partly reflecting the growing importance of Coventry as a centre for higher education, with annual enrolments at the city's two large universities growing by more than 8500 in the four years from 2014 alone. Residents who were born overseas now make-up around one-quarter of the city's population. Historical and contemporary patterns of migration are reflected in the diversity of Coventry. The city has a relatively large Asian/Asian British population, particularly Indian and Pakistani communities. Newer waves of migration include migration from the 'Accession states' of central and eastern Europe. In respect of migration flows then, Coventry has a long history of international linkages, but with a changing set of predominant flows and different drivers of these.

Short-term mobility, commuting, has also played an important part in Coventry's post-industrial experience. Increased commuting played a modest but important role in offsetting some of the loss of industrial jobs. The Coventry TTWA has grown to include Rugby, reflecting the greater sub-regional economic integration. The city became less 'self-contained' during the 2000s as commuting flows (both in and out) increased. In 2011, more than 50,000 workers commuted into Coventry from the surrounding area. However there are distinct occupational commuting patterns. Of all the almost 40,000 managerial and professional occupation jobs within the city (the highest paying occupational groups) more than half are filled by in-commuters. Many of these commuting flows, to the universities, health and parts of advanced manufacturing, are to organisations which are embedded in international networks. For lower-paid occupations there is a predominance of local residents filling jobs. Commuting patterns are also reflected in the nature of the sub-regional housing market, with Coventry's 'housing offer' being particularly oriented to lower value housing, although new developments are beginning to alter this.

It is also worth noting that graduate retention in the city is weak reflecting both the comparatively limited opportunities, outside of the large employers in education, health and parts of advanced manufacturing, as well as the quality of housing offer in the city. An important challenge for the city moving forward is translate the success of its educational institutions and their role in human capital development into long-run economic development and the expansion of good jobs and opportunities across a broad base of the city's population. Coventry is an open city, embedded in regional, national and international networks—this openness brings important benefits, but the city would also benefit from some additional 'stickyness' around graduate retention to support its ongoing transformation.

This is the central challenge as Coventry moves forward. The industrial base has been transformed but there is still a sharp distinction between the professional labour markets, which rely to a significant extent on in-commuting and which are driven by sectors such as education, health and other parts of the public sector, and the opportunities available to many residents. Important parts of the city's economy have seen growth which has attracted a more highly qualified population to work in, if not necessarily live in, the city. However these remain pockets of economic activity, and the city maintains a significant incidence of deprivation and disadvantage—communities which have not benefited significantly from these changes. There is a more self-contained Coventry, where residents are reliant on the opportunities of the very local labour market. For the city to truly thrive, economic development needs to pay greater attention to this, and to issues of local employment opportunities and job quality across the board base of employment, balanced against the ongoing strive for a new knowledge economy.

References

Beatty, C., & Fothergill, S. (1996). Labour Market Adjustment in Areas of Chronic Industrial Decline: The Case of the UK Coalfields. *Regional Studies, 30,* 627–640.

Beatty, C., Fothergill, S., Houston, D., Powell, R., & Sissons, P. (2009). A Gendered Theory of Employment, Unemployment and Sickness. *Environment and Planning C: Government and Policy, 27*(6), 958–974.

Benito, A., & Oswald, A. (2000). *Commuting in Great Britain in the 1990s: The Warwick Economics Research Paper Series (TWERPS) 560.* Department of Economics, University of Warwick.

Campbell, L. (2007). Paper Dream City/Modern Monument: Donald Gibson and Coventry. In I. B. Whyte (Ed.), *Man-Made Future: Planning, Education and Design in Mid-Twentieth-Century Britain* (pp. 121–144). London and New York: Routledge. ISBN 9780415357883.

Centre for Cities. (2017). *The Great British Brain Drain: An Analysis of Migration to and from Coventry*. London: Centre for Cities.

Coombes. (undated). *Alternative Travel to Work Areas.* Accessed from http://ons.maps.arcgis.com/apps/MapSeries/index.html?appid=397ccae5d5c7472e87cf0ca766386cc2.

Coventry City Council. (2012). *Strategic Housing Market Assessment.* Accessed at http://www.coventry.gov.uk/download/.../id/.../lp42_coventry_shma_2012_-_gl_hearn.pdf.

Ewart, H. (2011). 'Coventry Irish': Community, Class, Culture and Narrative in the Formation of a Migrant Identity, 1940–1970. *Midland History, 36*(2), 225–244.

Gould, J., & Gould, C. (2009). *Coventry Planned: The Architecture of the Plan for Coventry, 1940–1978*. Somerset: Gould and Gould Architects. https://www.coventry.gov.uk/downloads/file/19166/gould_report_coventry_planned_april_2009_revision

Green, A. (2009). *Geography Matters: The Importance of Subnational Perspectives on Employment and Skills*. Wath-Upon-Dearne: UKCES.

Healey, M., & Clark, D. (1984). Industrial Decline and Government Response in the West Midlands: The Case of Coventry. *Regional Studies, 18*(4), 303–318.

Healey, M., & Dunham, P. (1994). Changing Competitive Advantage in a Local Economy: The Case of Coventry, 1971–1990. *Urban Studies, 31*(8), 1279–1301.

Hill, D. (2010). *The Functional Economic Geography of the Coventry, Solihull & Warwickshire Sub-Region*: Coventry & Warwickshire Economic Assessment TOPIC PAPER 1. Accessed at https://apps.warwickshire.gov.uk/api/documents/WCCC-688-17.

King, R., Strachan, A., & Shuttleworth, I. (1989). The Irish in Coventry: The Social Geography of a Relict Community. *Irish Geography, 22,* 64–78.

Office for National Statistics, General Register Office for Scotland, Northern Ireland Statistics, and Research Agency. (2005). *2001 Census Aggregate Data* (Edition: 2005). UK Data Service. http://dx.doi.org/10.5257/census/aggregate-2001-1.

Office for National Statistics, National Records of Scotland, Northern Ireland Statistics and Research Agency. (2016). *2011 Census Aggregate Data*. UK Data Service (Edition: June 2016). http://dx.doi.org/10.5257/census/aggregate-2011–1.

Office for National Statistics. (2001). *Census: Special Workplace Statistics (England, Wales and Northern Ireland)* [Computer File]. UK Data Service Census Support. Downloaded from: https://wicid.ukdataservice.ac.uk.

Office for National Statistics. (2011). *Census: Special Workplace Statistics (United Kingdom)* [Computer File]. UK Data Service Census Support. Downloaded from https://wicid.ukdataservice.ac.uk.

Office of Population Censuses and Surveys, General Register Office for Scotland, Registrar General for Northern Ireland. (1997). *1991 Census Aggregate Data*. UK Data Service (Edition: 1997). http://dx.doi.org/10.5257/census/aggregate-1991-1.

Office of Population Censuses and Surveys, Registrar General for Scotland. (2000). *1981 Census Aggregate Data* (Edition: 2000). UK Data Service. http://dx.doi.org/10.5257/census/aggregate-1981-1.

Shenfield, A., & Florence, P. (1944). Labour for the War Industries: The Experience of Coventry. *The Review of Economic Studies, 12*(1), 31–49.

Thoms, D., & Donnelly, T. (1985). *The Motor Car Industry in Coventry Since the 1890's*. London: Routledge.

Turok, I., & Edge, N. (1999). *The Jobs Gap in Britain's Cities: Employment Loss and Labour Market Consequences*. York: Joseph Rowntree Foundation.

'The City of Coventry: Social History from 1700'. In W. B. Stephens (Ed.), *A History of the County of Warwick: Volume 8, the City of Coventry and Borough of Warwick* (1969) (pp. 222–241). London: British History Online. http://www.british-history.ac.uk/vch/warks/vol8/pp222-241.

'The City of Coventry: Introduction'. In W. B. Stephens (Ed.), *A History of the County of Warwick: Volume 8, the City of Coventry and Borough of Warwick* (1969) (pp. 1–23). London: British History Online. http://www.british-history.ac.uk/vch/warks/vol8/pp1-23.

8

Occupational Structure and Change in Post-war Coventry

Jason Begley

Globalisation is not a simple term to engage with. Over the last number of decades it has been ascribed an importance that has captured popular public attention. It has been alternatively presented as a Ricardian tool for closer cooperation and growth while forcing down inflationary forces through trade with developing countries, or as a trap that increases inequality and limits the capacity of the state to deal with same (Martin and Schumann 1997). In more recent years luminaries such as Joseph Stiglitz and Paul Krugman have begun to question whether the globalising process, or more accurately the unrestricted movement of goods and labour or trade globalisation, has in fact gone too far, arguing that advocates overestimate the benefits and underestimate costs, particularly for the standards of living of those in advanced countries with limited skills (Krugman 2016; Stiglitz 2017). It is this skills and occupational component that arguably deserves greater focus when considering the impact of globalisation on a city such as Coventry.

J. Begley (✉)
Coventry University, Coventry, UK
e-mail: aa0070@coventry.ac.uk

J. Begley et al. (eds.), *Revival of a City*, Palgrave Studies in Economic History,
https://doi.org/10.1007/978-3-030-22822-4_8

For economic historians a further challenge after identifying what to focus on is an appropriate period for examination. For example Williamson famously drew comparison between the late nineteenth and mid to late twentieth century in his examination of growth, globalisation and convergence (Williamson 1997). In later work with O'Rourke, the pair focussed on one dimension of globalisation, the integration of international commodity markets through three broad periods running right up until the twentieth century (O'Rourke and Williamson 2002, 2004). In the particular instance of Coventry there is considerable value in focussing on structural and occupational change in the period after the Second World War. It was during these years that the city became dominated by one large industry, the motor industry, while simultaneously becoming a major export centre for volume produced vehicles when the demand for these goods sky rocketed as economies moved increasingly toward easily affordable motorised private conveyances. However, by the 1970s, global demand was increasingly being met by international rivals, with the UK motor industry and in particular the West Midlands becoming the biggest casualties of the success of Japanese, American, German and French automakers. This chapter explores this sequence of events by examining occupational change, considering how labour specialisation would give away to significant economic and skills changes wrought by globalising forces, forcing the city's economic base to adapt to new circumstances of industrial and structural organisation.

Structural economic change in Coventry is considered by examining longitudinal variations in the allocation of the labour force across a range of industrial sectors in the post-WWII period. Structural change forms an important part of the way in which modern economic growth has been described and analysed. For example the three-sector hypothesis of Fisher and Clark divides the economy into broad occupational activities related to extraction, manufacturing and services provision (Primary, Secondary, tertiary). Lewis' two-sector model of economic development with unlimited supplies of labour, also known as the dual-sector model, perceived economic development as the movement of labour from agriculture to manufacturing processes. Kuznets identified six characteristics of modern economic growth and ascribed the transformation of a pre-industrial economy to a modern one to aggregate growth, structural change and international spread (Kuznets 1971; Broadberry 2016). Chenery et al. also posited a typical pattern of change in economic structure as countries experience economic development.[1] These analyses explain economic development as a set of inter-related structural changes as economies move through higher levels of GDP per capita. Structural change manifests itself both in sector output, but also in changes in the employment of the labour force across sectors. By focussing on the changing sector allocation of the Coventry labour force the chapter will demonstrate how new circumstances of production and trading, influenced by shifting global markets and emerging economic activities, instigated a development transition in the local economy. This change has impacted the workforce, altering both its composition, but also its character, creating new forms of labour engagement.

Coventry Before the War

In the years before the Second World War Coventry city's economy had become dominated by vehicle manufacturing and engineering. As discussed by Collis and Donnelly, vehicle production in the UK was heavily influenced by industrial and occupational shifts that occurred in Coventry at the turn of the Twentieth century. In the 1890s in Coventry textiles and watchmaking gave way to the manufacture of cars and their components as major firms like Daimler, Rover, Standard and Siddeley established themselves in and around the city. By 1911 vehicle and metal industries absorbed approximately 41% of Coventry's occupied population (Thoms et al. 2000). This had the effect of changing structures of work organisation and production, necessitating larger enterprises comprised of more specialised labour. However, the work remained largely craft-based, with skills yet to be superseded by assembly-line activities.

[1]Clark, C. The conditions of economic progress; Lewis, 'Economic Development with Unlimited Supplies'; Kuznets, 'Modern Economic Growth'; Chenery et al., 'Patterns of Development'; Chenery, 'Structural Change and Development'.

Income figures are difficult come by for this period, though the perception of the time was they were generally good (Thoms et al. 2000). This is borne out by the Medical Officer's annual reports for the City, showing as they do an improvement in general health and pointing toward rising living standards during the period (CHC, Medical officer reports).

In the year before the outbreak of the First World War production of motor vehicles in Britain had increased to 34,000 cars and commercial vehicles per annum (Maxcy and Silberston 1959). This was matched by an increase in registered vehicles in Britain from 23,192 in March 1906 to 132,015 in 1914 (Richardson 1977). However, the growth of the industry was curtailed somewhat by the start of the, initially, European conflict, as American exporters were able to take advantage of markets for private vehicles vacated by British firms supplying government contracts (Richardson 1977). Concerned industrialists lobbied the government for protection from international competition, resulting in the introduction of duties on luxury imports by the Chancellor of the Exchequer, Reginald McKenna. These levies of 33.3% were in place until 1956 and allowed British motor manufacturers to capture home markets during the interwar years, nullifying international rivals' attempts to enter the UK market. The importance of the McKenna Duties was made clear during the brief period they were waived from 1924 to 1925. The then Minister for Labour, Thomas Shaw, estimated the number of workers engaged in the branches of trade affected, directly or indirectly, by these duties was in the region of 200,000 (Hansard 1924).

Shielded by tariff protection, the motor industry made enormous gains in the domestic market in the Interwar years. The sector supplied 97% of the home market by 1937 and was second only to the US for exports (Thoms et al. 2000). Coventry city was no exception to this expansion of the motor trade and by 1939 the automotive industry accounted for 38% of Coventry's total labour force (of approximately 100,000 workers). However, from 1935 to 1936 onwards preparation for war fundamentally changed the nature of the industry. The establishment of the Shadow Factory Scheme(s), designed to increase aircraft production using motor industry technology and skills, was largely centred in the West Midlands.

The outbreak of war in 1939 saw the industry as a whole becoming almost entirely dedicated to armament production (Foreman-Peck 1995). By the middle of the war as the Shadow Factory Scheme(s) expanded its operations, vehicles, engines and aircraft production accounted for over 60% of employment in Coventry, while the closely related sector of general engineering employed a further 20%. What emerged during these years was rapid specialisation in production, labour and skills in the city, running parallel to rapid decline in other sectors (Thoms and Donnelly 1985). As discussed in Busch's chapter, earlier in this text, a variety of factors accounted for this growth, not least of which was firms' seeking to take advantage of clusters of skilled labour and supporting services. The demand for skilled labour created by this expansion of activity had a concomitant effect on wages, which remained high during the war years (Thoms and Donnelly 1985).

Post-war Wages and Occupations in Coventry

During the war years the Conditions of Employment and National Arbitration Order (Order 1305) ushered in a new era of work relations in the UK as labour disputes were brought to an arbitration panel. Though the act restricted strike activity, the unions chose to cooperate closely with government and employers, organising production, target setting and general planning. The act remained in place until 1951, when it was replaced by the Industrial Disputes Order, relaxing the sanctions on strike actions.[2] During the immediate years after the war Trade Union membership also rose rapidly, as successive governments strove to establish good relations with worker representatives. By the beginning of the 1950s the scene was set for rapid industrial growth, particularly in the motor sector as the move toward mass motoring in the post war era gathered pace.

---

[2] A fuller description of the Industrial Disputes Order can be found in Hansard Aug 1951, vol. 491, cc1624-30. https://api.parliament.uk/historic-hansard/commons/1951/aug/02/industrial-disputes-new-order

Table 8.1 Industrial groups of employees in Coventry

Group	1952		1966	
	No.	%	No.	%
Primary	3760	2.4	2067	1.0
Metal working	101,669	64.7	123,458	60.4
Other manufacturing	11,598	7.4	12,379	6.0
Construction	6717	4.2	9187	4.5
Utilities	6067	3.9	6307	3.1
Services	27,429	17.5	51,110	25.0
	157,240	100	204,508	100

Source Thoms and Donnelly (1985)

In Coventry, industrial expansion was largely absorbed by vehicle manufacturers and engineering. Table 8.1 shows a breakdown of workers by sector.

Much of this activity was directly employed in either motor or aero production, with the latter declining in significance during the 1960s.[3] For example, the motor sector accounted for 31.3% of total Coventry employment in 1951, dropping slightly to 29.5% in 1971. By comparison the national share of the Motor industry only accounted for 2% of the economy (Rosser and Mallier 1981).

A number of factors helped explain this growth in the motor industry in Coventry. First, and most obvious, was the industrial heritage and the advantages offered by the concentration of industry that occurred in the years before the war, but also established as a result of rearmament. Additionally, in the post-war period UK manufacturers were able to focus on pent up demand and burgeoning domestic markets. The only major international producers unaffected by the war were located in the US, who were still subject to tariffs under the McKenna agreement. Furthermore, the market for American models was substantially different to UK markets (with longer distances to travel) and the models they

[3]During the 1960s a number of significant closures in the in aero production occurred, resulting from government policies of rationalisation and defence considerations, leading to a 60% reduction in employment in the sector in Coventry, with the remainder focussed largely on aerospace engine production (Mallier and Rosser 1982).

produced were not entirely suitable for UK markets (Rosser and Mallier 1981). For example, imports only accounted for 3% of new registration during the 1950s. By 1969 this figure had risen to 10%, but by 1977 they accounted for 50% of new registrations. During the early decades after the war, what faced automotive producers was negligible external competition, high demand domestically and easy export markets. Little wonder that the industry grew rapidly in Coventry, with its strong base in engineering and manufacturing and specialised, skilled workforce. Growth in vehicle manufacturing also, almost inevitably, served to attract heavy inward migration, drawn by the prospects of well-paid, accessible employment opportunities.

The City's population went through a growth phase after the war. By 1948 the population of the city stood at 250,900. Three years later it had increased to 258,245. By 1961 the population had grown again to 305,521 and a decade later had gone as high as 335,235. Much of this increase was driven by inward migration of workers looking for work opportunities in a city that was deemed to be booming. In 1931 there were only 1100 migrants to Coventry. By 1935 this number had increased by 40% and was largely composed of UK workers from surrounding towns and cities (Lancaster and Mason 1986). The pace of migration increased after the war, and from 1951 to 1961, 44.5% of population growth was accounted for by new arrivals. Table 8.2 gives a breakdown of Coventry's population by origin.

Table 8.2 Birthplace Coventry residents

	1951	1961[a]
England	223,432	252,415
Wales	10,558	10,983
Scotland	7747	10,277
RoI	7521	14,802
N. Ireland	2294	4020
Commonwealth	1831	4285
Foreign	4471	4851
Other	391	2409

[a]Ewart (2011). Ewart's figures for population differ from Lancaster's by about 1000 persons, despite both referencing census reports as sources of data
Source Ewart (2011)

By the end of the decade this flow had slowed somewhat, with migration dropping to 5.8% compared to 19% of the previous decade. In fact, 1968 saw outward migration of 0.1% (Lancaster and Mason 1986).

What drove this migration into Coventry during the decades of the 1950s and 1960s was not only work opportunities. Wages were also exceptionally high for skilled and semi-skilled labour. In 1940 the Coventry and District Association of the Engineer Employers Federation agreed to set both piecework and toolroom rates at the same level for its employees, in a bid to halt the drain of toolroom workers to piecework (Brown 1971). A weighted average was taken of the standard hourly earnings of the skilled workers in twenty to thirty leading firms and the resulting figure set as the prevailing rate known as the Coventry District Toolroom Rate (Knowles and Robinson 1969). By the mid-1960s the Toolroom Rate effected approximately 10,000 workers. The agreement would remain in place until the end of the 1960s and would become a barometer of wage levels for a wide range of engineering and heavy metal labour. For example, Brown, using regression analysis, calculates that by 1958 only 28% of the Coventry Toolroom rate was accounted for by national agreements, with the rest being negotiated locally by trade union representatives (Brown 1971).

The impact of the toolroom rate on wages was considerable. Coventry workers earned 50% above the national average in 1942. This figure had dropped to 30% by 1948 with the end of wartime production. Over the ten-year period to 1963 earnings rose 76% compared to a national rise of 74% (Knowles and Robinson 1969). Brown (1971) notes that pieceworkers determined wage movement in all engineering factories. Even in a period of national wage increases, the growth in earnings in Coventry was exceptional (Flanders 1957). This was matched by a period of low unemployment in Coventry, 0.9% compared to a national average of 1.8% from 1953 to 1966 and 2.8% compared to a national average of 3.1% in 1967–1968. Tellingly Brown (1971) opines that wage increases were not matched by productivity and profitability changes.

Growth in earnings and job opportunities served to legitimise the establishment of migrant communities in the city according to Ewart. In her research on Irish communities (Ewart 2011), she notes "a change of status of the Irish migrant". No longer were they restricted to unskilled labouring jobs no one else wanted, they instead were able to increase their income through access to skilled work that served to integrate them into British occupational and social structures. As one migrant noted,

> You could walk in and out of work. You could take your pick of four jobs in the morning and, if you didn't like it, you could walk out at lunchtime and be in another by the afternoon. (Ewart 2011)

However, such access only came through personal connections, or community associations. This had an 'exclusionary closure' effect according to Parkin (1983), which created silos in terms of communities in the city. For example in 1954, the Indian Workers' Association complained to the Coventry Trades Council that they suspected a colour bar was being operated by Coventry Transport even though the company denied this (Ewart 2011).

Decline and Structural Change

By the end of the 1960s the Coventry economy was beginning to experience a slowdown in economic growth. This was not just a citywide experience. Regionally the West Midlands was also beginning to diverge from the South East of the country. Geary and Stark make productivity and GDP per capita estimates for UK regions for 150 years. Using wage and sectoral analysis they demonstrate that sigma and beta convergence[4] described a U shape during the years under examination. Between 1931 and 1951, the gap between productivity in the South East and the rest of the country (including the West Midlands) narrowed noticeably, stabilised until the 1970s, then increased after this date before rapidly diverging in the 1990s. GDP per capita followed a similar pathway

[4]Sigma convergence is based on neoclassical theory of economic growth. The theory states that all countries converge to the same level of advancement, i.e. economic output. Beta convergence is similarly theoretically grounded and points to poorer countries exhibiting faster rates of growth than richer countries, leading to economic catch-up over time.

(Geary and Stark 2015). The Coventry case was no different, though arguably the city endured a harsher low than the West Midlands generally, as will be discussed.

Considerable literature has been given over to explaining why this downturn occurred. For Coventry and the car industry in particular, the reasons most frequently offered cover low levels of investment, a lack of economies of scale, poor profitability, low productivity, government policy and volatile labour relations, all of which contributed to a downwards spiral of decline (Rhys 1972; Bhaskar and Rhys 1979; Dunnett 1980; Whisler 1999; Thoms et al. 2000). Foreman-Peck argue that the failure by British firms to rationalise plant and product meant that businesses were left with low volume models and plants with excess capacity (1995). Bowden et al. note that the UK motor industry as a whole had garnered a reputation for strikes, poor product quality, low productivity growth and wage drift.

The authors, echoing Church, point to the failure to address the piece rate system in Coventry as a prime example of such challenges facing the industry that were never dealt with at a local level (Bowden et al.; Church). Ultimately, though, the problems facing the car industry in Coventry and more widely in the West Midlands cannot be separated from the impact of de-industrialisation after 1970 juxtaposed to internationalisation and subsequent globalisation of the industry after the Second World War (Donnelly et al. 2017). The example of Rootes, one of the big six producers demonstrates the challenges brought about by increasing market penetration by international competitors. Even before the end of the 1960s, Rootes had been posting profit warnings (Table 8.3).

Profitability in 1968 could only be achieved after a round of rationalisation occurred under the new owners, as well as the sale of underperforming assets.[5] These losses can be partially explained by difficult trading conditions during the decade, including unofficial strike activity.[6] Important,

[5]PA 2616/2/1-14 "Rootes Motors ltd Annual report and statement of accounts 1970," Coventry Archive and Research Centre.

[6]PA 2616/2/12 "Rootes Motors ltd Annual report and statement of accounts 1962," Coventry Archive and Research Centre.

Table 8.3 Annual report 1968: Rootes Motors ltd

	Sales to public	Net earnings/loss	Depreciation
1959	108,000	4164	1317
1960	126,000	7081	1454
1961	115,000	1105	1635
1962	105,000	−1826	1555
1963	137,000	166	1951
1964	170,000	1974	2374
1965	175,000	−2226	2412
1966	178,000	−3291	2994
1967	171,000	−10,716	3559
1968	176,000	3804	4646

Source Chrysler Corporation, "Annual Report 1968: Rootes Motors ltd."

too, were the investment decisions taken by the senior management of the firm during these years.[7] Yet, notably the Rootes Group Chairman identified external factors like fluctuating domestic economic conditions and the failure of the UK to gain entry to the common market in 1967 as being central to the declining fortunes of the firm.[8] Growing competition from abroad was beginning to impact on Coventry firms even by the middle of the 1960s. The next two decades brought deindustrialisation and depression, with a concomitant impact on the structure of labour in the city.

Between 1975 and 1982 the city lost around 55,000 jobs, largely in manufacturing. Redundancies were at a rate of 46% in Coventry, compared to 32% for the West Midlands and 27% for the UK (Thoms and Donnelly 1985). Jobs were being lost in manufacturing faster than the growing service sector could substitute for. Moreover, key institutions in terms of public utilities, finance and distribution were located in Birmingham. Also concerning was that the population did not have readily transferable skills to attract alternative industrial activity, nor were there third level educational institutions in place until 1965 to offset these problems by upskilling the local population, resulting in a drain of talent and youth from the city. As Mallier and Rosser notes, Coventry's reputation as a producer of cars came from the fact that final assembly

[7]PA 2616/2/1-14.

[8]Ibid.

occurred there; components were typically assembled elsewhere, with the notable exception of Dunlop. The necessary pool of skilled labour for component manufacture was not available in Coventry, meaning Coventry was not only over specialised in terms of the motor industry, it had also focussed on passenger car assembly. This made Coventry more vulnerable to market forces, whereas components enjoyed a steadier demand across a range of models and brands (Mallier and Rosser 1982).

Part of what exacerbated the depth of the depression in Coventry was the transient nature of key firms located in the city. During the 1960s major employers in Coventry followed a trend of merging with larger partner groups, both nationally and internationally (Rosser and Mallier 1981). Firms such as Rootes, with their headquarters in the city, were being taken over by international automakers like the American firm Chrysler. By the mid 1980s most of the major firms in the city were not locally owned and only had a fraction of their overall workforce located in the city (Healey and Clark 1984). Table 8.4 shows returns for the top 50 firms in Coventry at the start of the decade.

For all, excluding necessary services and utilities, the local component of the overall workforce was small to insignificant. This meant decisions around location, investment and development of enterprises in the city were not as impacted by local factors as may have been the case in earlier decades. Thoms and Donnelly argue that this process of merger and internationalisation served to take core management activities out of the

Table 8.4 Ownership of Coventry's top 50 firms[a] by location of head office

Ownership[b]	No. firms	No. Employees	Employees[c] as total % Coventry workforce
Private, HO in Coventry	4	1500	0.75
Private, HO in WM	4	2500	1.5
Private, HO UK	26	37,500	20
Government/NEB (inc. pub utilities)	8	42,000	22.5
Private, HO outside UK	8	17,500	9.5

[a]Excludes central and local government employment and construction industry
[b]Ownership 1980
[c]Employee no.s 1975
Source Rosser and Mallier (1981)

city. In part this can be explained by the size of the city. Coventry was the ninth largest city in UK at the time, but was significantly smaller than Birmingham which was in close proximity. Consequently the city lacked a principal administrative centre by the middle of the 1980s. Public utilities main headquarters, financial institutions headquarters, principal distribution centres and principal regional offices were found in Birmingham (Thoms and Donnelly 1985).

Fothergill and Gudgin (1982) also argued that firms in the city were inhibited in their development by constrained locations restricted by old-fashioned premises, hemmed in by existing urban development and with no room for expansion. This point was also confirmed by Donnelly (2018)[9] and further suggested that this problem pre-dated the war years themselves. This point is also discussed by Busch in his chapter, where issues around logistics and space related to the Shadow Factory Scheme(s) are touched on. Healey (1985) also points to evidence that industrial development in Coventry had been constrained in this manner, at least until the late seventies. As Morris and Collis also discuss in their chapters, Coventry city in the 1960s and 1970s suffered from a lack of industrial land in the city and a shortage of small factory units in particular.

During this period of malaise the impact of change on the occupied population was stark. From 1951 to 1971 the city's occupied population increased by a third. Much of this growth was in female labour; the occupied male population increased from 87,330 in 1951 to 104, 190 in 1971, compared to 34,918 female workers in 1951 increasing to 57,670 in 1971. After 1971 the total occupied population increase was in the female occupied workforce only (Rosser and Mallier 1981). Activity rates for men versus women also reflected this surge. 89.3% of the Coventry male population were active in 1951, declining to 85.2% by 1971. These same figures for women were 35.5% increasing to 45.9% by 1971. However, this growth in female labour was not concentrated in manufacturing, which was not perceived as a job for women. Instead, female employment largely found its way into services,

[9] Author's conversation with Prof. T. Donnelly.

which were under-represented in the city before 1971, but increased its presence in the industrial base during the following decades, albeit at a slower rate than the UK average (Rosser and Mallier 1981). By the 1980s Coventry's economy had come full circle from over a century earlier. All industries were in decline, with unemployment as high as 17% of the labour force, with a declining population and slowdown of inward migration (Thoms and Donnelly 1985). Unemployment was particularly severe on younger people, 22% in Coventry in 1977 (Mallier and Rosser 1982). By the following year, total employment had fallen by 18% approximately to 173,000, while employment in manufacturing had declined by over 25% to approximately 98,000 (Healey and Clark 1984). The greatest losses were not industry closures, rather in surviving plants which went through rationalisation and job cuts (Healey and Clark 1984). However, this depression was different to that of the 1860s.[10] Industries were still active outside of Coventry, unlike previously. Instead globalisation and external competition had wrought a period of decline and de-industrialisation for the city.

Structurally, occupational change was quite quick. The trough of the depression was sharp, with deep lows and rapid recovery to an extent. Employment shrank at a faster rate than the national average from 1971 to 1981, but at a slower rate than the national average from 1981 to 1989. By 1989 manufacturing still dominated Coventry occupations, but the proportion of labour employed in the sector had fallen from two thirds to just one third according to the Census of Employment and the Standard Industrial Classification divisions recorded therein. Services had generally increased, by the start of the 1990s; 16,000 new jobs were located in the Coventry service sector than had been the case in 1971. However, the nature of this work also translated into more frequent instances of part-time work to 24%, nearly double that of two decades previously. Women were the main beneficiaries of the growth of services, albeit at inferior levels of pay to those enjoyed by their male counterparts in previous years (Healey and Dunham 1994).

[10]See Chapter 2 by Donnelly.

A shift-share analysis undertaken by Healey and Dunham (1994) shows the sectors that underperformed in terms of regional national comparisons.[11] In their work they showed how vehicle and engineering industries had drifted upwards and downwards compared to their national and regional counterparts in the UK, losing approximately 17,844 jobs more than expected from 1971 to 1981. In other words competition was not just international in scope, it was also domestic. Distribution, Hotels, Catering and Repairs also struggled, declining by an actual difference of 2809 jobs more than expected during the same period. Offsetting these sectors were marginal gains in Banking, Finance, Insurance and other service sectors. From 1981 to 1989 this swing was more pronounced. During these years the expected rate of loss was slower in Metal Goods, Engineering and Vehicles (SIC code 3) than the previous decade, 4703 jobs. Distribution, Hotels, Catering and Repairs continued to decline at around the same pace, losing 2664 jobs more than expected. Banking, Finance and Insurance saw a loss of 784 more jobs than expected, however, Other Services (SIC code 9) grew much more rapidly than before, gaining 7232 jobs more than expected, substantially contributing to the slightly better than expected results for the decade as a whole. Figure 8.1 graphically illustrates the shift in occupational activities in Coventry during the 1980s.

The reduction in metal goods and vehicle manufacturing contrasts to the sharp rise in distribution and services. The backdrop to this change was a national economy that was diverging on regional lines. For example, in the West Midlands, the region in which Coventry was recorded as belonging to after 1964, similar trends emerged. In the years after the war the Midlands and the South East of the UK enjoyed growth in industry and manufacturing in contrast to the North East and Celtic components of the UK. From the 1970s onwards, however, the Midlands too began to slow down and atrophy. By the 1980s, the West Midlands had experienced an absolute decline in its economic

[11]A shift-share analysis is a standard approach to measuring economic growth or decline by determining how a particular metric has performed against national and regional comparators. It has limitations due to its focus on job growth only, but allows analysis of change, particularly at high levels of disaggregation.

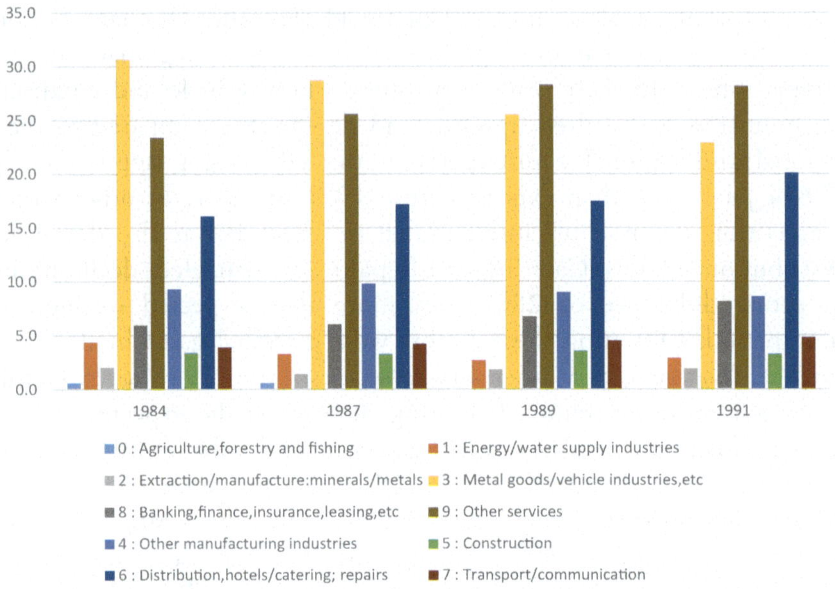

Fig. 8.1 Occupational change in Coventry, 1984–1991 (*Source* Census of Population, 1991, Office for national Statistics)

well-being compared to the other UK regions (Healey and Clark 1984; Geary and Stark 2002). Financial deregulation from the 1990s onwards also saw significant divergence of output per capita of the South East from the rest of the UK as all other territories began to lag behind (Geary and Stark 2002; O'Rourke and Williamson 2004).

By the turn of the Millennium structural change in Coventry was becoming even more marked. The shift to service occupations, visible in the 1980s as shown above, became even more pronounced. Figure 8.2, taken from the Labour Force Survey, aggregates occupations across industrial sectors into broad categories of activity. Allowing for overlaps between occupations, where certain roles intersect, demonstrates the shift toward tertiary activities during the decade before the new Millennium. Table 8.5 which follows uses the Standard Occupational Classifications (2000) to show the growth in unskilled and other classes, largely at the expense of craft and related occupations.

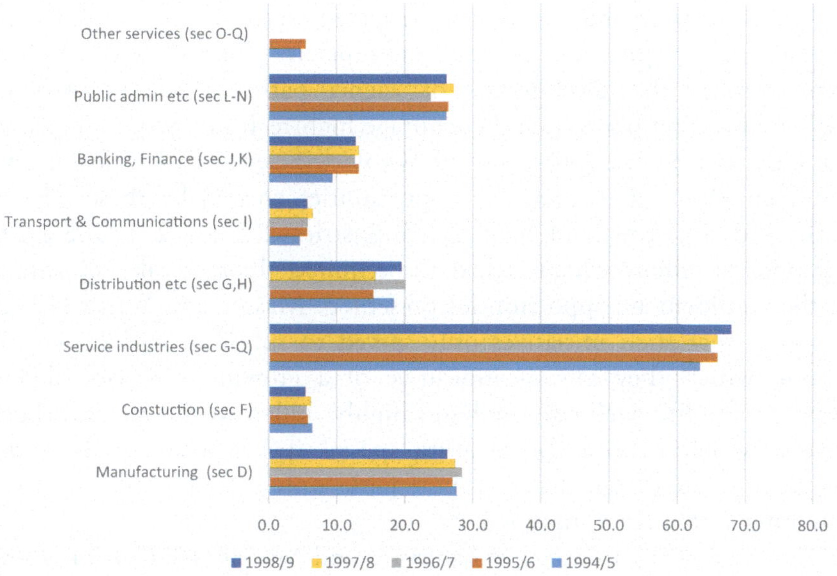

Fig. 8.2 Occupations identifiable under differing categories of activity (*Source* Annual Population Survey and Labour Force Survey, 1990–2001)

Table 8.5 Occupations as percentage of all in employment[a]

Industrial sector	1994/5	1995/6	1996/7	1997/8	1998/9
Managers and administrators	11.7	13.0	11.6	11.4	12.0
Professional occupations	8.9	11.1	10.7	13.6	12.1
Professional and technical occupations	9.2	10.1	9.6	9.1	9.6
Clerical, secretarial occupations	14.9	16.1	16.2	17.2	15.9
Craft and related occupations	14.3	15.1	17.3	17.4	11.2
Personal, protective occupations	12.4	8.9	7.5	9.3	9.9
Sales occupations	9.0	7.1	8.4	6.7	8.8
Plant and machine operators	8.6	10.5	10.8	9.8	9.8
Other occupations	9.2	7.2	7.4	5.6	10.6
Unskilled occupations	5.8	4.9	4.8	–	6.5

[a]Due to rounding of numerators these percentages do not add up to 100%
Source Annual Population Survey and Labour Force Survey, 1990–2001

Against this milieu, Coventry struggled in terms of employment creation and population decline. Attempts to generate new employment sparked the development of science parks to link industry to higher education research and encourage high-tech industry to locate in the city, such as the University of Warwick Science Park (Healey and Dunham 1994). However, the opportunities created by these science parks and the growth of high-tech industries did not serve the existing pool of labour which lacked the required skills to take advantage of the employment opportunities presented. Massey and Wield (1992) observed that such initiatives only served to subsidise mobile, skilled labour, which they saw as indicative of a growing UK-wide divide between an elite, well-educated and highly-skilled workforce and those that were left behind. By creating special spaces where such workers were isolated from the rest, these parks only served to silo the local economy, rather than support it.

This echoed the findings of Lancaster and Mason (1986) from a few years before, when he noted that skilled non-manual workers were more mobile and capable of leaving for better opportunities, differentiating them from the rest of workforce. Furthermore, Lancaster and Mason contended that the major employment challenges of the 1980s and 1990s was generational in character. He argued that many of the thousands of workers that migrated to Coventry in the 1930s and 1950s were ready to retire by the 1970s or take redundancies. It was the following generation that lacked the opportunities of their parents, and were unable to take their skills elsewhere (Lancaster and Mason 1986). This division, commonly associated with technological advances and globalising forces encouraging greater labour mobility, emerged in the period of internationalisation in Coventry, debatably creating a two-tier economy of skilled and unskilled activities. Set against that is the argument that the arrival to Coventry of more and more national and international investment served to provide safe havens for those workers able to find employment, as opportunities in traditional industries shrank.

Procter, writing at the end of the decade, observed the impact these changes in occupation and economic structure had on the working classes located in the city. In a study of Ivybridge in Coventry from 1990, the author examined whether the impact of the restructuring of capital and labour had served to break community ties and erode a sense of local identity. In a dissenting view to the widely held belief at the time, that the working classes had become increasingly isolated and privatised, Procter observed a strong sense of localism amongst the working class in Ivybridge, with participants indicating their dependence on friends and family for financial support and access to job opportunities. In describing them as such the picture that emerges of the 42 respondents is of a close knit community, in regular contact with family and neighbours. Conversely, interaction with groups outside this circle were more limited. While there were obvious size limitations to the study, the findings were still noteworthy, speaking of a community not benefitting from affluence in other areas of the city (Procter 1990).

New Growth for the New Millennium

By the beginning of the new century, approximately two generations after the war, Coventry's economic base and occupational groupings had changed substantially, a trend that was to be maintained over the next two decades. Perhaps the most noticeable change was in terms of population and ethnicity. In terms of population growth, the city was initially static in terms of growth and expansion. Perhaps surprisingly, considering the credit crisis of 2008 and the austerity measures that followed, the city enjoyed a sharp rise in residential numbers over the last decade as shown in Table 8.6.

Simultaneously there has also been considerable changes in the ethnic makeup of the city. Asian and African communities have begun to firmly establish themselves in Coventry, as shown by the returns from the 2001 and 2011 censuses. Increasingly the manifestation of these ethnic minorities in Coventry's environs, occurring during a period of population growth, are being driven by international migration flows, rather than internal movement of persons, as shown by local area indicators in Tables 8.7 and 8.8.

During the same period as the population was increasing, unemployment rates for those between 16 years and 64 years of age were also rising. From a figure of 5.1% in 2004, unemployment rates for the

Table 8.6 Coventry city population since the Millennium

Year	Population
2001	302,804
2002	301,295
2003	300,665
2004	298,174
2005	298,386
2006	300,129
2007	301,429
2008	305,186
2009	307,393
2010	311,674
2011	316,915
2012	322,504
2013	328,423
2014	335,018
2015	344,288
2016	353,215
2017	360,149

Source Census of population (2000–2018), ONS

economically active population rose to 7.1% in 2008, after which date the city saw a steady rise of workless jobseekers to 9.5% in 2012 and again in 2013. After this date unemployment figures dropped off over the next number of years until it hit 3.8% in 2017. However, in 2018 it once again increased to 5.8 percentage points, a level higher than that of the year 2004. Explanations for the waxing and waning of employment can possibly be found in problems associated with the credit crisis and subsequent business concerns around the decision by the UK to leave the EU trading bloc. However, it is more difficult to explain how inward migration flows and population growth appear so untouched by the relative fortunes of the local economy.

One partial explanation potentially relates to the perceived disconnect between certain economic activities and economic groups in the city of Coventry. The arguments put forward by Massey and Wield in relation to Science Parks may also have resonance in the new structures of economic development in Coventry. Table 8.9 outlines the changes to Coventry's occupational groupings, allocating workers across 9 broad categories using Standard Occupational Classifications from 2010.

Table 8.7 Ethnicity and Coventry in the new Millennium

Ethnicity[a]	2001		2011	
White	252,643		234,029	
English/Welsh/Scottish/Northern Irish/British		235,632		211,188
Irish		10,401		7305
Gypsy or Irish Traveller				151
Other White		6610		15,385
Mixed/multiple ethnic groups	5163		8230	
White and Black Caribbean		2453		3672
White and Black African		271		943
White and Asian		1605		2388
Other Mixed		834		1227
Asian/Asian British	37,630		51,598	
Indian		24,177		27,751
Pakistani		6169		9510
Bangladeshi		1741		2951
Other Asian		1823		7658
Chinese[b]		2183		3728
Chinese: other		1537		
Black/African/Caribbean/Black British	5412		17,764	
Caribbean		3314		3317
African		1679		12,836
Other Black		419		1611
Other ethnic group			5339	
Arab				2020
Any other ethnic group				3319
Total	300,848		316,960	

[a]Changes of definition from 2001 to 2011 mean comparisons are not exact
[b]Figures for Chinese respondents were recorded separately in 2001
Source Census of Population, 2001 and 2011, ONS

The picture that emerges for Coventry over the last two decades is growth at either end of the classification system. An increase in professional occupations, and to a lesser extent an increase in associate professional and technical occupations. At the same time there has also been in increase in elementary occupations. There has also been significant drops in numbers for those workers in the categories 'Managers, Directors and Senior Officials', 'Administrative and Secretarial occupations' and 'Skilled

Table 8.8 Origin of migration flows in and out of Coventry, 2007/8–2016/17

	Long-term international migration		Internal migration (within UK)	
	Inflow	Outflow	Inflow	Outflow
2007/8	6921	1927	13,575	15,062
2008/9	6548	3172	13,974	15,329
2009/10	7455	2787	14,700	15,646
2010/11	9043	3837	14,802	15,576
2011/12	7050	2576	16,392	17,384
2012/13	7330	2737	15,671	16,267
2013/14	8043	3105	16,912	17,176
2014/15	10,757	2845	16,774	17,153
2015/16	10,416	2764	17,042	17,543
2016/17	8674	2368	20,125	21,139

Source Local area migration indicators, UK, ONS (2018)

trades occupations'. The emergence of two discernible groups of skilled and unskilled labour engaged in elementary and professional occupations is an important trend for the city. In comparable recent cases unskilled labour has struggled to progress to higher tiers of employment without the presence of intermediate employment opportunities (Velthius 2019).

The expansion of middle management and professionals is in keeping with previous trends in the city where main offices and business headquarters began to locate outside the city due to mergers and acquisitions by corporate firms with a global reach. The growth of services and decline of craft workers is also in keeping with previous trends, shifting the economic base from specialised industrial activities seeking to export goods, to services supporting the local population. However, the growth of elementary and other service occupations could potentially point to a growing number of workers who find employment servicing professional classes in low-skilled, low paid, menial activities. Wage data for Coventry is unavailable or underdeveloped. However, Gross Disposable Household Income (GDHI) at current basic prices, though not an ideal measure due to its lack of detail for sectoral returns, does offer some important insights to working lives and standards of living in Coventry, not least because of the picture painted by the figures themselves. Figure 8.3 outlines GDHI for Coventry for two decades starting in 1997.

Table 8.9 Standard Occupational Classifications (2010) for the Coventry area, 2000–2018

	Managers, Directors and Senior Officials	Professional occupations	Associate profes-sional and technical occupations	Administrative and secretarial occupations	Skilled trades occupa-tions	Caring, leisure and other service occupations	Sales and customer service occupa-tions	Process, plant and machine operatives	Elementary occupations
2000[a]	11.8	11.2	7.6	17.1	12.5	13.2	7.3	10.6	8.7
2001[a]	14.1	12	8.5	17.4	12.7	11.4	7.1	9.7	6.8
2002[b]	11.9	11.7	12	13	12.7	6.2	10.7	10.8	10.9
2003[b]	10.9	12	12.3	12.6	11.8	8.6	9.3	10.9	11.1
2004	8.9	17.1	11.1	12.5	10.8	8.6	9.4	8.1	12.8
2005	7.2	17.3	11.3	11.8	11.3	7.6	9.1	8.6	14.8
2006	6.3	17.2	11.6	14.3	10.0	7.0	9.4	9.0	14.6
2007	7.1	16.7	10.6	13.5	10.8	9.5	8.9	8.7	13.7
2008	6.9	15.0	12.0	16.1	12.5	8.2	6.8	9.0	12.7
2009	7.3	19.4	11.3	10.7	10.4	7.6	9.0	8.3	15.3
2010	6.6	18.7	11.7	10.6	11.1	8.8	9.7	7.9	14.3
2011	6.6	21.4	10.6	11.1	9.5	8.7	9.1	7.0	15.2
2012	6.2	17.8	11.6	13.0	10.5	9.0	10.7	7.0	13.8
2013	6.6	15.0	13.2	12.0	11.4	8.1	9.4	7.8	15.8
2014	8.2	17.8	13.2	10.4	12.6	8.3	7.4	6.8	13.9
2015	5.6	19.8	12.0	11.5	10.3	10.7	7.5	8.4	14.0
2016	6.5	17.7	13.1	9.5	11.1	9.5	7.3	8.7	16.2
2017	6.9	17.2	12.9	10.5	8.3	10.4	7.5	8.1	17.7
2018	6.8	20.8	12.3	9.6	9.1	10.1	7.8	8.2	14.5

[a]Figures for 2000–2001 taken from Local Area labour Force Survey. Changes to definitions and categories post-2001 mean comparisons must be treated with caution for these years

[b]Figures for 2002–2003 use averages from the Labour Force Quarterly Survey

Source Annual Population Survey and Labour Force Survey (2000–2018), ONS

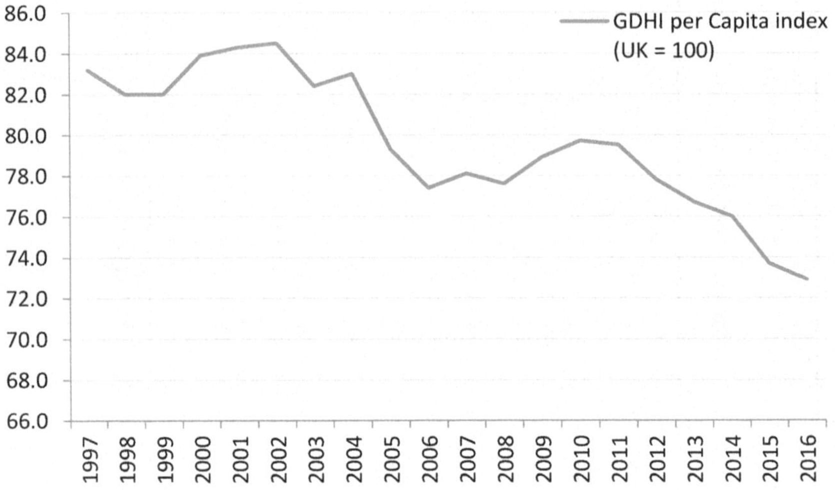

Fig. 8.3 Regional gross disposable household income (GDHI) at current basic prices (*Source* Gross Disposable Household Income [GDHI], ONS [2019])

Looking at figures for Coventry pegged against UK GHDI per capita (index 100) what has occurred over two decades until the most recent data is available has been a steady decline in incomes in Coventry. This fall, from 83.2 to 72.9, has been even sharper and deeper than for the rest of the West Midlands which has dropped from 91.1 to 86.3 compared to the rest of the UK during the same period. While these figures must be treated with caution as explanations for this divergence is multifaceted, when juxtaposed to the occupational and economic structural changes that have occurred in the city during the same period it points to a city that has seen relative decline within its region and more broadly within the UK since the start of the century. It would appear that the increases in instances of professionals and associate professionals have not been enough the offset the decrease in frequency of managers, directors and senior officials working in the city, nor the swell in numbers of elementary occupations.

Part of the explanation for this fall has been the changing demography of the Coventry population, which has seen a growing youthful profile driven primarily by education opportunities increasing within the city's main educational institutions. A study by Swinney and Williams (2016) examining where graduates moved to on completion of their degrees included data for Coventry graduates, as did work by Piazza (2017), which built on these figures to offer some analysis of patterns of change within the city from the perspective of the graduate job market. From 2009 to 2015, 107,480 people moved into Coventry and 113,050 people moved out, resulting in a net outflow of 5570 people during these years (ONS 2009–2015). According to the Census for 2011, this flow was inward from London and outward to Birmingham and was dominated by 16–21 year olds who accounted for 10% of the city's population but 41% of inward migration and 25% of outward migration. The next largest group who accounted for outward migration after this was 22–25 year olds (8% and 23% respectively) and then 31–45 year olds (17% and 19% respectively) (ONS 2011).

Effectively what was happening was a body of young people coming to Coventry to attain an education but then moving afterward to avail of employment opportunities elsewhere. These graduates were lost mainly to cities across the rest of the West Midlands, though London accounted for the largest share of graduates (HESA 2013–2015). Coventry has struggled to attract and keep those arriving for education from outside the city. Coventry retained just 15% of such graduates, the fourth lowest number compared to any other city in the UK. Piazza described this phenomenon as 'bouncing', with 90% of Coventry graduates moving immediately after finishing their education. In part this is driven by wage concerns, with graduate wages starting on average at just £23,960 in the city of Coventry, which placed Coventry at twelfth amongst UK cities (Piazza 2017; HESA 2013–2015). Despite these trends, Coventry's population has seen a growth in graduate numbers overall, but these are primarily Coventry youths returning from education at institutions elsewhere. Coventry has been relatively unsuccessful at attracting new graduates with no connection to the city (HESA 2013–2015).

The impact of this growth in graduates has been a corresponding increase in those with a level 4 National Vocational Qualification

Table 8.10 Index of persons aged 16–64 recorded as having a NVQ 4 award, 2004–2017

Year	Coventry	United Kingdom	West Midlands
2004	100	100	100
2005	108	103	102
2006	111	107	107
2007	103	113	111
2008	106	117	114
2009	112	123	117
2010	129	129	123
2011	121	135	124
2012	125	142	131
2013	141	146	134
2014	156	150	140
2015	147	155	149
2016	170	161	151
2017	178	163	153

Source ONS (2019)

(NVQ) in the city.[12] In 2004, 45,300 people in Coventry were recorded as having a certificate of higher education or equivalent. By 2017 this number had increased to 80,800. The rapidity of this increase outstripped regional and national figures, as shown in Table 8.10.

Using 2004 as a base year the index shows changes to graduate numbers over time. Unlike the steady growth shown regionally and nationally, increases in graduates in Coventry have come in waves, with dips in 2007, 2011 and 2015, being offset by rises in 2006, 2010 and 2016. Coventry made a surprisingly large leap after 2016 in particular, surging ahead of the rest of the West Midlands from a comparable level (ONS 2019). The greatest gains have been made by women; female graduates in Coventry have nearly doubled since 2004, from 19,900 to 38,700 in 2017. This compares to 25,400 male graduates in 2004 increasing at a slower rate to 42,100 in 2017. In terms of graduate occupations, the

[12]National Vocational Qualification are competence based qualifications. There are five levels, with level 4 (used here) corresponding to certificates of higher education. They were replaced by Regulated Qualifications Framework in 2015, but the corresponding certificate level remains the same.

public sector accounted for the bulk of these workers, 54% compared to the UK average of 46% (HESA 2013–2015). This is in keeping generally with economic activities in the city with Coventry City Council and the University Hospital Coventry and Warwickshire being the most prominent employers, alongside both major research institutions.

Arguably Coventry now has a bigger pool of skilled labourers available for work engaged in more diverse activities, focussed much more in the tertiary sector, a hallmark of a modern, knowledge-based economy as noted at the beginning of this chapter. The gender imbalance is also far less pronounced in terms of skills and occupational activity; where previously males dominated engineering, the largest industrial sector in the city, male and female workers are now more evenly spread across service activities. Set against this interpretation is the fact that earnings for new graduates and household incomes overall are lower than regional and national levels. What has occurred since the war has been the growth of a comparatively higher skilled, but lower paid workforce employed largely in public sector services due to deindustrialisation of core economic activities in the city since the 1970s.

Concluding Remarks

Industrial decline, malaise and slow recovery of a local economy has been the prism through which the post-war experience of Coventry has been perceived. Central to this understanding has been the experience of manufacturing in the city, most notably that of vehicle production, tool-making and engineering, and, to a lesser extent, the aero industry. Interpretations and analysis have concentrated on issues of productivity, labour relations, national policy-making and structural weaknesses in the sector. Perhaps less appreciated has been the story of occupational change and how it demonstrates the fragility that was inherent within Coventry's economy. Most notable was the comparatively late shift to service based activities within the city, compared to trends perceptible at regional and national level.

Even when the local economy began to manifest signs of developing the service sector it did not arise as part of a growth pathway. Instead low-skill services filled the vacuum left by deindustrialisation. While the growth in tertiary activities opened new opportunities to female workers it was, arguably, not matched by financial reward. While specific evidence of sectoral wage decline after 1971 is unavailable, GDP per capita and, by extension, earnings, all declined sharply during the latter part of the 1970s and 1980s, at both regional and local level. Travel to work patterns are discussed elsewhere in this book by Sissons, but suffice to say that outward migration and declining output, allied to increased frequency of low-skilled work opportunities, would point to a period of income decline.

In part this stemmed from the nature of manufacturing in Coventry. As observed by Mallier and Rosser (1982) the emphasis in Coventry was on final assembly, rather than earlier tiers of production. For example component suppliers were infrequent in the city; had they been in greater abundance then perhaps Coventry could have more effectively weathered market forces that saw British vehicles falling out of favour with domestic and international consumers. Effectively Coventry depended on a narrow, overly specialised base of industrial activity which was even more niche than just vehicle production alone. When tertiary activities increased their presence in the local economy, it was as a replacement for these declining industries rather than as a response to their emergence. The type of service activities and occupations that emerged in Coventry are not indicative of a strong cluster of industrial support.

This decline was matched at a regional level, but arguably the nature of Coventry's industrial base meant the downturn was sharper than the rest of the West Midlands, as the city was more vulnerable to demand-side shocks at domestic and international level. Attempts to mitigate the downturn included investment in Science Parks; however, such initiatives were comparatively small in scale due to the problems associated with the enormous loss of manufacturing jobs. Furthermore, as Massey and Wield contend, investment in Science Parks only served to artificially embed these activities in the city, attracting mobile skilled labour from outside due to the skills gap apparent in the local populous. It would not be to the mid-to-late-1990s that a conscious decision was made to develop a knowledge economy in Coventry, leading to renewed efforts to upskill Coventry workers and place third level education institutions at the heart of the city's economic base.

What has occurred over the last decade or so as a consequence of this decision is a growth in the education and skills sector, but with a corresponding change to the nature of immigration into the city. Immigrants now come to the city at a young age with a view to receiving an education. However, retention rates in the city remain low, with most of those upskilling passing through and seeking work opportunities elsewhere. While their contribution to the local economy in terms of rent, subsistence and recreational activities is important, it is seasonal in nature. Instead it is Coventry sons and daughters who are returning from education elsewhere that are increasing the prevalence of third level graduates in the city.

Globalisation and increased competition has played an important role in the economic restructuring of Coventry. While there were numerous causes for the failure of key industries in the city, rival international companies undoubtedly hastened their collapse. Instead of well paid opportunities for low skilled, entry level workers, employment opportunities are now concentrated in services, with elementary occupations accounting for a greater share of low skilled labour. Work by Velthius (2019) suggests that in such a scenario it may prove difficult for labour to find intermediary employment opportunities to progress to higher-skilled and better paid work. It may be that there are two discernible tiers of work life emerging in Coventry city.

References

2011 Census of Population, Office for National Statisitics, UK.

2011 Census: Key Statistics and Quick Statistics for Local Authorities in the United Kingdom. Office for National Statistics. 2011.

Annual Population Survey and Labour Force Survey. (1990–2001). Office for National Statistics.

Annual Population Survey and Labour Force Survey. (2000–2018). Office for National Statistics.

Bhaskar, K., & Rhys, G. (1979). *The Future of the UK Motor Industry*. London: Kogan Page.

Broadberry, S. (2016). 11: The Great Divergence in the World Economy: Long-Run Trends of Real Income. In *A History of the Global Economy: 1500 to the Present* (p. 35). Cambridge: Cambridge University.
Brown, W. (1971). Piecework Wage Determination in Coventry. *Scottish Journal of Political Economy, 18*(1), 1–30.
Census of Population. (1991). Office for National Statistics.
Chenery, H. B. (1979). Structural Change and Development Policy (No. 04; HD82, C4).
Chenery, H. B., Syrquin, M., & Elkington, H. (1975). *Patterns of Development, 1950–1970* (Vol. 75). London: Oxford University Press.
Clark, C. (1957). *The Conditions of Economic Progress* (3rd ed.). London: Macmillan.
Conditions of Employment and National Arbitration Order (Order) at Hansard Aug 1951, Vol. 491. cc1624–30. https://api.parliament.uk/historic-hansard/commons/1951/aug/02/industrial-disputes-new-order.
Coventry History Centre, [Coventry City] Medical Officer Reports, Annual.
Coventry History Centre. Chrysler Corporation. Annual Report 1968: Rootes Motors ltd. PA 2616/2/1-14.
Coventry History Centre. Chrysler Corporation. Rootes Motors Ltd Annual Report and Statement of Accounts 1970. PA 2616/2/1-14.
Coventry History Centre. Rootes Group. Rootes Motors Ltd Annual Report and Statement of Accounts 1962. PA2616/2/12.
Donnelly, T., Begley, J., & Collis, C. (2017). The West Midlands Automotive Industry: The Road Downhill. *Business History, 59*(1), 56–74.
Dunnett, P. (1980). *The Decline of the British Motor Industry: The Effects of Government Policy, 1945–1979*. London: Croom Helm.
Ewart, H. (2011). 'Coventry Irish': Community, Class, Culture and Narrative in the Formation of a Migrant Identity, 1940–1970. *Midland History, 36*(2), 225–244.
Flanders, A. (1957). Wage Movements and Wage Policy in Postwar Britain. *The Annals of the American Academy of Political and Social Science, 310*(1), 87–98.
Foreman-Peck, J. (1995). *The British Motor Industry* (Vol. 1). Manchester: Manchester University Press.
Fothergill, S., & Gudgin, G. (1982). *Unequal Growth: Urban and Regional Employment Change in the UK*. London: Heinemann Educational Publishers.
Geary, F., & Stark, T. (2002). Examining Ireland's Post-Famine Economic Growth Performance. *The Economic Journal, 112*(482), 919–935.

Geary, F., & Stark, T. (2015). Regional GDP in the UK, 1861–1911: New Estimates. *The Economic History Review, 68*(1), 123–144.

Graduates in the UK Labour Market. (2019). Office for National Statistics.

Gross Disposable Household Income (GDHI). (2019). Office for National Statistics.

Hansard, Deb 14 May 1924 vol 173 cc1324–6.

Healey, M., & Clark, D. (1984). Industrial Decline and Government Response in the West Midlands: The Case of Coventry. *Regional Studies, 18*(4), 303–318.

Healey, M. J., & Dunham, P. J. (1994). Changing Competitive Advantage in a Local Economy: The Case of Coventry, 1971–90. *Urban Studies, 31*(8), 1279–1301.

Healey, M. J. (1985). Industrial Decline in a Local Economy: The Case of Coventry, 1974–1982. *Environment and Planning A, 17*(10), 1351–1367.

Higher Education Statistics Agency, Destination of Leavers Survey, 2013/14–2014/15.

https://api.parliament.uk/historic-hansard/commons/1924/may/14/mckenna-duties.

Internal Migration, England and Wales: Year Ending June 2015. Office for National Statistics. 2015. Available at https://www.ons.gov.uk/peoplepopulationandcommunity/populationandmigration/migrationwithintheuk/bulletins/internalmigrationbylocalauthoritiesinenglandandwales/yearendingjune2015.

Knowles, K. G. J. C., & Robinson, D. (1969). Wage Movements in Coventry. *Bulletin of the Oxford University Institute of Economics & Statistics, 31*(1), 1–21.

Krugman, P. (2016, March 14). Globalization and Growth. *New York Times*.

Kuznets, Simon Smith. (1971). Modern Economic Growth: Findings and Reflections. Nobel Prize Lecture. https://www.nobelprize.org/prizes/economic-sciences/1971/kuznets/lecture/.

Lancaster, Bill, & Mason, Tony (Eds.). (1986). *Life and Labour in a Twentieth Century City: The Experience of Coventry*. Coventry: Cryfield Press.

Lewis, W. A. (1954). Economic Development with Unlimited Supplies of Labour. *The Manchester School, 22*(2), 139–191.

Mallier, A. T., & Rosser, M. J. (1982). Skill Shortages in a Local Labour Market—The Coventry Case. *Personnel Review, 11*(1), 23–30.

Martin, H.-P., & Schumann, H. (1997). *The Global Trap: Globalization and the Assault on Prosperity and Democracy*. London: Zed.

Massey, D., & Wield, D. (1992). Evaluating Science Parks. *Local Economy, 7*(1), 10–25.
Maxcy, G., & Silberston, A. (1959). *Automobile Industry and Trade*. London: Allen & Unwin.
Office for National Statisitics. (2018). Local Area Migration Indicators, UK. https://www.ons.gov.uk/peoplepopulationandcommunity/populationandmigration/migrationwithintheuk/datasets/localareamigrationindicatorsunitedkingdom.
Office for National Statisitics. (2009–2015). Local Area Migration Indicators, UK.
O'Rourke, K. H., & Williamson, J. G. (2002). When Did Globalisation Begin? *European Review of Economic History, 6*(1), 23–50.
O'Rourke, K. H., & Williamson, J. G. (2004). Once More: When did Globalisation Begin? *European Review of Economic History, 8*(1), 109–117.
O'Rourke, K. H., & Williamson, J. G. (2004). Once More: When Did Globalisation Begin? *European Review of Economic History, 8*(1), 109–117.
Parkin, F. (1983). *Marxism and Class Theory*. New York: Columbia University Press.
Piazza, G. (2017). A More Detailed Look at the Movement of University Students and Graduates. The Centre for Cities.
Procter, I. (1990). The Privatisation of Working-Class Life: A Dissenting View. *British Journal of Sociology, 41*(2), 157–180.
Rhys, D. G. (1972). *The Motor Industry: An Economic Survey*. London: Butterworths.
Richardson, K. (1977). *The British Motor Industry 1896–1939*. London: Springer.
Rosser, M., & Mallier, T. (1981). *The Economic Base of Coventry*. Coventry: Dept of Economics, (Lanchester) Polytechnic.
Standard Occupational Classification (SOC 2000) and NS-SEC on the Labour Force Survey, Office for National Statistics. Available at https://www.ons.gov.uk/employmentandlabourmarket/peopleinwork/employmentandemployeetypes/methodologies/standardoccupationalclassificationsoc2000andnsseconthelabourforcesurvey.
Stiglitz, J. E. (2017). The Overselling of Globalization. *Business Economics, 52*(3), 129–137.
Swinney, P., & Williams, M. (2016). *The Great British Brain Drain*. London: The Centre for Cities.
Thoms, D., & Donnelly, T. (1985). *The Motor Car Industry in Coventry Since the 1890s: Origins. Development, Structure*. London: Routledge.

Thoms, D., Donnelly, T., Beaven, B. J., Carr, F., Holme, A., Perkin, H., et al. (2000). Militancy and Organization: Women Workers and Trade Unions in the Motor Trades in the 1930s. In *The Coventry Motor Industry: Birth To Renaissance?* (Vol. 48, No. 4, pp. ix–ix). London: Lanchester Polytechnic.

Velthius, S. (2019). *Occupational and Wage Progression Among Low-Paid Workers*. Unpublished thesis, Coventry University.

Whisler, T. (1999). *The British Motor Industry, 1945–94: A Case Study in Industrial Decline*. Oxford: Oxford University Press.

Williamson, J. G. (1997). Globalization and Inequality, Past and Present. *The World Bank Research Observer, 12*(2), 117–135.

9

The Rebirth of the Phoenix City—Sectoral Shifts and the Evolution of Coventry's Economic Base

Myles Mackie

In less than five years, the economy of Coventry collapsed. For a century, Coventry had been at the forefront of economic growth but in 1979–1983 the city was plunged into an unprecedented recession and became a depressed area. Few in 1983 would have believed that within a generation, Coventry would be ranked by PWC eighth out of 42 UK cities for having '*Good Growth*'[1] or ranked as the eighth mid-sized European city of the Future in 2018–2019[2] with a transformed prospering economy and a very different economic base from the post war years.

The collapse came not without forewarnings, most of which were met with disbelief or only a minimal response. The Job Seekers' Allowance[3] (JSA—dole) in 1950 had around 1000 signing on. The count doubled in the late 1950s with the relaxation of wartime economic controls and

[1]PWC (2016) *Good Growth for Cities*.

[2]FDI magazine European Cities and Regions of the Future 2018–2019. *Financial Times*, March 2018. Population between 200,000 and 350,000.

[3]The definition has changed over the years, so the chart is illustrative but remains indicative of the strength of the local economy.

M. Mackie (✉)
Coventry City Council (Retired), Coventry, UK

J. Begley et al. (eds.), *Revival of a City*, Palgrave Studies in Economic History,
https://doi.org/10.1007/978-3-030-22822-4_9

reduced reconstruction spending. From the 1960s international comparisons showed that British manufacturing was undercapitalised and uncompetitive in international markets. Tolliday (1988) showed that fixed assets in British Leyland were only £920 per worker compared to over £2500 in its major foreign competitors. This made it impossible to gain significant economies of scale as output expanded.[4] Foreign imported cars were generally seen as better quality and more reliable than their British equivalents.

Perhaps, the first dramatic warning of Coventry's economic vulnerability was in 1966 with the closure of the Armstrong Whitworth aeroplane design and manufacturing business with over 2000 redundancies. This ended fifty years of aircraft production in the city. It was a shock[5] but as the car industry was still booming, little was done. The JSA count doubled again. The 1973 oil crisis and the lax budgetary policy of 1972–1974 caused inflation to rise to record peacetime highs.[6] The inflationary decade of the 1970s basically stagnated the economy with businesses and workers seeking to protect themselves from the adverse impact of price rises and the competition. The JSA count doubled yet again. Coventry's economic base, like much of the local economies across England, was by 1979 already in trouble: the boom years were over. Businesses were under-capitalised, in poor industrial buildings; overly labour intensive, had poor management teams; with poor industrial relations, undertaking little research so were technologically behind and were generally uncompetitive internationally. Siren voices raised the issue of the deindustrialisation of British economy.[7]

The dramatic closures in 1980 of Rover Group manufacturing activities of British Leyland (20,000 redundancies) and Alfred Herbert Machine Tools (3500 redundancies) combined with the impact of recession arising out of the heavy deflationary policies of the Thatcher government led to the collapse of many SME's and big reductions in employment in those surviving companies. Coventry was not alone in

[4]Tolliday (1988, pp. 63–77).

[5]Mayoral conferences were called to discuss the situation led to ideas but little action. Planes were built in Coventry since WWI.

[6]OPEC quadrupled the price of oil and Chancellor Barber's budgets of 1972–1973 generated an inflationary spiral.

[7]See Singh (1977), Healey and Clarke (1984), and Healey and Dunham (1994).

facing this collapse which is still felt across much of the UK outside the South East and London.

By 1983 unemployment in Coventry had risen to over 17% with some areas of the city like Foleshill Ward recording over 30% on JSA benefits. For Coventry, these were the worst unemployment figures since 1920 and the post WWI recession. The city had a business estate that had been built in the inter-war or immediate post war era which no longer met modern business needs and the city's image looked severely tarnished.

After the Fire and Death—The Baptism of a New Economic Paradigm

The post-war economic paradigm of corporatist collaboration and state involvement ended in the 1970s. The recession of 1979–1983 coincided with major change in the economic climate, the scale of which was probably not fully appreciated at the time. Five major waves of change started to be felt from 1980:

1. **Globalisation**: The post-war settlement aimed to free up trade under the aegis of the GATT.[8] By the 1970s this began to expose UK business to international competition leading to the globalisation of trade under the World Trade Organisation in 1996. Coventry companies have been helped to develop trade markets by the local Chamber of Commerce. Globalisation has helped FDI flows to develop and this has helped Coventry in its recovery but has also contributed to a more competitive environment.
2. **The rise of neoliberalism** and displacement of Keynesian economics. The reliance on private sector markets to determine socio-economic outturns replaced much government economic control and regulation. This led to deep policy and institutional changes ending Corporatism and state interventionism in the economy. For Coventry, with a third of jobs in the public sector this meant a significant step change.

[8]General Agreement of Tariffs and Trade which oversaw a series of trade negotiations (called Rounds). The Tokyo Round 1973–1979 significantly liberalised trade. In addition, the EU Single Market came into force in 1986.

3. **The explosion of technology** and the Third Industrial Revolution started in the 1970s and fundamentally altered production lines and products—old skills became redundant; work digitalised; greater market connectivity through the internet; the production of intangible knowledge-based products; the growth of universities; better designed products etc. Coventry, along with much of the UK economy, was initially unprepared for the changes.
4. **The fall of Communism** and the end of the bi-polar global world. The reforms of Deng Xiaoping in 1984 started the rise of Chinese capitalism followed by opening of eastern Europe in 1989 and the collapse of the Soviet Union in 1991. This permitted the expansion of the EU and the development in a globalised world of the Chinese economy which has become a major trading and FDI partner for Coventry.
5. **Human generated Global climate change** and the ending of the carbon-based economy has led to the development of renewable electricity generation and reduced dependence on fossil fuels and wrought fundamental change for the automotive sector. It has also created jobs in the development of energy saving systems, electric vehicles and batteries etc.

Coventry being a medium sized city in the UK, an open market economy, had no option but to accept these changes head on as their implications came to the fore. A city like Coventry is in no position to successfully challenge these sweeping changes which in the 1980s tended to be unfavourable to the local economy but with time the city has adapted and has, somewhat, benefitted from the changes.

The New Local Economy Is Very Different from the Old

The 1979–1983 recession was a major disruption which, having exposed the weaknesses of the old one, meant that things had to change. What was not recognised in the 1980s was how large the impending structural change in the economy would be. Coventry had always been a manufacturing centre and despite the concerns of the 1970s, most felt that it would remain a manufacturing centre with the automotive sector its core even if it was desirable to diversify and reduce dependences on one sector and increase some service sector presence.

In 2017 employment in the city had, after a gap of forty years, returned to the levels of the late 1970s but the composition and its occupational workforce structures has changed. Manufacturing which accounted for 93,700 jobs or 57% of all jobs in 1978 had fallen to 18,000 or 11% in 2017. Manufacturing's ranking fell from the largest to the fifth largest sector in the economy. The service sector expanded and its share of jobs rose from 39% in 1978 to 83% of all jobs in the city.

This decline in the manufacturing sector had started in the 1966 when the Armstrong Whitworth aircraft factory closed. The inflation and increased competitive pressures, labour unrest, poor management and relocations of production and high oil prices caused significant damage to the city's manufacturing sector. Change was opposed as it would mean job losses though strategies[9] were being drawn up and concerns over de-industrialisation[10] voiced. There were some little noticed beginnings of change during the 1970s as businesses started to think and develop anew the ideas and technologies of that time but economic pressures and lack of investment ensured that they remained on a small scale.

The Thatcher government's austerity generated the 1979–1983 UK recession which was the deepest since the 1929 crash and saw unemployment rise to over 3 million. Coventry saw its unemployment rate rise to over 17%[11] and investment including depreciation investment collapsed. UK car production fell by 40%; Rover Group output fell by 45% between 1978 and 1983. Matters were not helped by the increasing pace of technological change and competition from abroad which exposed the backwardness of Coventry's businesses. In effect, the recession was a major disruption in Coventry's economy which was not helped by the cultural changes taking place. Businesses closed as sales dried up while at the same time the government enforced closures to cut losses and denationalised the state manufacturing companies (Table 9.1).

[9]These included the closure of the Standard Triumph works in 1978 (7500 jobs) which was vigorously opposed and shelved.

[10]See Singh (1977), Healey and Clarke (1984), and Healey and Dunham (1994).

[11]JSA rate rose to 17% from 6% in 1978 but many people retired and/or left the city led Sheffield Hallam University to estimate it as effectively over 20%. In St Michaels and Foleshill Wards the JSA rate rose to 35%.

Table 9.1 Number of jobs in Coventry 1978–2017

Number	1978	1984	1991	1995	2000	2005	2010	2015	2016	2017
Manufacturing	93,702	60,930	41,992	32,452	32,450	20,533	15,000	19,000	19,000	18,000
Utilities	1811	2522	2284	2591	2248	1426	500	3200	3300	4500
Construction	3952	3850	3298	2715	2388	3280	4000	3500	3000	4000
Distribution	20,914	19,381	23,977	17,398	22,336	25,381	25,000	24,000	25,000	24,000
Hotels and Restaurants etc.	1976	5177	5709	5059	6181	8128	8000	8000	8000	9000
Transport Storage and Comm.	4611	4513	5201	4936	7164	6702	9500	11,000	11,000	11,000
Finance	2800	3186	4567	4812	6321	6417	8000	6000	4500	5000
Real estate and Business Services	5434	6106	7992	12,956	17,419	21,103	22,000	32,000	31,000	30,000
Education	8728	8761	16,746	18,138	18,964	21,531	20,000	20,000	20,000	22,000
Health	6587	6505	7612	11,599	12,783	15,970	19,000	19,000	21,000	22,000
Government	9387	10,487	6724	6540	5900	7130	7000	6000	6000	6000
Other	4117	1195	634	4072	6321	5133	4000	5255	6190	6000
Total (000's)	165	132	127	123	140	143	142	157	158	162

Source Census of Employment, Annual Business Inquiry, Business Register ONS
Small sector changes may be a result of firms being reclassified

The recession began to ease in the mid 1980s as monetary and fiscal policies were relaxed, and businesses began to invest in changes and new technologies. In manufacturing, this is evidenced by the adoption of digital machinery and streamlined production lines raising labour productivity. The closures and new technologies led to productivity growth of over 5% p.a. for over a decade with some individual factories including Peugeot at Ryton being able to cut employment levels by half. Computerisation led also to increased productivity and changed the nature of office jobs logistics, stock management and marketing as well as creating new economic activities such as software, games, business administration etc. Many of these jobs being integrated in manufacturing concerns became classified as service sector. Business management culture had to change as new ideas dating from the 1960s began to be widely adopted following the 1979–1983 recession which, in turn, significantly improved efficiencies and competitiveness.

For Coventry, the Council developed an economic development strategy that recognised that market solutions were failing to solve the unemployment crisis in the city. The strategy aimed at creating jobs which captured the changed trends of the 1980s—new technologies, green business parks (i.e. desirable locations); working in partnership and seizing any opportunity that could help. This strategy was helped by the two universities, the Chamber of Commerce and Warwickshire local authorities. The 1990–1993[12] recession hit Coventry hard, but the impact was cushioned by the council policies and inward investing businesses[13] which created over 10,000 new jobs in the city between 1987 and 1993.

It was following the 1990–1993 recession and the long period of growth to 2008 that enabled Coventry to consolidate change and to grow. The number of jobs in Coventry reached a low of 119,000 in

[12]The collapse of the Lawson boom accompanied by the First Gulf 1990–1991 War which generated a global oil price shock. Iraqi owned Matrix Churchill Machine Tool company (600 jobs) was taken over by the Bank of England and sold off, work on Kuwaiti Sovereign Fund financed Cathedral Lanes shopping centre was halted.

[13]Including Barclays Bank HQ functions, RSA Examinations Board (OCR), Fanuc Robotics, Walkers Snack Foods.

1993 after twenty years or so of decline. By 2008, just before the global financial crisis, jobs in the city had risen to 141,000, a rise of 18% despite over 6500 redundancies with the major closures of Agco/Massey Ferguson, Courtaulds, GEC-Marconi and downsizing of Peugeot.[14] These closures could have happened at any time and reflects globalisation and a neo-liberalist business environment where any government involvement was minimal.

The city's new growth path rested on the revitalisation of the rump of the automotive manufacturing sector, mainly Jaguar Land Rover, and the component manufacturing companies; the rise of the education/knowledge economy in business services and company research and development. The new management approaches of outsourcing and supply chain management led also to the growth of the business service sector and logistics. The relaxation of fiscal policy led to a consumer boom which in turn led to growth in retailing in the form of retail parks and new city centre shopping precincts. Underlying this growth was a continued stream of inward investing businesses which both strengthened and diversified the economic base of Coventry. The development of science, technology and business parks provided a powerful stimulus in the attraction of inward investing companies.

The technological changes began to take place across most sectors in the city. This is best symbolised in 1992 by Fanuc Robotics establishing a base in the city and in 1993 Peugeot installing robots on the Ryton production line. In the 1980s, it was possible for business managers to not know how computers worked but by the 1990s, the usefulness of the internet and new computer software combined with new management cultures meant that computers could no longer be seen just as typewriters or adding machines. The 1990s saw the nature of work and occupational status change as well as the impact of lean production added pressure to reduce labour costs. By the 2010s this had become a major concern over equalities and worker rights. CIPD (2017) demonstrated the complexities of the law showing that

[14]The Ryton factory which closed (2200 job losses) in 2006 is in Warwickshire—The Peugeot offices in Coventry were downsized.

'worker' can be most difficult to define legally and consequently gives uncertain status in legal rights and pay.[15]

The labour force has had to change as a result of new management cultures, new technologies, new processes and new products many of which are intangible. Holmes and Mayhew (2012) noted that nationally the middle ranking occupations have been squeezed as work has become less routine. In Coventry the proportion of the labour force employed in the top three occupational levels has doubled to 39% since the early 1980s while the three middle grades have squeezed as a proportion from 46% to 30%. The bottom three grades have fallen to 30% from 35%. The main contributing factor of this decline has been the sharp decline in plant operator jobs which have disappeared with the growth of robotic production lines.

This changing pattern has led to significant changes in the nature of work away from routine and repetitive jobs towards jobs requiring knowledge skills rather than basic elementary skills. Since the 1980s the proportion of the work force qualified to NVQ4+ levels have doubled to over a third whereas people with no qualifications has shrunk from over 35% in the late 1970s to under 10% in 2017. This has implications for labour mobility, pay levels, inequality, health and social cohesion as pressures on workers and their families increase.

In Coventry, this has become apparent since the 2008 global financial crisis and impact of austerity on communities and the widening of inequality. The 2010s has been overall a period when the city achieved 'economic lift off' as the big structural and business changes of the long period of expansion between 1993 and 2008 started to mature. The Universities expanded on a broad front in terms of student numbers, research and partnership working with businesses. Coventry companies during the 1980s and 1990s caught up with their competitors by adopting new management methods, new technologies and embracing change. Coventry's growth led to heavy investment in business infrastructure and training of both managers and workers.

---

[15]In the 2010s people have been defined as working if they are employed for only 1 hour a week. This is a result of politicking partly to hide the dislocating impact of technological and employment change.

The Components of Change in Coventry's Reborn Economy

1. The Council's response to the crisis

A city like Coventry in an open economy is dominated by the changes taking place in the wider economy. The election of the Thatcher government favouring the market as the arbiter of economic change and not state intervention frowned on any local attempts to overcome the negative consequences of the recession for fear it create economic distortions. Bailoni (2014) analyses the broad based semi-political approach adopted by the Thatcher government which saw the abolition of the West Midlands County Council in 1986 and the repeal of the 1952 Coventry Corporation Act which provided a legal basis for much of the Council's economic development activity. Coventry recognised that at best the Council could only have strategic but marginal impacts on the local economy and in doing this, resolved to avoid any conflicts with central government.

In the search for a way out of the crisis, the Lord Mayor called a series of roundtable conferences in 1980 to discuss the crisis and find positive steps to ease the position. This was the start of the Council having an active economic development policy though there was little confidence in any outcomes. It would be true to say that Coventry was feeling its way for positive outcomes as the crisis was seen as overwhelming with no obvious solutions. The aim was to generate new jobs and centred on:

- To work in partnership with organisations and companies.
- Make loans and grants to help businesses to generate new jobs, modernise and improve their premises.
- The development of new employment land and premises including incubator units for new start businesses.
- Work with the universities and support the development of science and technology parks.

- Gain national and European regional assistance for companies and infrastructure projects.
- From 1986 a campaign to attract inward investment and broaden the city's economic base.

With hindsight the strategies seem comprehensively planned but in practice the Council took advantage, not always successfully, of any opportunity that arose, but it did not seek to return to the past or to waste limited resources in generalised wage subsidies or exotic regeneration schemes.[16] It was keeping an open mind and being flexible that helped the Council to make a positive contribution to the economic recovery, for example, undertaking speculative investments such as Westwood Business Park and making high risk loans to SME's.[17]

The Council's slogan of *Invest in Success Invest in Coventry* appealed mostly to non-manufacturing businesses attracted to the city by lower costs, availability of staff and the prospect of a growing labour force. Some UK businesses wanted to have a base away from the South East for fear that there would be not enough young people to fill jobs[18] in the 2000s as well as the continued congestion and pollution of London. Coventry could also play on being relatively close to London. The first firms to move into the city were a software company moving into the University of Warwick Science Park from Birmingham, Itech (later taken over by Admiral Computing) and Sun Hydraulics in 1985 from Florida which built a new unit at Seven Stars Industrial estate.

The Council's inward investment campaign proved to be successful and attracted in the first five years over 10,000 new jobs to the city. The new inward investors included Barclays Bank, RICS, Brose, George Fischer, Eon, Camping and Caravanning Club, Fanuc Robotics, and many companies wanting to work with the universities and/or to be

[16]This was done in some areas including S Yorkshire and Liverpool.

[17]High risk loans demand promises to repay—the Council made losses as did some individuals. However, the local tax income generated and employment offset much of the costs.

[18]Barclays Bank agents frequently asked for the number of unemployed office staff in the city. The inward investment team kept a running total (unemployed workers minus new jobs created plus jobs lost). Lower UK birth rates and ageing population forecasts drove these concerns.

inside the European Single European Market.[19] By the mid 1990s a flow of inward investing businesses in both services and manufacturing operations moved into the city until the 2008 financial crisis.

Although the Council bid to be the location of Toyota and Nissan car plants, Coventry failed to attract them. The main reason given was the city's poor image.[20] When the plants opened in Sunderland and Burnaston, Coventry benefited as component suppliers based in the city benefited from orders as have the city's universities which have undertaken joint working on projects with them.

2. **The business management changed**

Surviving businesses from the early 1980s recession had to adjust to the new economic paradigm of globalisation, neoliberalism and technological change. Initially, these firms followed the traditional route of closing-down costly/inefficient sites. This was a factor leading to the ending of Rover Group production in Coventry and concentrating production at Longbridge, Birmingham. Nationally and locally, this saw a rise in labour productivity and improved competitiveness without much investment as it was the most inefficient and costly establishments that were closed.[21] However, this was not sufficient to turn around the fortunes of many firms and it was obvious further action was needed in both large manufacturing concerns and SMEs.

Four significant changes in the way management operated began to take hold in the recovery from the 1979–1983 recession though each had begun to be adopted from the late 1960s. These changes represent a generational change as many mangers retired as businesses closed or transformed.

[19]This was a common reason why Japanese and American firms were looking for a base in Europe.

[20]Poor labour relations, inefficient production units, old fashioned employment buildings etc.

[21]The Ryder Report (1975) noted that BL had 7 foundries and '*productivity levels are judged to be less than half those in plants which use more modern equipment*,' p. 30.

- **Decentralising of businesses** following the US consultancy McKinsey advice in the 1960s and popularised by Porter (1979, 1985) amongst others which saw businesses as a compartmentalised whole with each section being a profit centre. This led many Coventry businesses to question '*what business are we in?*' and beginning to specialise. Peugeot, for example, sold off it bus manufacturing business in 1986.
- **Total Quality Management** (TQM) to over the chronic quality issues facing manufacturing in the city. The approach was developed by Ishikawa (1968) and Feigenbaum (1961) by recommending the analysis of cause and effect in production processes. Companies were encouraged seek and gain standards accreditation, typically ISO 9001 though Klassen and McLaughlin (1993) argue that TMQ goes well beyond that standard.
- **Procurement** had been recognised in the 1970s as a problem area. John Egan, as head of Unipart before becoming the MD of Rover Group, found that a quarter of bought-in componen*ts had faults and were often late.*[22] From the 1980s OEM businesses identified suppliers by competitive tendering and made orders electronically.[23] A number of Coventry supply companies did not make the grade and closed.
- **Deregulation** by the Thatcher government transferred a wide number of responsibilities to the private sector under the political acronym 'popular capitalism'.[24] This included: prices and income controls, health and safety (businesses had to take on more responsibilities for health and safety), product safety and corporate governance.[25] In addition, the implementation of the European Single Market in 1986 brought in new regulations which affected business management.[26]

---

[22]The Ryder Report (1975) Chapter on procurement.

[23]This ended the buyers and the use of brown envelopes.

[24]Bolick (1995) extols the Thatcher government's deregulation record but Booth (2015) is less sanguine.

[25]This is summarised by the Code of Best practice in the Cadbury Report: Committee on the Financial Aspects of Corporate Governance 1992.

[26]Although the EU Commission is blamed for their complexity—UK governments have tended to 'gold plate' the regulations by adding in extra conditions.

The impact led to major changes in the way businesses operated and more importantly their priorities. This, in turn, helped change Coventry's economic dynamic and structure.

3. **Ownership: privatisation and shareholder value**

The general weakness of the British economy was apparent as the country emerged from wartime controls and the first liberalisation of trade presaging globalisation. This general weakness was broadly reflected in the undercapitalisation of business which was worsened by the continuing relatively slow national economic growth and lack of competitiveness. The inflationary decade of the 1970s and general economic stagnation led to company failures and strategic and major businesses being nationalised e.g. Rolls Royce in 1972 and British Leyland in 1975 both companies having a large presence in Coventry.

The Thatcher government in 1979 issued new directives to the nationalised industries with the aim of improving efficiency and, therefore, profitability, led to rationalisations in the Coventry state companies. British Leyland/Rover closed the Morris Engines Plant and the Standard Triumph works cutting its Coventry labour force in 1980 by 20,000. The business was split up into its component parts and privatised: Jaguar (acquired by Ford in 1991), Rover (acquired by British Aerospace in 1988), Unipart (management buyout from the Rover Group in 1987) Alvis (sold to United Scientific in 1982 forming new company renamed Alvis plc). Alfred Herbert Machine Tools was sold off to Tooling Investments Ltd in 1980 and dissolved in 1982 although six small start-up companies came out of the ashes of the closure. Rolls Royce was privatised in 1987 having reduced its presence in the city by more than half. By the mid 1980s three state companies and successor companies employed some 16,000 people—a 60% cut. The closures led to some 20% of factory space in Coventry becoming empty—300,000 sqm of factory space on the market—much of it was in a poor state of repair. A further estimated 300,000 sqm was left occupied but basically unused.[27]

---

[27]This includes much of the Humber Road factories; Standard Triumph works and the Telephone Works.

Another non-market aspect of ownership has been the rise in shareholder power under the deregulated financial markets. This empowered shareholders, particularly institutional shareholders, to optimise their financial holdings often by using consultancy reports on companies or in reaction to comments by the commentariat. Local suppliers and employees had no part in this process.

The decision to demerge Courtaulds in 1990 and split-up GEC in 1998 were taken in the mistaken belief that it would maximise shareholder values. GEC employed 8900 workers and Courtaulds 3100.[28] The experience for Coventry of the demergers was essentially the disappearance of two leading employers, the loss of jobs and innovative companies. By the end of the 1990s demerging of companies was not seen generally as an attractive proposition. The ultimate result of the demerging was to leave the city with a few remaining departmental operations such as Coventry based SFM Ltd (Speciality Fibres & Materials) and vinyl flooring business Amtico Co Ltd. GEC after being demerged saw Marconi, its last significant presence in the city, fail in the Dot Com crash of 2001 and end up being taken over by Ericsson, renamed as Telent and relocated to Warwick. There was a net loss of 1000 jobs.

Perhaps a more market-based decision was the closure by the headquarters of the US owned Agco (Massey Ferguson) and Peugeot Ryton plants. Agco facing surplus capacity decided to close the Coventry plant shifting the work to Beauvais in France. The reason for this was that it was the most cost-effective option for the multinational business.[29] The closure cost 1200 jobs. The second major company closure was that of Peugeot Ryton in 2006. Again, company overcapacity and long logistical chains led to the work being transferred to France with the loss of 2200 jobs. These ownership decisions were taken without consideration of local issues or, perhaps with the exception of Peugeot, the welfare of the workforce.

[28]Mackie (2008a, p. 26).

[29]Other reasons given by commentators were that it was easier to sack British workers than French ones; the UK was not joining the Euro and the sale of the UK site was more likely to raise more.

4. Inward Investment

Inward investing companies from abroad over the last 30 years have also helped to transform the local economy. FDI businesses have had two significant impacts on the local economy. The overall impact has had spill over effects by which local companies have altered and changed their operations as a result of business interactions and networking in various forums such as the Chamber of Commerce, conferences or through third parties such as accountancy firms. Coventry has benefited from both takeovers and greenfield FDI. For example. German company Brose bought in 1988 and diversified the failing component Sheridan Engineering company of Durbar Avenue, transforming the business into a Tier 1 supply company and trebling employment to 900.[30] A greenfield example is US Mexican Mission Foods employing 600 people in the manufacture of tortilla chips and snacks that moved onto the Coventry Business Park in 1997.

It was inward investing firms which helped Coventry recover from the 1979–1983 recession originating from, at first, France and Germany but later Japan, China and India. By 1990, foreign inward investment took off partly as a result of Ford's acquisition of Jaguar in 1992. Under Ford, Jaguar was able to expand its product range but failed to make expected profits. In 2000, Jaguar with Land Rover[31] along with Aston Martin and Volvo cars[32] became the Premier Automotive Group. Ford's own problems led to Jaguar and Land Rover being put up for sale with Tata Motors[33] taking over in 2008. After a sticky start, Jaguar Land Rover boomed under Tata after the financial crisis becoming a global company and setting up plants in Brazil, China, India, Slovakia with partners in Austria and Hungary.

---

[30] 2018 figure after 30 years presence in the city.

[31] Bought from BMW (owners of Rover Group) in 2000.

[32] Aston Martin was sold off in 2007 to a consortium led By Prodrive based in Banbury and Volvo Cars based in Torslanda, Sweden in 2010 was taken over by Geely Group of China.

[33] It is thought that Lord Bhattachyyrya of WMG—UW, a friend of Ratan Tata, played a key role in the take-over and the subsequent JAGUAR LAND ROVER success.

In recent years China has been a significant FDI investor following capital overseas investment reforms in 2003–2005 which enabled substantial investment in Coventry with the takeover of London Taxi Company—London Electric Vehicle Company: LEVC by Zhejiang Geely Holding Group Co. of Nanjing in 2013 and the development of a new 37,000 sqm research and production unit at Ansty producing electric taxis. The struggling body-in-white manufacturer Stadco Ltd was taken over by Cad Cam Automotive[34] in 2013. A £300 m investment programme in joint venture with China Red Sun Group, will see 1000 new jobs in the 2020s in a new energy and research centre. Not all projects have been successful, however, as Shandong Yongtai Group took over Covpress in 2013 but for various reasons Covpress fell into administration and was taken over by the UK Liberty House Group in 2017. Chinese investment has also led to substantial property investment in the city's student accommodation building boom.

5. **Size**

The act of splitting companies up and privatising them has changed the structure of the city's business community. Before 1979, Coventry's economy had been dominated by big companies, a big City Council and big trade unions. In 1978 just over two thirds of jobs in the city were in the top 10 companies and the City Council. In 2017 this had fallen to under one job in five, a fall of 70%. The Council has shrunk from 27,250 to 4500 over the same period reflecting the independence of Coventry Polytechnic in 1988 and out-sourcing activities, particularly after the onset of austerity under the Cameron—May governments when over 10,000 posts were outsourced or made redundant. For the first time in over 30 years, the Council lost its top spot (Tables 9.2 and 9.3).

---

[34]Former name Motor Panels Coventry based in Holbrook Lane.

Table 9.2 The 10 largest employers in Coventry by number of jobs in the Coventry area

Rank	1978		1984		1997	
1	British Leyland	27,258	Coventry Council	18,860	Coventry Council	16,142
2	Coventry Council	21,500	Jaguar Cars	9688	Jaguar Cars	4206
3	GEC	16,166	GEC Telecoms	8878	Peugeot	3673
4	Chrysler - Talbot	12,531	NHS	4919	University of Warwick	4350
5	Rolls Royce	8307	Rolls Royce	4266	Walsgrave Hospital	4489
6	Massey Ferguson	6014	Peugeot - Talbot	3453	GPT (ex GEC)	3000
7	Dunlop	5749	Courtaulds	3069	Rolls Royce	2334
8	NHS	5600	Dunlop	2805	Agco = MF	2225
9	Courtaulds	3786	Austin Rover	2525	Coventry University	2578
10	Alfred Herbert's MT	3469	University Warwick	2315	BTR	1562
	Total Top 10	**110,380**		**60,778**		**44,559**
	Percent of all	67.3%		48.6%		33.8%
	All jobs in Coventry	**164,000**		**125,000**		**132,000**
Rank	**2007**		**2011**		**2017**	
1	Coventry Council	17,458	Coventry Council	16,900	University of Warwick	6100
2	University Hospital CW	6000	University Hospital	6450	Jaguar Land Rover	6000
3	University of Warwick	4734	University Warwick	5400	University Hospital CW	5700
4	Coventry University	2280	Coventry University.	4600	Coventry University	5400
5	Jaguar Land Rover	2104	NHS Partnership	3500	Coventry Council	4500
6	NHS PCT	2705	Jaguar Land Rover	2500	NHS Partnership	3000
7	Barclays Bank	1992	Barclays Bank	2350	Severn Trent	2100
8	Royal Mail-Parcelforce	1889	Severn Trent	1950	LEVC	1500
9	Tesco	1547	Tesco Stores	1570	WM Police and Fire	1150
10	WM Police and Fire	1456	PSA Group	1220	Royal Mail Parcelforce	1100
Total		**42,165**		**46,440**		**36,850**
Percent of		30.1%		32.5%		22.2%
All jobs in Coventry		**140,000**		**143,000**		**160,000**

Source Coventry City Council in conjunction with ONS and business reports

Table 9.3 Number and average size of workplaces in Coventry

No. of employees	1986	1996	2006	2016
Under 10	3460	6681	7501	9465
10–49	1245	1225	1286	1515
50–99	178	188	235	240
100–249	94	99	127	132
250–499	53	77	86	73
Over 500	33	25	26	30
Total	**5063**	**8295**	**9261**	**11,455**
Average size of workplace	28	16	16	14
Concerns with 10+jobs	80	72	75	45

Source ONS NOMIS

The table shows the collapse of manufacturing in Coventry. In 1978, eight of the top 10 spots were taken manufacturing concerns employing 77,266 people. By 2017 LEVC and Jaguar were the only companies engaged in manufacturing with some 2500[35] engaged purely in manufacturing activities. The table shows the rise of the universities but does not yet reflect the growth of the knowledge economy in the city. The later lists will already change as Amazon (1500 jobs) and Meggitt Aerospace (1200 jobs as a result of consolidation of activities into Coventry) are building facilities in or on the edge of the city in Warwickshire which are due to open during 2018–2019. Inward investment has played a significant part in the listings with Severn Trent moving its HQ to Coventry and Jaguar Land Rover and LEVC expanding under new owners.[36]

6. **The business estate renewed**

The recession of 1979–1983 exposed the poor quality of the city's industrial estate. Post war regional policies restricted the construction of new factory buildings in Coventry by the Industrial Development

[35]This includes Jaguar's employees at Whitley HQ and Ryton but excludes company HQ functions staff while LEVC has also research staff at its plant.

[36]The trade war between the US and China may slowdown investment.

Certificates system[37] which enabled the government to direct investment to areas of high unemployment. This, in effect, led to factory buildings not being modernised. The Rootes Group located a car plant in 1963 at Linwood, Scotland and not Coventry under this regulation. The dramatic closures in the early 1980s led to some 25% of employment properties being vacant or underused.

Much of the business estate, both in use and on the market, was in poor condition,[38] with low eave heights and, often, leaky roofs and pillars too close together making it unsuitable for the new technology production lines. It was hard in the early 1980s to appreciate that most of the city's business estate needed to be replaced. It was recognised that there was insufficient space for small businesses and start-ups and the Council took the lead in developing new small units of under 500 sqm. Given the size of property on the market, the private sector needed the Council to demonstrate that there was any demand for new property.

The Council successfully developed small units in the City Centre[39] area and provided sites at the new Seven Stars Industrial Estate. In addition, the Council converted in 1984–1985 a former Courtaulds factory in Little Heath into small space units and provided on-site business support. In 1988 it developed the first office business park in the West Midlands at Westwood and with surprising speed the sites were taken up by national companies such as Barclays Bank and Eon,. It was only by the late 1980s that the private sector had accepted that investing in new properties could be profitable and started to invest and developed Leofric and Cross Point Business Parks, as well as upgrading and re-developing the old Armstrong Whitworth buildings at Siskin Drive into the Middlemarch Business Park (Table 9.4).

---

[37]The IDC's originated form wartime controls and incorporated into peace time by the 1947 Town and Country Planning Act. Most government used its powers until 1981 when the Thatcher government suspended its use.

[38]Wickmans on Banner lane had a leaking roof and has to stop work during heavy rain showers.

[39]Short Street on Parkside, in Hillfields and at Hornchurch Road. Around 40 all under 5000 sqm.

Table 9.4 Employment land related development in Coventry since 1980

	Ha	%
Employment land gone to housing	189	16.4
Employment land redeveloped	572	49.7
Greenfield land to employment	390	33.9
Total	1151	100.0

Source Mackie (2008a) and updated

The prospect of a revival in demand in the early 1980s seemed small considering the depth of the recession, the collapse in manufacturing combined with Coventry's poor image. Unseen, at first, was the potential demand from new businesses and inward investors which was met by the government and EU regional funding, helping the Council to develop new properties, meeting this new demand from businesses originating mostly from both the service sector and the new knowledge businesses.

From the mid 1980s to the present, Coventry business estate has been replaced with over 80% of Coventry workers operating in new premises with modern facilities built in the last 25 years. Without public investment in property development, the recovery of the city's economy would have been severely handicapped. In the 2010s, the recovery of the city's economy has made private sector development the norm though there is still some reticence for commercial developments in the city centre.

Over the last 30 years the city has redeveloped or built over 1150 hectares of new employment related developments. This equates to 11% of the total area of Coventry or 17% of the built-up area.[40] If new housing is added well over a third of the present-day city has been developed in little more than a generation. The recovery and inward investment

[40]These figures include development immediately outside the city limits taking these out would reduce them to 9 and 15%.

led to a big demand for business properties and sites with occasional shortages of employment property.[41]

Inward investing companies from abroad expect prestigious high-quality properties for the business and for their key workers moving with the business. Sun Hydraulics from Florida was the one of first business to be attracted into the city. The company rejected taking an existing unit preferring a site meeting the company's preference to build a modern unit. The success of the inward investment campaign[42] attracted property companies and property facilities management companies to the city as well as investment finance.[43] This in turn, helped the city to attract international companies to set up in the city by providing services to their establishment and any subsequent expansion.

7. **Outsourcing**

The breakdown of business into processes enabled managements to reduce non-mainstream business operations costs by outsourcing operations. Some companies have developed entirely (or are working to develop) subcontracting for all their operations—administration, production, logistics, sales and marketing etc.[44] This led to a debate in the 1980s as to whether vertically integrated businesses had had their day. In the long run vertically integrated businesses are, generally, more efficient[45] but in times of disruption and rapidly changing technologies, outsourcing offers more flexibility, lower costs and reduced risk. The rise of outsourcing, at first, led to work being placed with specialist

---

[41]One German inward investing company in 1989 described the property position as a *verkäufermarkt* and went elsewhere.

[42]The Council has participated in, for example, MIPIM, the international property event, since the early 1990s.

[43]Property development and facilities companies include Prologis, Goodmans, M & G with finance provide by many international banks.

[44]An early example of this in World War 2 was Coventry based Hawker Sidderley (parent company of Whitworth Armstrong) subsidiary Gloster Aircraft Co. assembled Albemarle. Gloster from individual parts and sub-assemblies produced by about 1000 subcontractors.

[45]Francine Lafontaine and Margaret Slade (2006, August) Vertical Integration and Firm Boundaries: The Evidence. *Journal of Economic Literature*, discusses the issues surrounding businesses limits.

companies, but as more activities became routinely outsourced to independent specialist companies new service activities were created, such as cleaning, maintenance, delivery and warehousing etc.

All these activities transferred out of large manufacturing concerns had their classification in their new company format switched from manufacturing to the relevant services sector.[46] When Peugeot Ryton closed in 2006, the factory had 73 non-production related suppliers engaged in logistics, cleaning security, and catering.[47] By the mid 1990s some 10,000 jobs in Coventry were effectively transferred out of manufacturing into the service sector simply through out-sourcing activities.

As the connectivity between management, company branches and suppliers improved outsourcing has led to moving production closer to markets abroad. Outsourcing abroad started in the 1990s with some Coventry call centres work being moved to firms in Bangalore as VoIP,[48] dramatically reducing call costs. With globalisation becoming stronger production lines were built abroad in order to gain lower production costs, reduced logistical costs, better taxation rates and proximity to customers. Jaguar Land Rover for example has outsourced production in Austria, Brazil, China, India and Slovakia and hopes to produce in the USA.

Logistics, perhaps the largest outsourced activity, has become an industry in its own right with specialist firms like DHL, Gefco, Unipart Logistics (the former in-house BL subsidiary) providing bespoke solutions for companies across all the sectors. A third of the take up of warehousing in Coventry and Warwickshire has been taken by third party logistics firms[49] and in addition companies have located their own standalone logistics operations such as Network Rail, Co-op and Amazon. Jaguar Land Rover has a complex supply chain inherited in part from previous owners of the company prior to Tata Motors. It has some 350

[46]The main activity of an establishment generally determines its classification supporting activities may not match that classification.

[47]See Mackie (2008b).

[48]Voice over the internet protocol—technologies for the delivery of voice communications and multimedia sessions over Internet. This outsourcing was not seen as the issue it was to later become.

[49]CWLEP—CBRE Employment Land Study, p. 86.

UK and 450 European based suppliers with further supply chains linked to overseas factories. Using lead logistics providers, the company has combined almost its entire inbound network and integrated it under the control of DHL, which manages transport, stock handling and line feeding at the three plants.[50] Similar control has been arranged with speciality provider Priority Freight for premium freight movements.

As time has passed, these systems have and will continue to become increasingly more efficient and more sophisticated and tailor-made to meet specific business needs. The Single European Market, for example, meant the sector had to operate across borders as frictionless as possible in order to meet the needs of business in the 28-member states.[51] The European Commission established in 2007 an action plan to tackle problems that had built up as a result of the increased complexity of supply chain management across the European single market and the need to reduce avoidable barriers.[52] The logistics industry within the Coventry area has more than doubled in size over the last thirty years.

This led to a big increase in demand for warehouse space. In Coventry, planners were, at first, reluctant to approve warehouse developments owing to their large size and relatively small employee numbers. It was felt that they were better at strategically located specialised distribution parks at Crick and Lutterworth by the M6 – M1 junction. However, it was soon realised that the limited development of warehouses meant that the costs of a new business park infrastructure could be met and help release sites for other uses[53] as well as the new logistics companies engaging in warehouse product operations such as some assembly work or packaging creating more jobs.

---

[50]See Ludwig (2012) *Secrets of a success story at JAGUAR LAND ROVER.* Automotive Logistics. https://automotivelogistics.media/intelligence/secrets-of-a-success-story.

[51]This is a significant Brexit issue.

[52]Ecorys, Fraunhofer, TCI, Prognos and AUEB-RC/TRANSLOG (2015) *Fact-finding studies in support of the development of an EU strategy for freight transport logistics Lot 1: Analysis of the EU logistics sector European Commission*—CONTRACT NUMBER FV355/2012/MOVE/D1/ETU/SI2.659384

[53]The best example of this was the development of the Toys R Us 60,000 sqm. warehouse and 4000 sqm. retail unit on the c. 50 ha. Cross Point Business Park in 1989–1990.

8. The Third Industrial revolution

By the 1980 technological changes had begun to take hold in the mainstream economy. In Coventry, new technologies were being adopted in factories and offices with what today would be called primitive automatic machine tools and computers (even if they were used as typewriters and adding machines). The University of Warwick established Warwick Manufacturing Group (WMG) in 1980 to help businesses become competitive and modernise. The University of Warwick Science Park started in 1983. These developments combined with the creation of the Coventry University Technology Park in 1996 enabled Coventry and West Midlands businesses to gain access to and adopt the new management and technologies that were coming on stream as well as developing new tangible and intangible products.

Government grants and privatisation of learning developed a market in learning—knowledge had become an intangible commodity. This is signified in Coventry by the formation in 1990 of RDI distance learning company which in 2015 became the University of Arden based in Coventry. Local accountancy firms, private training companies and the Chamber of Commerce took advantage of this new market. By the 1990s learning had become a major employment sector in the city.

By the late 1980s University student numbers started to grow and after 2000 they grew rapidly. The success of the universities is marked by the growth in their student numbers. In 2016–2017 there were 56,735 students attending the two universities[54]: 25,705 undergraduates and 5985 posy graduates at Coventry and 16,110 and 8935 respectively at the University of Warwick.[55] These numbers have grown since 2000 when there were 31,875 students at the two universities, a rise of 78%. By far the biggest subject area growth was in Business & Administrative studies accounting for 14,090 students or about one in

[54]The official statistics in the 1980s may have for some series the University of Warwick may have been put in Warwick District statistics. Coventry Polytechnic until the 1988 Education Act was part of the city council and some Polytechnic jobs may be classified as local authority.

[55]Higher Education Statistics Agency data.

four. Engineering and computer science accounted for a further 7130 or one in eight. Some 7000 students are engaged in medicine and allied subjects. The number of foreign students in 2016–2017 was 7425 and formed around one in eight of the Coventry student body. This compares to around one in five who live within computing distance from their homes.

The universities work also, in partnership or for many major businesses providing valuable feedback and knowledge inputs to businesses which enables the universities adapt and apply knowledge applications to other areas. Although engineering faculties are, often, headline departments, other university departments like business studies, arts and design and the sciences help businesses to meet the special needs of companies. Altogether over 2000 businesses work with the city's two universities. This cooperation has positive feedbacks and has put the two universities amongst the best in the UK.

Coventry has evolved out of the 1979–1983 recession by adopting and helping develop the new industries of the twenty-first century. With luck and considerable investment, Coventry and its surrounding environs can look forward to a long period of sustained growth in these industries of this century as much as it did at the new industries at the start of the last century. Much will depend on the city remaining competitive and investing in innovation.

Conclusions

The last forty years has not been a story of some Schumpeterian disruption[56] followed by a positive creative spasm of recovery. The disruption was a result of government deflationary policies coinciding with an oil crisis and a global downturn. The traditional solutions of closing

[56]Schumpeter disruption is popular in neo-liberalism and refers to sudden deep adverse changes enabling firms to re-energise by improving productivity and dynamism of the business. Chile in the 1970s and Poland after 1980 are often cited as examples.

capacity—inefficient capacity—made the disruption worse and led to heavy job losses. For a city like Coventry dependent on manufacturing, there was no simple market led solution to the crisis except to build on what was left of the city's economic assets: engineering traditions, skills and the two universities.

The 1979–1983 recession obliterated the post-World War II economy and the fledgling companies[57] that might have flourished in a normal recovery. The city needed external stimuli and investment. It was companies moving into Coventry, particularly from abroad, combined with the universities' knowledge and expertise in production and product development, that restored the city's competitiveness and established strong links to the global economy, putting Coventry on a strong growth path. The process was not without some collateral damage, as many Coventrians were scarred by unemployment, the unfamiliarity of the nature of the new work and the technology.

Coventry is a city based in a national market which itself is deeply embedded in the international economy. The city had no choice but to face the full impact of European and globalised competition and the continuing changes which have been unrelenting over the last thirty years, but as the 2020s approach equally daunting challenges still face Coventry. International uncertainty and the technological revolution is likely to continue to change business parameters. Two factors stand in the city's favour—the experience of the past and, unlike after 1980, Coventry has competitive and dynamic businesses and institutions with which to face a further period of all-inclusive change. Coventry has developed resilience out of thirty years of fundamental change.

[57]These include Norman Butter Robots Ltd in its original form; Noel Penny Turbines and software companies.

References

Bailoni, M. (2014, April 2). The Effects of Thatcherism in the Urban North of England (O. Waine, Trans.). *Metropolitics*. https://www.metropolitiques.eu/The-effects-of-Thatcherism-in-the.html.

Bolick, C. (1995). Thatcher's Revolution: Deregulation and Political Transformation. *Yale Journal on Regulation, 12*(2) article 6. https://pdfs.semanticscholar.org/f8c5/e9cbbccd7f992bd9345f19ccbab3bf50e889.pdf.

Booth, P. (2015). *Thatcher: The Myth of Deregulation* (Discussion Paper 60). Institute of Economic Affairs. https://iea.org.uk/publications/research/thatcher-the-myth-of-deregulation.

Chartered Institute of Personnel and Development (CIPD). (2017, June 30). *Annual Report and Accounts.*

Coventry City Council. (1980–1987). *Economic Monitor Department of Planning & Economic Development.*

Coventry City Council. (2016). *Coventry Local Plan 2011–2031 Publication Draft.*

Coventry & Warwickshire Local Economic Partnership. *CBRE Employment Land Study.*

Daly, G., & Gulliver, K. (2018, March). FDI Magazine European Cities and Regions of the Future 2018-9. *Financial Times.*

Feigenbaum, A. V. (1961). *Total Quality Control.* New York: McGraw-Hill.

Healey, M. J., & Clarke, D. (1984). Industrial Decline and Government Response in the West Midlands: The Case of Coventry. *Journal of Regional Studies, 18*(4), 303–318.

Healey, M. J., & Dunham, P. J. (1994, October). Changing Competitive Advantage in a Local Economy: The Case of Coventry, 1971–90. *Urban Studies, 31*(8), 1279–1301.

Holmes, C., & Mayhew, K. (2012). *The Changing Shape of the UK Job Market and Its Implications for the Bottom Half of Earners Commission on Living Standards* (Resolution Foundation Paper).

Ishikawa, K. (1968). *Guide to Quality Control.* Tokyo: JUSE.

Klassen, R. D., & McLaughlin, C. P. (1993). TQM and Environmental Excellence in Manufacturing. *Industrial Management and Data Systems, 93,* 14–22.

Klein, N. (2007). *The Shock Doctrine: The Rise of Disaster Capitalism.* New York: Metropolitan Books, Henry Holt LLC.

Lafontaine, F., & Slade, M. (2006). Vertical Integration and Firm Boundaries: The Evidence. *Journal of Economic Literature XLV* (September 2007), 629–685.

Ludwig. (2012). *Secrets of a Success Story at JLR.* Automotive Logistics. https://automotivelogistics.media/intelligence/secrets-of-a-success-story.

Mackie, M. L. (2008a). *Coventry's Economy 1976–2026* (Research & Strategy Paper). Coventry City Council.

Mackie M. L. (2008b). *The Work of the Peugeot Partnership and the Closure of the Ryton Plant* (Research & Strategy Paper 67). Coventry City Council.

Porter, M. E. (1979). The structure within industries and companies' performance. *Review of Economics and Statistics, 61*(2), 214–227.

Porter, M. E. (1985). Technology and competitive advantage. *Journal of Business Strategy, 5*(3), 60–78.

PWC. (2016). *Good Growth for Cities.*

Ryder, D. Sir (1975). *British Leyland: The Next Decade.* House of Common C (75) 53.

Singh, A. (1977, June). UK Industry and the World Economy: A Case of De-industrialisation? *Cambridge Journal of Economics, 1*(2), 113–136.

Tolliday, S. (1988). Competition and the workplace in the British automobile industry, 1945–1988. *Business and Economic History*, 63–77.

Tolliday, S., & Zeitlin, J. (Eds.). (1987). *The Automobile Industry and Its Workers: Between Fordism and Flexibility.* Edited by Steven Tolliday and Jonathan Zeitlin. *Business History Review, 62*(4), 720–722 (1988).

10

Toward a New Knowledge Economy?

David Morris

Introduction

This chapter takes a forward, and positive, look at the economic prospects for Coventry. As with many cities there is a recognition that economic success will be based on building a strong knowledge base which supports innovation and technological development leading to commercialisation of new products. But that aim could be applied to many cities and begs the question as to why Coventry should be successful in the face of strong competition. The answer is unsurprising, but none the worse for being so. Coventry, like many cities, has survived by reinventing itself–several times over. That process of renewal must recognise the city's strengths, a medium-sized UK city cannot do everything and should not ignore its history. This chapter does not pretend to offer a plan of what Coventry should do. Nor is it set out as an options appraisal. What it can do is summarise some current

D. Morris (✉)
Coventry University, Coventry, UK
e-mail: ecy037@coventry.ac.uk

J. Begley et al. (eds.), *Revival of a City*, Palgrave Studies in Economic History,
https://doi.org/10.1007/978-3-030-22822-4_10

thinking on the ways in which local economies in general might prosper in the future and see how Coventry measures up. Such a discussion cannot, of course, confine itself to Coventry as an entity. The city is a major part of the West Midlands region, particularly in economic terms, and the discussion needs to recognise that. Coventry is also surrounded by Warwickshire and for many purposes it is artificial to separate the two. But the focus is firmly on Coventry.

The chapter explores three main themes. Firstly, it asks how clusters of economic activity in specific areas change in response to economic, political and other external pressures. This discussion bears directly on the effect of fundamental changes in the traditional automotive industry as it faces the challenges posed by the move to more environmentally acceptable vehicles, shifts in power train technologies away from the internal combustion engine (ICE), changes in the way mobility is provided and people access it and consequent re-composing of vehicle value chains. Secondly, how is the expected role of the city's two universities changing to meet the knowledge requirements of the changing automotive industry? Thirdly, given that knowledge in a digital world cannot be confined to specific places, do place-based economic development strategies work at all?

Clusters

Clusters are not new; they have always played a major part in the distribution of economic activity. In the past they were mainly based on the presence of particular factors of production, for example raw materials or natural resources. Local demand conditions and the development of specialised markets for skilled labour and financial capital also played a major role. The emergence of global markets for capital and professional labour, the increasing importance of knowledge-based industries as creators of wealth and competitive advantage based on the capacity to innovate have changed the nature of clusters rather than provoked their disappearance. In simple terms clusters are concentrations of interconnected firms and institutions at a regional or national level. They encompass an array of linked industries and other entities important to competition, and affect competitiveness within countries as well as across national borders. Often clusters also extend downstream to distribution channels and customers, to manufacturers of complementary products and to companies in sectors related to development of skills, technologies, or common inputs. Many clusters, including the West Midlands automotive industry, also include governmental and other institutions, such as research institutes and universities.

There is a general acceptance that the concept of "cluster" is useful in developing economic policies at the regional level. In the European Competitiveness Report of 2012, clusters are defined as

> ...geographically co-located firms and other institutions engaged in economic activities in a set of related industries, connected though externalities and other types of linkages.....

Note the reference to "geographically co-located" here. Morosini (2003) defined "industrial cluster" as

> ...a socioeconomic entity characterized by a social community of people and a population of economic agents localised in close proximity in a specific geographic region. Within an industrial cluster, a significant part of both the social community and the economic agents work together in economically linked activities, sharing and nurturing a common stock of product, technology and organisational knowledge in order to generate superior products and services in the marketplace...

Although this definition appears broader than that adopted by the EU there is still an emphasis on place and localization. However, it also recognises that clusters are not coterminous with industries or sectors as conventionally defined. Commonalities and complementarities, including knowledge relationships, are not limited to industry or sector boundaries and change dynamically as innovations in technology, business models and markets occur. Thus, clusters have constantly changing (porous) boundaries and membership. The main advantage of clusters is that they offer the possibilities of promoting increased competitiveness and sustainable competitive advantage at the regional level through advances in productivity, innovation, increased flexibility and enabling the successive creation of new businesses. It is the dynamic benefits gained from clusters rather than any static advantages that are important.

Cluster organisations formalise and develop these links (internal and external) for the collective good of cluster members. They are frequently developed and promoted by external policy interventions; a hallmark of successful cluster organisations is active involvement by local government agencies. Networks often operate across clusters to pursue specific objectives which will benefit from collaboration. These may be particularly effective where new "enabling" technologies are being overlaid on a given application area. For example, the development of electric vehicles is dependent on the application of technologies, for example batteries, which are outside those associated with conventionally powered vehicles. Similarly, smart mobility developments are dependent on a wide range of ICT applications which are derived from outside the automotive industry, for example environment sensing, GPS tracking and cybersecurity prevention.

Clusters can be driven by combinations of the following:

- History: particular regions may, as a result of their pasts have particular strengths, capabilities and resources (human and physical) and cultures which can be exploited to develop new competitive advantages. Regions promoting cultural, heritage or eco-tourism are an example. History is also a compelling factor underpinning Coventry's revived fortunes as a centre of automotive expertise and economic activity.
- Presence of distinct physical resources: which is, perhaps, of relatively little importance in the case of Coventry.
- Research capabilities: research-driven clusters build on, inter alia, the strengths of universities and research institutes. This is a factor of growing importance to Coventry and its immediate neighbours as witnessed by the presence of international research centres of excellence such as Horiba-MIRA and the Warwick Manufacturing Group.
- Innovative milieu: the grouping of a dynamic mix of economic, social, political and cultural elements and (social) interrelationships

which occur in a specific, predominantly physical space. Examples include industries relying on creativity, design and artistic skills or some combination of them.
- Adversity: the need to overcome negative economic circumstances, for example the decline of traditional industries in a region or long-term under-investment, is often the trigger for concerted effort to rebuild the industrial, business and commercial base of a region. The Coventry petrol engines industry of war and post-war times is a stark example. Clusters based on "green" industries, for example low-carbon vehicles, driven by environmental concerns are a new example.
- Technology: the exploitation of particular technologies and the associated supply chains, innovation networks and specialised labour markets is perhaps the best-known instance of clustering. An archetypal example, but one under threat from rapidly changing technology, is provided by the conventional West Midlands automotive industry. However, technology-based clusters can be rapidly eroded by technology change as Coventry's experience with the telephone equipment industry showed in the wake of the transition from mechanical exchanges to electro-mechanical ones.

Explaining how clusters start is not always easy, but not necessary in practical terms. The important issue is to understand how they change and develop, and, in turn, can be fostered and supported. The following elements are widely accepted as being necessary for successful cluster development:

- Networking: cluster growth involves networking and fostering the growth of social capital. Often, the more generic social capital within a region must develop within (cluster-) specific networks if clusters are to grow.
- Circumstances: cluster growth develops when the "right" market circumstances are present; these include elements of rivalry, cooperation, openness to international markets, the presence of demanding lead customers, etc.

- Interaction: interacting with labour markets, higher education institutions, research laboratories to enhance labour factor specialisation and upgrading, and cater for increasing demand sophistication.
- Links with institutions: a multitude of linkages across institutions, as well as the transformation of public science into private science and the commercialisation of new knowledge.
- Links with markets: a growing cluster involves linkages to international markets, both factor markets and final goods markets. Cluster growth needs an inflow of people with different skills, inward investments, imports of materials, components and products, and new technologies.
- Mobility of people: where scientists and industry experts can operate in a number of domains and career paths are flexible enough to generate cross-fertilisation between industry and research, policy-making bodies and productive enterprises and so on. Technology transfer between universities and research institutes and industry is well-developed. Cluster-specific institutions evolve.
- Political texture: cluster growth takes place within a particular political setting. Regulations and political actions cover competition policies and market regulation and regional, industry, and science and innovation policies. More general policies affect the overall attractiveness of a region to people (housing, transportation, recreation and culture) and companies (land, investment attraction packages, skilled people).

Can government policy interventions intentionally create clusters? The alternate views (to intentional creation) suggest that, either, governments can only create conditions in which clusters might emerge through the bottom-up actions of private firms, or that clusters begin to emerge on their own (autonomously), but once they have started they can be encouraged to grow through targeted policy interventions. However, innovative clusters will not emerge automatically and a number of facilitating conditions need to be present. Prominent among these are the ability of clusters to reduce the costs of co-ordinating complementary but dissimilar activities and the presence of network-innovation. Network-innovation occurs when different economic actors with distinct competencies combine their skills to improve existing products or processes or create new ones. Network-innovations do not always occur through a planned process or programme of research and development, but do require the co-operation of multiple organisations along the value chain. Cluster initiatives are public-private actions designed and resourced to strengthen clusters. Note the word "strengthen" rather than "create". Again, the implication is that initiatives can only develop something which has already begun to emerge rather than build something new where there was previously a gap. Cluster initiatives concentrate on particular aspects of cluster policy, for example developing commercial and research collaboration. Upgrading human resources and the business environment are also important.

Technology and innovation are intimately connected to each other in successful clustering. Some innovations are, at least partly, the outcome of a process of transferring technology between cluster members through university education, training, specialised technology transfer offices and incubators, joint R&D projects and regional public-private organisations that focus on networking and commercialising new discoveries. Innovation is enhanced in environments where different resources can constantly be redirected efficiently and effectively. The reshuffling of critical resources is facilitated by the development of diverse avenues of technology sharing. This is particularly important when inventions and innovations do not always find use where they first emerge, but need to be migrated to other environments to be fully exploited; batteries in the EV market and ICTs in the smart mobility arena are examples. Innovation in mature industries is based on a process of incremental reduction of technical and economic uncertainty, technologies are modified and adapted and business models adjusted. Knowledge is tightly controlled and often privatized.

The goal of economic development is the inclusive one of achieving prosperity for all. Productivity and productivity growth determine economic growth. Innovation is a key driver of productivity growth, and clustering supports both productivity and innovation. Once a cluster is formed, the group of industries becomes mutually supportive. Thus, clusters can affect competition by increasing companies' productivity and driving the direction and pace of innovation. Being part of a cluster allows companies to operate more productively in sourcing inputs including knowledge, accessing information, technology and institutions, coordinate Universities and businesses share spaces and are spatially distributed and, in general, co-location is interpreted to mean physical proximity. However, increasingly our notions of space are being broadened to include virtual as well as physical spaces. For many sociologists, for example Thrift (2008), the notion of space has distinct characteristics that many people might find surprising and conceptually challenging. Firstly, everything is spatially distributed, including economic activity, knowledge, and research and innovation effort. Secondly, all spaces are porous and there is no such thing as a fixed boundary. Thirdly, all spaces are in constant motion. Fourthly, there are many kinds of space that interact with each other. Innovation spaces need to be dynamic, have multiple inter-locking dimensions (economic, political, social, technological and so on), exist in a given form only temporarily and are both leaky and sponge-like. In contrast, the conceptual frameworks underpinning local economic development plans are often based on place, that is, the physical locations, layouts, facilities and other concrete manifestations of presence. Recognition of the wider dimensions of space is usually somewhere down the list of challenges to be met.

However, new challenges are emerging all the time and will form part of the future agenda for cluster development. The recognition that modern clusters overlap with each other, have permeable boundaries and may be time-limited in their effectiveness has important consequences, particularly as dominant technologies change, markets become even more globalized and megatrends such as ageing of society, increasing inequalities in the distribution of wealth and environmental concerns weigh even heavier. How do the new clusters, which develop in response to these forces, interact with those which are already entrenched, well-organized and integrated and powerful? For example, how do low carbon vehicle (LCV) and electromobility clusters interact with established (ICE-based) automotive OEMs and their supply chains? Given the major importance of SMEs as employers and sources of potential innovation–how do we ensure that they benefit from cluster initiatives? And, who is going to ensure that the new clusters work, prosper and develop?

Promoting Innovative Regions

A minimalist and unproductive view of economic development policy treats regions as spatially proximate, historically-determined collections of autonomous entities pursuing their own incremental agendas to the exclusion of all else. But regions are not simply co-located collections of isolated autonomous firms; firms are parts of industries, supply chains, value chains and innovation networks. Nor are regions co-terminous with clusters. Indeed, regions which overlap with specific clusters may be vulnerable to changes in technology, large-scale market entry by new producers, emerging scarcity of key resources and shifting global forces, priorities and threats. The West Midlands automotive industry is a highly visible example as it fights to develop in response to global and national pressures for more environmentally friendly vehicles, acquiring and adapting unfamiliar, to the industry at least, technologies for power trains and countering cyber-security threats. However, it would be foolish, short-sighted and probably politically and socially unacceptable to ignore the experiences, capabilities and resources which regions have built up during their long histories of successful competition. The challenge, for Coventry and elsewhere, is to discover new outlets for the surviving assets and meld them with new ones.

The economies of many regions and cities have changed in fundamental ways, resulting in competitiveness being based on foundations in addition to cost efficiency, product quality and differentiation, control of strategic resources (including intellectual property) and the close integration of supply and value chains. The notion that recombining existing resources, that is resource recombination or RR for short, rather than the acquisition of new ones, is an important source of innovation and value creation for firms is far from new. However, the logic of RR is equally persuasive when applied beyond the boundaries of the firm. Here, the term "enterprise" is used to recognise that innovation as a process is often the result of concerted activity by groups of economic actors pursuing a common goal which has market value. It becomes even stronger when knowledge is recognised as potentially the most dynamic and valuable of productive resources. The region can be seen as a dynamic reservoir of skills, competences and knowledge resources rather than a portfolio of businesses and products.

The modern car is a complex electro-mechanical construct connected to the Internet-of-Things (IoT). The technologies which are core to designing and developing the "connected car", and the self-driving ones of the future (AVs-autonomous vehicles), are a combination of familiar automotive ones and ICTs. Over the next ten years the cost of a new car accounted for by electronics components could rise to 50%. These technologies largely reside with IT "giants" such as Google, Apple and Microsoft rather than the familiar car makers such as Ford, VW and Jaguar. As a result new alliances and networks are being created and new entrants to the automotive industry emerging.

The innovation process is largely determined by synthesising, coupling and cross-fertilising existing knowledge and experience rather than being the product of radical breakthroughs. Local economies and firms have to continuously strive to change their internal asset structures and external relationships to develop skill in new technologies and exploit new market opportunities; such dynamic capabilities are the ways "by which firms achieve new resource configurations as markets emerge, collide, split, evolve and die" (Eisenhardt and Martin 2000, p. 1107). Or, put another way, "the firm's potential to systematically solve problems, formed by its propensity to sense opportunities and threats, to make timely and market oriented decisions, and to change its resource base" (Barreto 2010, p. 271) is vital for survival and ensuring prosperity. This capability is important where the rate of change technological change is slow and incremental, but even more so when, as now, rapid change is endemic. Consequently, learned organisational processes, which possess a strong degree of path dependence, may become a burden rather than a strength. The current technological revolution in the automotive industry is a major example.

Knowledge: A Key Resource

Enterprises possessing a high degree of technical knowledge have developed sophisticated skills in product and services design, optimisation of productionisation and improving functionality and reliability. Market knowledge is the guide which stimulates enterprises to apply their technical knowledge in profitable, customer-centric, directions. Knowledge quality is usually taken to have two dimensions, knowledge breadth, the range of relevant and potentially useful sources of knowledge enterprises can access, and knowledge depth, the level of sophistication of that knowledge. Technological and market knowledge breadth taken together can enhance innovation performance by promoting the ability to identify and fill market gaps and opportunities (Zahra 2008). Resource complementarity, as contrasted with resource supplementarity, refers to the ways in which different domains of knowledge can be combined with each other and the other resources available to the enterprise to generate synergistic RRs.

Resource renewal reflects the balance between existing and newly acquired resources. Whilst the possession of a strong portfolio of existing resources is a potential source of RRs, "there are limitations with reliance solely on resources internal to the firm for generating new productive resource combinations because it is unlikely that the exact same set of resources can be used to develop new and more valuable combinations over and over again" (Wiklund and Shepherd 2009, p. 195).

Organisations need the dynamic capability to exploit opportunities and deploy resources effectively. Dynamic capability can be disaggregated into three different capacities; sensing, seizing and transformational (reconfiguring). Sensing new opportunities is very much a scanning, creation, learning, and interpretative activity. Seizing capacity is the ability to address new opportunities through new processes, products, services and business models. Transformational capacity relates to maintaining competitiveness through reconfiguring resources. Taken together these capacities enable the enterprise to find and exploit new value-enhancing opportunities. Innovation is promoted in environments where resources can constantly be redirected efficiently and effectively. The movement of critical resources, knowledge and people is facilitated by the development of diverse avenues of product and technology sharing. This is particularly important when inventions and innovations do not always find use where they first emerge, but need to be migrated to other environments to be fully exploited.

The Triple Helix

Firms, as consistently argued here, are not the only actors in economic development. The Triple Helix formulation (see Etzkowitz 2008), stresses the roles of governments, businesses and (higher) education forming a research nexus working in concentration to create what is often characterised as an innovative milieu. Universities and research institutes provide highly skilled labour and a stream of commercial spin-out opportunities from their research activities. When this sector works in harmony with government and entrepreneurs, as a "Triple Helix", the constellation can lead to an innovative milieu and a dynamic economy. A feature of the Triple Helix approach is that regional development processes are conceived of as being interactive rather than linear and eventually becoming endogenous rather than having some exogenous elements to them (for example central government decisions to relocate particular activities to a region). In principle, therefore, the helix should develop a growth momentum of its own. This does not mean that a continued stream of both inward and domestic (at the regional level) investment is not required; however, the processes which generate the continued flow of investment will come from within rather than needing to be orchestrated from outside. In essence the Triple Helix is an evolutionary model of development which generates a high rate of both product and process innovation leading to the creation of new businesses as clusters evolve through time (Fig. 10.1).

There are many different ways of describing the economic development relationships between government, industry and universities. The Triple Helix is sometimes encapsulated in a simple Venn diagram form of the type shown in Fig. 10.1. This representation emphasizes the multiple roles of the three domains in local economic development. All three have roles in their own right, the non-overlapping elements of the circles point to the self-evident realization that a strong triple-helix cannot be built around weak strands. Bilateral relationships are also important, there needs to be productive overlaps between pairs of main actors. Finally, the area in the middle where all three domains overlap underlines the role of "social concertation" and pro-activity on

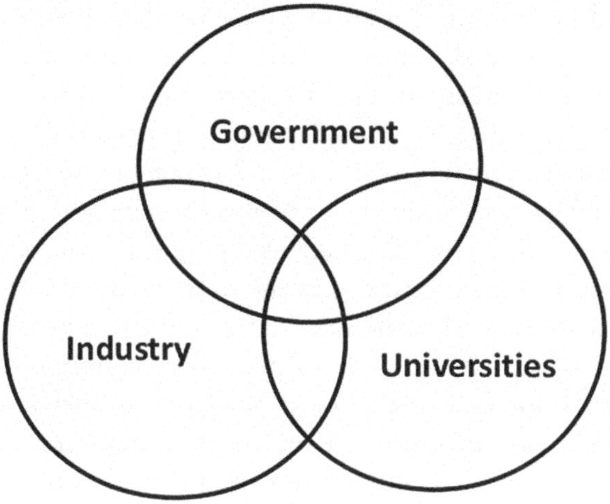

Fig. 10.1 The main actors in economic development

the part of partners in promoting economic development at the regional level. In this view, successful economic development requires a concerted effort to ensure conscious co-ordination between the different parties to work towards the same aims. Such social integration requires a high degree of communication and trust between the parties. Whilst sharing a common cultural background is a useful context for social integration, it is not enough. Conscious effort directed towards coordinating activity is also required, economic development at the regional level does not "just happen" nor is it the product of external forces such as national development policies. Nor can a strong whole be built from weak parts. Innovation is rooted in a process of continuous interaction across organizations and creating "thick ties" to build social capital.

Three main configurations in the positioning of the university, industry and government institutional spheres relative to each other can usefully be distinguished. A statist configuration is one where government plays the lead role, driving universities and industry, but also limiting their capacity to initiate and develop innovative transformations. A laissez-faire configuration, characterised by limited state intervention in the economy, is present to some extent in some EU countries; here, industry is the driving force and the other two spheres act as ancillary support structures and have limited roles in innovation. Universities are essentially providers of skilled human capital, and government is a reluctant regulator of market mechanisms. However, the creation of an effective and proactive Knowledge Society requires a balanced configuration, where universities, research institutes and other knowledge institutions act in partnership with industry and government and may even take the lead in joint initiatives. The balanced configuration offers the most important insights for innovation, as the most favourable environments for innovation are created at the intersections of the spheres.

Figure 10.2 shows another way of picturing economic development. Whilst Fig. 10.1 focused attention at the institutional level, Fig. 10.2 highlights the major processes involved. In a balanced configuration the circles in the two diagrams do not map directly onto one another. So, the role of industry is not simply confined to knowledge exploitation any more than modern universities limit, or are expected by society at large to confine, themselves to knowledge generation. Note also that these processes are not seen as being linearly or sequentially related, rather they are overlapping, dynamic and synergistic. They are also

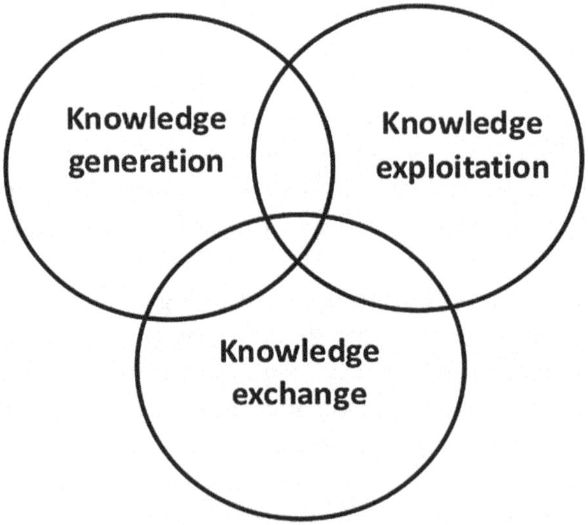

Fig. 10.2 Knowledge processes

long-term with one aim, among others, being to develop a collective understanding of the unique value which a cluster or region can generate. Improving a region's competitiveness depends on adopting an holistic approach to policy which outlives transient political administrations.

In practice, firm level interventions aimed at improving sustainable regional economic performance are very costly and distort the competitive workings of the economy, whilst policies directed at broad levels of the economy will have little effect. "Meso-level agents" have been found to be effective and have a significant performance enhancing effect for firms located in regions of advanced countries. Meso-level agents are those which sit in the middle of the economy between the micro-level actors, such as individual firms, and the macro-economic agencies such as governments. Examples include regional or industry development agencies, standards organisations, national research institutes and so on.

We also need to question whether Triple Helix processes will successfully persist over the long term in the absence of external (exogeneous) pressures and influences. The three main parties to the helix have different motives and do not naturally respond to the same set of incentives. Government actors will be motivated by political survival and, more optimistically, the democratically inspired pursuit of social welfare. University researchers are often motivated by curiosity and may be de-motivated by pressures to justify their work in terms of its short-term commercial application. Businesses will be motivated by commercial returns. The survival of the helix requires continued promotion of research at the same time as responding to the external pressures to maintain the competitiveness of the local economy. This is a delicate balance, particularly as (curiosity-driven research) does not reflect the same spatial boundaries as local economic competitiveness.

Smart Specialization

"Smart Specialisation" is a means of priority setting for regional innovation strategies in order to achieve economic transformation by developing competitive advantage through promoting strength in R&D, exploiting the unique characteristics of a region and matching those with business needs. Although Smart Specialisation is still a place-based approach, the notion of "place" transcends physical proximity to include virtual space. It entails focussing on a limited set of priorities for any region and attempts to avoid duplication and fragmentation of effort at the EU level in order to promote global competitiveness. Smart Specialisation should also exploit new forms of innovation including "open" and "user-led" approaches. The challenge is to match research effort and investment with market potential, business needs and capabilities. We need to develop links between sectors, cooperation between regions and promote "superclusters" based on collaboration between existing and emerging clusters.

Development of a Smart Specialisation strategy must be grounded in a strong evidence base gathered from a number of sources. The process of developing competitiveness, which is more than ever based on the capacity to generate and exploit innovations, is an incremental and cyclical one. However, we cannot afford to keep going round the same cycle. Cluster development strategy needs to be incremental in building on a rich existing evidence base to generate new insights into likely future sources of competitiveness and cyclical in that it helps to move us up an expanding spiral. Within clusters, it is important to have economic actors who complement each other. Successful clusters are not "towers of Babel" of companies all trying to do the same things, the competition to be heard may defeat attempts to organise clusters for the pursuit of collective aims. A balance between compactness, giving a clear focus, and complementarity, promoting cooperation, may provide the best option.

However, the continuing long-term success of a specialised cluster depends on its ability to change and adapt to a dynamic global competitive environment, emerging technologies and shifting customer demand. Clusters and their host regions that are over-specialised may be vulnerable to external market shocks and will find rapid adaptation difficult. However, changes in the macro-environment also present opportunities which emerging clusters can exploit. In some cases such clusters may be based on thematic networks; themes could be economic activity directed towards "green" products and services, for example LCV, or smart mobility. Whereas product clusters are often developed, at least initially, bottom-up and autonomously through the natural processes of agglomeration and exploitation of economies of scale, thematic clusters are often created through policy interventions and exploit economies of scope rather than scale. Of course, some successful clusters will have both product and thematic elements.

The transport industry clusters of the future will not simply build on or replicate existing automotive industry clusters based on ICE technologies. Mature clusters are often anchored by a small number of very large firms at the top of supply chains. The existing West Midlands auto industry cluster is no exception. It has well developed, historically tested and refined, lean, agile supply chains. But new suppliers and innovators find it very difficult to break into the established industry structures. Intellectual Property is highly protected. Technology is mature and advances incrementally. Many SMEs see the electro- and smart mobility sectors as opportunities to work outside the existing automotive supply chain and innovation network structures. On the other hand, they also see the need to interact with a larger grouping of diverse agents and actors in order to access the resources, markets and expertise which they need to be successful. In particular they value collaboration, creativity and opportunity above competition even if this means a greater degree of sharing of their own knowledge assets than is common in an established cluster.

Recent research undertaken by Coventry University identified four major barriers to SME participation in the West Midlands low carbon transport sector. Firstly, a lack of financial support for new product development. Secondly, innovation being stifled by successful SME's being bought out by larger companies and, in the process, closing off routes to market for innovative developments. Thirdly, a lack of a strategic lead from economic development agencies and major companies. Fourthly, a shortage of skilled engineers and technicians. The barriers to productionisation stage were very high in the view of those SMEs which even managed to reached this stage of product development.

There is also a strong realisation that no one place is likely to be able to provide all the inputs needed for collective success. Each region has its own unique mix of history, culture, resources, institutions and strengths on which it can build. Weaknesses can be counteracted by opportunities for collaborating with others who have complementary strengths. Threats can be countered through mutually beneficial collaboration rather than unproductive competition. New electro- and smart mobility clusters need to be based in a philosophy and strategy of smart specialisation, focusing on existing strengths but collaborating with other clusters working in the same area and with complementary strengths.

Glocalisation

It is a commonplace observation that knowledge and the pace of innovation are growing exponentially whereas our capacity to increase output is, at best, growing linearly. The leap from, "local and linear" to "global and exponential", sometimes summarized in the somewhat ugly term "glocalization", has to be based on the specific contributions regions can make within a global economic environment characterized by cooperation as much as competition.

Glocalization means local production made possible through sharing knowledge in a much more open way than has been the case in the past. By focusing on key sectors where they have an advantage, regions can enable their SMEs to play a key role in innovation and compete globally. Creating such a system will require new policy and funding approaches. The global technology-sharing element of glocalization has the potential to cut engineering and development costs to a level much lower than they have been. Production can be made simple, fast and affordable everywhere and attuned to different local needs and markets. Local production will be based around integrated supply chains featuring a high degree of SME participation. But this outcome, in turn, depends on sharing the best practice and knowledge on a global and open basis.

The new generation of clusters will be based not just around technical innovation but also institutional and system innovations. Institutional innovation must create networks of scientists, firms, universities, public authorities and users engaged in the processes of co-creation. Systems innovation will re-shape networks and practices to embrace far greater openness, collaboration and knowledge sharing. Whilst innovation systems are becoming more complex, innovation processes will need to become more distributed and may have distinct local characteristics. Taken together these shifts will result in the transformative innovation required to meet the challenges of sustainable development.

Clusters and Spatial Proximity: Does Place Matter Anymore?

A potential criticism of the proposition that clusters are an effective force in regional economic development is the emergence of more globalised industries that are knowledge-based and the ubiquity of technologies that promote and enable communication and collaboration over virtual spaces. In such cases physical co-location of cluster activities is not necessary and may bring unnecessary costs. But it can be argued that virtual communication technologies and developments in global transportation and logistics have made localisation economies more, not less, critical to the competitive performance of firms. Virtual communications and similar technologies have highlighted the importance of tacit knowledge and close personal relationships between economic agents (people) as key determinants for the competitive success of firms. At the same time, global logistics have made access to basic production factors such as capital and non-specialised labour largely open to all, whereas flows of specialised knowledge and the rich knowledge interactions that lead to valuable innovations remain stronger between agents in close physical proximity to one another than among geographically dispersed firms. On the other hand, knowledge does not recognize the boundaries of physical space and developing communication technologies are allowing "rich" knowledge sharing and development to take place effectively across and within virtual spaces.

The key question is what binds clusters together and, by implication, whether these binding forces are stronger across physical than virtual space. "Cluster glue" can occur in a number of forms. It could be the cooperative activities of a cluster organisation, (funded) projects or programmes can also play a productive role. Glue can arise from inside the cluster based on mutual recognition of common interests, strong and accepted leadership, communications events, interactions and rituals or be provided externally through policy interventions. Often both forms are needed, but externally injected glue can at best be a catalyst to help boost the effectiveness of internal glue. Unless there is some commitment of members of the cluster to a common cause and trust between them external interventions will not work.

The strongest component of cluster glue will be the development of a common stock of knowledge and its accompanying technical language. Knowledge interactions employing highly developed and specific mechanisms for sharing key technical and business knowledge across research centres, universities and other cluster partners through executive workshops, secondments and other events are key. Knowledge sharing and trust are the vital underpinnings. If the knowledge to be shared is predominantly tacit rather than explicit, then localization may be the preferred outcome. A related issue, of potentially major significance in the case of Coventry, is the role of "anchor" firms. Anchor firms deliver wide economic advantages to their regions by acting as hubs in supply chains, are more likely to be active in global trade, and invest more in research and development.

Universities and the Coventry Local Economy

Expectations of what a university should do and be like have changed in recent times and will continue to develop. This is nowhere more obvious than in the relationship between universities and the areas where they are located, particularly if that area is a city. Old and outworn distinctions and enmities between town and gown have long since been marginalised as universities have become major economic, social and political forces in city centres and beyond. Government industrial strategy now has major expectations of HEIs as deliverers of national repositioning, whether the UK leaves or stays within the EU. Local leadership teams recognise universities' central roles in promoting innovation, developing workforce skills, building fit-for-purpose knowledge and research infrastructure, enhancing the business environment, and place-making. The University of Warwick, for example, has identified three major dimensions determining its relationship to place; leadership, partnership, and citizenship. The central role of universities as anchor institutions in local growth and development is now a given. Their local interventions should now be undertaken in genuine partnership with local role players and beneficiaries, rather than being driven solely by academic requirements. And they need to be a consistently 'good citizens' in the way they engage with their host communities, including managing any potential downsides contingent on their activities.

The overwhelming importance of the higher education sector to the Coventry economy is self-evident as the figures given below emphasise. They relate to the period 2015–2018 and will change over time. They are given here to provide a background against which the discussion of the role of universities play in local economies and not as definitive statements of the position at any point in time. However, the overall message is clear. Higher education is now a major economic force within the West Midlands and, given the spatial concentration of Coventry University in the city centre, particularly Coventry.

Coventry University has 30,000 students, supports 12,200 jobs across the UK and contributes almost £800 million in annual gross value added (GVA) to the economy. Graduates of Coventry University, which is the fasting growing higher education institution in the UK over the last 15 years, will contribute £560 million to the UK economy over their lifetime, while one in every seven higher education students in the West Midlands attends the university. The local impact is, of course, proportionately greater. One in 25 jobs in Coventry is supported by the university; in terms of direct employment one in every 46 jobs in Coventry is with the Coventry University Group. Full-time students from outside Coventry spend more than £145m p.a. in the city resulting in 1500 additional jobs. 83% of Coventry University students move into a high skilled occupation after graduation, compared to the national position of 45% and Coventry's students are among the most entrepreneurial in the UK, creating 250 graduate start-ups and more start-up social enterprises than any UK university. The economic impact is not just limited to students. The University employs approximately 3330 staff, 45% of whom live in the city and 86% regionally.

University employees inject more than £82 m p.a. into the UK economy, of which 46% is retained in Coventry.

Warwick University has over 26,000 students. Some 7000 of these come from outside the EU and a further 2500 from inside the EU but outside the UK. The university employs some 6640 academic and professional staff and supports a further 9245. Just over 40% of these live in Coventry and a further 21% in the Warwickshire towns and villages immediately south of the main campus. Overall the university contributes over £1 billion GVA per annum to the economy, only 13% or so of this is accounted for by UK student fees. It owns and cares for over 700 acres of prime land covering part of the southern area of the city and Warwickshire.

However, 56,000 students, 21,000 jobs and £1.8 billion GVA is only the start. Universities are also major investors. Coventry and Warwick combined had plans to invest over £1 billion over period 2016–2020. The bulk of this was on buildings for academic, research and student accommodation purposes in the city and south Warwickshire. As of May 2018, it was estimated that there were plans to build new accommodation to house 6000 students in the city centre or very close by. Much of this is private sector investment and adds a further estimated £370 million to the £1 billion direct investment spend by the universities themselves. These investments are transforming the city landscape, physically, economically, socially and culturally.

But a concentration on the economic impacts of universities, particularly innovative and successful ones such as Coventry and Warwick, only tells a part of the story. For example, student volunteering enriches and promotes community projects and builds links between students and local people. Around 1000 Warwick students provide 13,000 hours each year in local help. Firm data is not available for Coventry students, but several hundred are known to be actively involved. The Warwick Arts Centre is the major cultural and entertainment facility in Coventry and Warwickshire and has over 300,000 visitors a year. Both universities' sports facilities are progressively, as they are being renewed and upgraded, being made accessible to the public. The two universities are also taking major roles in *Coventry 2021 City of Culture* programmes. The Warwick Science Park, part of Warwick University, supports over

140 small businesses on site and provides virtual tenancies and facilities for many more. The Coventry University Technology Park houses start-ups, divisions of major established businesses and enterprise agencies.

A Motor City Reborn?

The 2019 automotive news agenda has been dominated by job cuts, lay-offs, shifting of production to other countries and seemingly endless uncertainty over the UK's future in the EU. These themes can crowd out a broader and more positive narrative. Whilst this book is not meant to be a celebration of Coventry's history, although there is much to be proud of, it should take a positive view of the city's longer-term future. The city has, like many others, been subject to cyclical forces beyond its immediate control; adversity has been a driver of change. But adversity creates opportunities as well as threatening the prosperity of existing activities. Currently (early 2019), the market attractiveness of conventional ICE vehicles, particularly diesels, is waning in the face of pressures to reduce their negative environmental impacts. The switch to EVs entails exploiting new power technologies which are not the familiar home ground of the car producers such as JLR. On the other hand, the rapid rise of connected vehicles and the race to develop (fully) autonomous vehicles provides a major impetus for the industry, particularly in the smart mobility arena. The car may be different in the future, but it shows little sign of going away. The question is whether Coventry is able to benefit from these major changes in technologies and markets. The signs are promising.

The West Midlands region benefits from several competitive advantages in the electric vehicle and smart mobility sectors, based on its historical traditions in the automotive industry, the presence of large OEMs (JLR and BMW) and automotive suppliers, and universities and R&D centres with advanced automotive engineering programmes and complementary research specialisms. This is supported by national and regional policies, economic development agencies and grants for the reduction of CO_2 emissions and related technology innovations in low carbon transport.

The early 2019 auto industry headlines were dominated by the announcement that JLR was to cut its global workforce by 10%. Worrying as this may be, it is worthwhile noting that the company's workforce grew from 17,255 in 2011/2012 to 43,224 in 2017/2018. At the same time as job losses were announced in 2019, JLR announced major investment in EVs including a battery plant to the west of Coventry. Much of JLR's Coventry presence is in research and development, advanced engineering, product testing and activities other than vehicle assembly. JLR is an archetypal anchor firm and has a major impact on Coventry.

Warwick Manufacturing Group (WMG) is a world leading research institute which has been widely held up as a model for how universities and business can successfully collaborate. WMG has a £100 million collaborative research programme with JLR, a £19 million LCV Technology Project and a £74 million p.a. high value manufacturing Catapult programme and many other thriving collaborations with industrial partners.

£150 million is being invested in the National Automotive Innovation Campus (NAIC) building and its research activities through a long-term commitment between Jaguar Land Rover, Tata Motors European Technical Centre, WMG and the University of Warwick, along with an expanding network of supplier companies. NAIC will enable academic/industry teams to work together in state-of-the-art buildings, with tailored equipment to create and integrate breakthrough technologies with a whole system approach crossing multiple disciplines. It will provide 1000 jobs and address the shortage of skilled R&D staff in the automotive supply chain, creating a pipeline of people into companies.

A consortium of Coventry City Council, Coventry and Warwickshire Local Enterprise Partnership, and WMG was recently awarded £80 million, to establish a new national facility for battery manufacturing development (UKBIC–UK Battery Industrialisation Centre); the centre will open in 2020.

The Institute for Future Transport and Cities (FTC) at Coventry University brings together world class expertise in disciplines across art and design, human factors, engineering, manufacturing, computer systems and business studies to deliver "safe and sustainable transport solutions fit for the cities of the future". Major dimensions of FTC's work will include research to demonstrate new technologies, training and skills development, and commercialisation of new technologies to deliver impact and business growth. The Institute builds on existing successful strategic partnerships with organisations such as Horiba-MIRA. The FTC is also home to the National Transport Design Centre (NTDC), a state-of-the-art facility dedicated to exploring new areas of transport design research and creating new technologies.

HORIBA MIRA (formerly the Motor Industry Research Association) is an independent automotive research and technology organisation based just north of Coventry. It has a staff of over 1000. MIRA provides research, development, certification, testing and engineering analysis services to automotive companies throughout the world. The services offered provide comprehensive coverage of all the disciplines required for automotive design and development, as well as for many other industries with similar requirements. HORIBA MIRA's activities include vehicle electrical system architecture and integration, system and software safety engineering, and automotive cyber security.

The Centre for Connected and Autonomous Automotive Research (C-CAAR) is a joint venture between MIRA and Coventry University located at the heart of MIRA Technology Park. It will provide an environment to stimulate test and evaluate the security and safety of connected and autonomous vehicles; undertake research to accelerate the development of new products and services in the CAV segment and produce a pipeline of talent to support growth of the CAV sector.

Coventry has a large population of small (less than 20 employees) SMEs but a relatively small number of large (>100) ones. In 2017 Coventry was the origin of the second (after Cambridge) highest number of patents per resident, significantly ahead of the third-placed city. It also had the fastest growing population. Fostering the new generations of Coventry SMEs is a major opportunity, but will depend on recognising the problems that they face, particularly in contributing to the motor industry.

Coventry's roots as a centre of the car industry began with a small, but growing, number of entrepreneurs adapting bicycles to become motorized passenger vehicles. The fledgling industry relied on the ingenuity of a skilled workforce engaged in craft production. The demand for small military vehicles in the First World War was a catalyst in the introduction of more reliable, cheaper and scalable methods of production ultimately leading to mass production methods. Coventry, along with other centres such Birmingham, Manchester and Oxford became a major site of vehicle assembly. However, new entrants to the market from Europe and later Asia, initially Japan successfully captured a substantial share of the market based on lower costs and improved product reliability. Success in the future will not derive from the ingenuity of mainly amateur engineers or the economies of scale of mass production, but from the design and development of vehicles which are environmentally sustainable, safer, smarter and accessible. The new economic, technological and educational developments in Coventry are well placed to lead the way.

References

Barreto, I. (2010). Dynamic Capabilities: A Review of Past Research and an Agenda for the Future. *Journal of Management, 36*(1), 256–280.

Eisenhardt, K. M., & Martin, J. A. (2000). Dynamic Capabilities: What Are They? *Strategic Management Journal, 21*(10/11), 1105–1121.

Etzkowitz, H. (2008). *The Triple Helix: University–Industry–Government in Action*. New York: Routledge.

Morosini, P. (2003). Industrial Clusters, Knowledge Integration and Performance. *World Development, 32*(2), 305–326.

Thrift, N. (2008). *Space*. Available at http://www.nigelthrift.files.wordpress.com.

Wiklund, J., & Shepherd, D. A. (2009). The Effectiveness of Alliances and Acquisitions: The Role of Resource Combination Activities. *Entrepreneurship: Theory & Practice, 33*(1), 193–212.

Zahra, S. A. (2008). The Virtuous Cycle of Discovery and Creation of Entrepreneurial Opportunities. *Strategic Entrepreneurship Journal, 2*(3), 243–257.

11
Concluding Remarks

Jason Begley, Tom Donnelly, David Jarvis
and Paul Sissons

Globalisation has powerfully shaped the evolution of places. Historically and contemporarily, Coventry has experienced significant economic shifts and changes of fortune as its place in the regional, national and international economy has changed. The contributions in this book demonstrate the complex and multifarious relationships which underlie Coventry's evolution, their links to globalising forces, and the positive and negative consequences of this. The opening-up of international markets and the accompanying flows of capital and labour have supported some of its most successful periods of the city's growth, but

J. Begley (✉) · T. Donnelly · D. Jarvis · P. Sissons
Coventry University, Coventry, UK
e-mail: Jason.Begley@coventry.ac.uk

T. Donnelly
e-mail: aa5962@coventry.ac.uk

D. Jarvis
e-mail: ecy037@coventry.ac.uk

P. Sissons
e-mail: Paul.Sissons@coventry.ac.uk

J. Begley et al. (eds.), *Revival of a City*, Palgrave Studies in Economic History,
https://doi.org/10.1007/978-3-030-22822-4_11

have also functioned in the opposite direction and are implicated in the deepest of social and economic troughs endured by the city. It is tempting, therefore, when considering the impact of these forces on the city to focus on key periods; when the city was at its most visible as an international actor, a major player in the world market for automotives at a time when such businesses were becoming so large as to be considered integral in their importance to economies. Alternatively, the focus might also be placed on the time when such globalising forces were themselves becoming more tangible in their import and effect on the city, having a profound impact on the culture, the character and even the structures of the city itself. In the last number of decades not only have instances of Foreign Direct Investment (FDI) and mobile labour become more prevalent in Coventry, but local and regional authorities have increasingly looked to external investment and markets to help revitalise the city.

Yet, as we have seen throughout the pages of this work, the influence of global markets have played a major role throughout Coventry's history. The city had enjoyed a period of prosperity in the second half of the nineteenth century, as it had benefitted from burgeoning markets for textiles and watches. This had seen the city grow in size, with an influx of migrant labour attracted by the comparatively well-paid work. Once these trades started to flounder, in large part resulting from competition from French, Swiss and Belgian importers, the city entered a period of depression. As Donnelly notes though, 'It [Coventry] had prospered due to the emergence of the textile industries, fell away due to its own failings'. In other words globalisation has offered Coventry opportunities to grow its local economy through exports such as textiles; subsequent decline is more attributable to the shortcomings of local firms. This would be a recurring theme in Coventry's relationship with globalising forces, the city would make early advances as the manufacturing vanguard of a technological wave only to lose out in the longer-term due to the rise of domestic and international competition in key industrial sectors. In the interwar period bicycle firms began to decline and in their stead motor vehicle manufacture came to the fore. Primarily this was because of the proximity of technologically advanced manufacturing firms with access to specialised, skilled labour being able to take advantage of emerging technologies. However, timing was also important as was access to capital reserves and the profitability of the firms making the switch. What drove this process was also important as bicycle firms, coming under considerable pressure from business rivals, were forced to diversify into new and emerging markets.

The war years and those in between marked something of a hiatus from the opportunities and pressures of international trade. Early in the Great War the decision was taken by Reginald McKenna to place a tariff on luxury goods such as cars, to protect English manufacturers from American firms seeking to fill niches left vacant by manufacturers now engaged in armaments and munitions production. Effectively this decision shielded auto manufacturers, a key sector at the time for Coventry, allowing them to expand their operations behind duties. The twenties and early thirties represented something of a golden era for Coventry's automakers, but this also represented something of a lost opportunity too. As Busch discusses, firms that grew up behind protective walls were not well placed to compete with external firms once this shield was removed and this was even more detrimental in the long-run.

Perhaps less appreciated in the literature is the key point of Busch's chapter, namely the suspension of market operations, either through tariff protection or through government intervention in the form of armaments production, was disadvantageous to the economic fortunes of a medium-sized city such as Coventry. As Stiglitz (2017) argues, to retreat from globalisation is a negative sum, or lose-lose situation. While globalisation has contributed to deindustrialisation in places such as Coventry, trying to mitigate these forces through tariffs, for example, can be even more detrimental to the success of local business. What comes through strongly in analysis of the Coventry manufacturing sector during the Second World War was the lack of preparation that was undertaken for the post-conflict world. This was despite the manufacturers themselves, across a range of interrelated industries being aware of the movements of their international competitors, who as early as 1941 were manoeuvring to be best placed to take advantage of post-war markets.

Coventry manufacturers, in contrast, were still focussed on armaments production and were willing to accept a period of difficult recovery in the aftermath of the struggle as the cost for rapidly increasing output. This was partly due to the rapidity of rearmament and the pressures of war. But a contributing factor was the extended period of protection followed by the guaranteed orders of wartime production. Immediately after the war the firms turned to outdated models to drive sales, while also depending on production facilities more suited to wartime production than peacetime, leaving an overly-specialised city with a major concentration of semi-skilled and skilled workers more vulnerable to market shocks.

Initially these problems did not manifest; in the buoyant markets of the post-war period Coventry's manufacturers succeeded spectacularly, becoming major international producers, with firms such as Rootes having numerous overseas operations to tap into American and European markets. However, this period of boom was deceptive; soon enough the inherent flaws in Coventry motor sector would be cruelly exposed, with international competition starkly demonstrating the shortcomings of the industry. However, it would be remiss to overlook Coventry's boom years, to ignore the significant social and economic changes that occurred in the city thanks largely to the profits generated by access to international markets, before the cycle of growth and decline, so evident at the beginning of the century, repeated itself once more.

Haynes discusses the changes brought about by the expansion and success of Coventry in these years, focussing on social and cultural changes as much as economic; and there were many. Looking at the period of the long boom, from circa the late 1940s–1970s, Coventry enjoyed a period of rapid change and growth. Population growth offers a simple but impactful metric, as does the growth in manufacturing employment and production. This translated into high wages and improved education opportunities required for training skilled workers. Labour travelled from far and wide to take advantage of high quality employment opportunities, and Coventry became a melting pot of different cultures and identities. It's easy now to underplay the boom because of the problems that followed, but over two decades of prosperity were experienced on the back of exports and the city was transformed. The language used to describe the city is a testimony to this; a symbol of post-war recovery, an architectural triumph that became a showplace for foreign dignitaries, a technological powerhouse and so forth. Economic success intersected with all facets of life, from buildings to bands. Flows of goods in and out became the life blood of the city, as global links deepened. This was perhaps the globalising vision made good, a place with a unique identity but plugged into a wider network of actors.

Nowhere was this more evident and, arguably, enduring, than in the changes to the cityscape in the latter half of the twentieth century. Up until the Second World War the city had remained largely medieval in character. Plans had been in place pre-war to overhaul key structures, widen streets and open up the city to take advantage of emerging transport technologies. Gibson had been at the forefront of this process, but the interruptions of war had put these plans on hold. The vagaries of the hostilities had seen the city bombed in the early 1940s, giving further impetus to the process of change. Post-war reconstruction reflected the new character of the city, embracing modernist architecture and redesigning the urban transport network. Though such plans borrowed from pre-war thinking, the city was still perceived, internally and externally, to have broken with its past and embraced more outward-looking ideas.

Kershaw captures this new spirit in his discussion of how the changes to the city were perceived by residents. The apparent departure from the old Coventry and the rise of the new was evident for those that lived through this period. Buildings that had been said to be 'quaint' and 'olde worlde' were to be replaced with new structures that were described as being futuristic and even reminiscent of science fiction shows. Even outside observers referred to Coventry as the 'City of the future'. While these changes were not always welcomed, nonetheless the spirit of the period was captured in these constructions and mostly viewed in a positive light by contemporaries. Though this initial enthusiasm would wane with time, it demonstrates how Coventry was changing in outlook and appearance during the era of the long boom.

However, as fast as Coventry grew, its competitors grew faster. Yet, it was not just international competition; Coventry businesses were also static in terms of domestic market share. By the mid 1960s the limits of the domestic markets had been reached and export was proving increasingly difficult. The city's automakers were struggling to compete against domestic and international products. One of the first firms to exhibit signs of the difficulties was the Rootes group, founded by Billie and Reggie Rootes in the late 1920s. Having made an enormous leap forward from dealership to manufacturing through acquisition, the firm had established itself as one of the 'Big Six' in motor manufacturing, supplanting Singer, by the outbreak of the war, during which the company distinguished itself in its contribution to arms production. This would not ultimately save the company though; by the mid 1960s it was losing profitability and three years of bad trading at the end of the decade saw it taken-over by the American firm Chrysler. Rootes was the first major motor firm to enter overseas ownership, in what would prove to be a difficult decade for Coventry.

During the 1970s the core of the Coventry economy, vehicle manufacturing and engineering, went into steady decline as extensive deindustrialisation began to occur. A range of reasons and perspectives were offered for this at the time and in post-event analysis; structural, managerial, poor industrial relations, a militant labour force, a technology and design gap, outdated production methods and growing international competition. The depth of the economic malaise that followed was severe. Subsequently, the collapse of motor manufacturing in Coventry has become seen as the departure point for enormous change in the city, as the entire economic base shifted, seeing industry decline significantly and being replaced by service activities. However, the city had endured such churn before, with industry being forced to diversify into new markets, taking advantage of new technologies and exploiting new opportunities. What differed with the deindustrialisation process of the 1970s and 1980s in Coventry was that it was part of a global shift, an ongoing reorganisation of economies and workforces to take advantage of new modes of production and exchange.

The decline of the motor industry in Coventry wasn't so exceptional an event as the context in which it occurred. Collis is careful to place the decline of Coventry in a wider setting, concentrating on waves of FDI, but seeing it as part of a series of events connected to globalisation generally. He stresses that Coventry's economic problems should be seen against the background of a weakening national economy and a declining level of international competiveness. Notably he observes that the city actually gained relatively more employment in the 1980s than it lost during the recessionary years as it moved from relative competitive disadvantage to relative competitive advantage, though for lower levels of remuneration. What, he argues, gravely weakened Coventry's local economy was the corporatist structure of many of the major firms, with subsidiary companies dominating the local economy as part of multi-plant enterprises and high concentrations of workers in relatively few businesses, making the city vulnerable to sudden changes in firm fortunes.

During this period the global motor industry itself was undergoing rapid restructuring, with increasing frequency of mergers and acquisitions mostly as a result of the reduction of trade barriers and FDI spreading, allied to technological change. Furthermore, assembly operations were increasingly shifted toward low cost areas; Coventry, as a city focused on final assembly, lost out in this process, as did the wider West Midlands and the national sector as a whole. Little wonder that government planning and intervention in the motor industry became a motif during these years. One example offered is that of the Massey Ferguson factory, at Banner Lane, the demise of which was inextricably related to the development of the company as a large transnational corporation; mergers in the early 1990s had seen the Banner Lane factory fall down the list of priorities for the company, eventually being deemed surplus to requirements. Set against such tales of decay are the positive impacts FDI has had on the city, the safeguarding of jobs by Geely, or the introduction of new plant by Chrysler at Ryton.

It is this point, that globalisation has brought change, good and bad, that dominates the remaining thematic chapters of the book. Sissons, Begley, Morris and Mackie repeatedly return to the mantra of transformation, showing how globalising forces brought about the reorganisation of business, labour mobility, occupations and above all education and skills, with a new emphasis on the knowledge economy and closer cooperation amongst business, government and education. In terms of occupational change, Begley focuses on the changing sector allocation of the Coventry labour force, and in doing so demonstrates how shifting global markets and emerging economic activities, played a key role in the transition from industry to service activities. What emerges in this analysis is the fact that the Coventry labour force, through increasing specialisation, had reached an economic cul-de-sac by the time the city's motor industry had entered a period of decline. The very skills that had given the city such enormous advantages in the beginning of the century were now no longer valued, not least because of changing production methods in the industry, with less emphasis on skills and more emphasis on knowledge of a range of simple tasks.

Many of the trends perceived in Coventry were matched across the West Midlands and nationally; however, specialisation and the unique character of the Coventry workforce meant the trough was deeper and the recovery slower. Attempts by local authorities to mitigate the worse effects of the downturn had a silo effect, with skilled, mobile workers locating in areas around the city rather than in it, to take advantage of new Science Parks located at the fringes of the city's limits. During this period the changing composition of the workforce was also important, with more women entering employment, particularly in part-time employment in the service sector. With the workforce now developing into concentrations of low-skilled, low-paid work and high-skilled professional work, government and local authorities responded by working with business and education institutions to upskill the existing Coventry workforce.

As Mackie shows, there was an enormous expansion of higher education offerings to support this, as the two major universities in the city became amongst the most important employers. Particularly noteworthy is his table, taken from city council research into employment patterns, which shows the incredible and relatively quick expansion of higher education employment, from hardly registering in the 1980s to being the city's largest employer in 2017. However, despite the large influx of students to the city graduate retention in the city is low.

Mackie, in his work on structural change in Coventry, writes extensively on the roll of the city council. His detailed account showcases the value of having a contributor that was part of the decision-making process when it came to local economic development during the 1980s and 1990s, into the new millennium. As he explains it, the council decided to pursue local economic development through changing trends, such as the greening of the economy for example, driven by inward investment. The new growth path also depended on revitalising the rump of the remaining motor industry, embedding them in higher education institutions through centres like the Warwick Manufacturing Group. They embraced new management practises of outsourcing and supply chain management, leading to the growth of the business service sector and logistics companies in the city. Mackie argues that this campaign was a success, attracting thousands of new jobs to the city through inward capital flows into the local economy. Interestingly he concludes that the disruption to Coventry's local economy was a result of government deflationary policies coinciding with an oil crisis and a global downturn. These factors certainly played their part, but structural change was also critical, as he demonstrates.

Possibly the most telling detail in this chapter was the change of business in evidence in Coventry. As Mackie shows in his table, the private sector has shown an enormous decline in the city, with the dominant employers being drawn from the public sector; government, health services and so forth. In conjunction with Sissons's work on commuting patterns into Coventry, showing as it does that professionals and management are predominantly living outside the city, while those in elementary occupations, for example, are residents, the picture that emerges of Coventry is substantially different to that of the 1960s and 1970s.

Sissons's draws a "a sharp distinction between the professional labour markets, which rely to a significant extent on in-commuting and which are driven by sectors such as education, health and other parts of the public sector, and the opportunities available to many residents"; arguing that the central challenge for the city going forward is to develop economic development policies which balance the needs for more local employment opportunities and better job quality among the wider labour force against the ongoing drive to develop a new knowledge economy. In response to concerns about the nature of 'housing offer' the City Council has made recent attempts to attract more highly skilled labour to locate in the city by providing better quality housing and amenities in the city centre through the Broadgate House public realm regeneration project.

More intriguingly the city now appears to be more embedded in regional and national economic activities, a factor Mackie cites as helping improve the resilience of the city at a challenging time of international political and economic turmoil. It is this final point that Morris addresses in his chapter, what the future holds for the city? If we are to assess the changes the city has endured over the last number of decades, then it is perhaps best determined through the prism of resilience. Is the city capable of avoiding or ameliorating large future shocks to the local economy, or has it merely exchanged one vulnerability for another? An economy dependent on one industrial sector for one dependent on public sector and educational institutions. Morris focuses on emerging trends in citywide prosperity and then considers how Coventry measures up against these. He does so by focussing on clusters, educational institutions and, finally, place-based economic development strategies. Key to all of these is innovation and smart specialisation. For example, technology and innovation are at the core of successful clustering.

Perhaps most tellingly Morris acknowledges that Coventry is not an economy with autonomy. Businesses are parts of supply and value chains, connected to networks of innovation. The Coventry economy is plugged into a broader range of economic actors, subject to churn and change but able to draw on its resources, historical experience and previous industrial success to forge a new path. The key then is to identify the most promising surviving assets and meld them with new ones. The conclusion that he reaches is that Coventry is well placed to lead the way in terms of technological and educational developments. It is promising then, that in the lead-up to the City of Culture celebrations that Coventry is set to enjoy in 2021 that the prospects ahead for the city are positive. While there are a number of issues still facing the city, the worse effects of the recession and long malaise that followed the 1970s and 1980s downturn are now behind Coventry. Central to this recovery has been the same forces that brought about change, namely globalisation, or now the process of glocalisation which Morris refers to, the transition from local and linear to global and exponential. While this change has not always been easy, it has ultimately moulded the city.

Reference

Stiglitz, J. E. (2017). The overselling of globalization. *Business Economics, 52*(3), 129–137.

Index

J. Begley et al. (eds.), *Revival of a City*, Palgrave Studies in Economic History,
https://doi.org/10.1007/978-3-030-22822-4

I

J

K

L

The manufacturer's authorised representative in the EU is Springer Nature Customer Service Centre GmbH, Europaplatz 3, 69115 Heidelberg, Germany. If you have any concerns regarding our products, please contact ProductSafety@springernature.com

Printed and bound by CPI Group (UK) Ltd, Croydon, CR0 4YY
05/10/2026
02228123-0004